The American College
and Its Teachers

The
American College
and Its Teachers

by Francis C. Rosecrance

DEAN, COLLEGE OF EDUCATION
WAYNE STATE UNIVERSITY
DETROIT, MICHIGAN

THE MACMILLAN COMPANY, NEW YORK
MACMILLAN NEW YORK, LONDON

© F. C. ROSECRANCE 1962

First Printing

Library of Congress catalog card number: 62-17485

The Macmillan Company, New York
Collier-Macmillan Canada, Ltd., Galt, Ontario
Divisions of The Crowell-Collier Publishing Company

Printed in the United States of America

DESIGNED BY HERMANN STROHBACH

To Dick

FOREWORD

This book was written for several reasons. First, many new college faculty members will be required to staff our colleges and universities during the next ten years. Fortunately, there seems to be an increasing interest in college teaching at this time.

Second, during the past fifteen years the writer has taught courses in higher education in three different universities. Some of the hundreds of students who were enrolled have said that these courses helped them to ask the right questions when being employed as college teachers and to understand the institution of which they came to be a part. It may be that some experienced college professors will find the reading of some portions of this book helpful.

Third, it has been the author's good fortune to be associated intimately with liberal arts and professional colleges on the campuses of Northwestern, New York and Wayne State universities. In addition, during these years he has had some significant connection with self-studies and surveys of sixty colleges located in the East, the South, the Midwest and the Far West. Data thus obtained, as well as those gathered as a member of visiting accrediting teams, have been immensely useful in writing this volume.

I am especially indebted to the presidents of the eight colleges whose special programs are described in Chapter five. They or their representatives took time to read, correct and approve the descriptions. Many additional persons have been of special help, foremost among whom are my colleagues in the three institutions in which I have served and the persons who have worked with me on college studies and surveys.

Particular mention is made of Dr. Thomas B. Stone, who read two chapters and gave me valuable criticism; and my wife

Marjorie N. Rosecrance, without whose patience, writing and editorial skills, and attention to the details of manuscript preparation, this book would not have been published.

FRANCIS C. ROSECRANCE

Grosse Pointe Park, Michigan

CONTENTS

ix

CHAPTER 1

Opportunities in
College Teaching

MAKE SURE OF YOUR TEACHER
AND FORGET ABOUT EVERYTHING ELSE.
                —*Charles Malik*

The modern television teacher may have a class of thirty thousand students. We might contrast this figure with a class of thirty, or with what James A. Garfield once described as his ideal of a college class—"a log with a student at one end and Mark Hopkins at the other." Hopkins, at one time Garfield's teacher, was for forty-two years a member of the faculty of Williams College and was its president for thirty-six of those years. President Garfield stated an ideal, but one could hope that at some time during every college student's school days he might have the experience of being at the other end of a log from a person like Mark Hopkins, who was not only broadly trained, but was also a moral philosopher interested in the development of the individual student. This ideal, of course, neglects the influence of the group on the individual and the important role which students play in sharpening the wits of one another, and it is, of course, unattainable except infrequently because of the tremendous increase in college enrollments and the consequent heavy demands on the teacher's time.

Enrollments. The following figures for the Fall enrollment in higher education in this country in 1960 and 1961 show something of the problem of providing enough college teachers:

TABLE 1

OPENING (FALL) ENROLLMENT IN HIGHER EDUCATION, 1961 AND 1960 [1]

			Change	
	Fall, 1961	*Fall, 1960*	*Number*	*Per Cent*
Total degree credit enrollment [a]				
Both sexes	3,891,000	3,610,000	+281,000	+ 7.8
Men	2,424,000	2,270,000	+153,000	+ 6.8
Women	1,467,000	1,339,000	+128,000	+ 9.5

3

TABLE 1 (cont.)

OPENING (FALL) ENROLLMENT IN HIGHER EDUCATION, 1961 AND 1960 [1]

| First-time degree | | | Change | |
credit enrollment [a]	Fall, 1961	Fall, 1960	Number	Per Cent
Both sexes	1,026,000	930,000	+ 96,000	+10.4
Men	596,000	543,000	+ 53,000	+ 9.8
Women	430,000	387,000	+ 43,000	+11.2

[a] Resident and extension. Does not include mail, radio or television.

In Table 1 the numerical extent of the problem of teaching college students can be seen. If, as has been predicted,[2] there will be six million students in public and private institutions by 1970 or before, it becomes evident that the problem promises to become even more difficult. If it is assumed that about 50 per cent of the college age population can profit by college attendance, then 6,800,000 young people might be expected to seek college entrance in 1970. If only 40 per cent of these young people are to be enrolled as full-time students, college attendance will be almost 5,500,000. And if as few as one-third attend, there will still be an enrollment of almost 4,500,000. This brings up the question of who should go to college, which will be considered in a later chapter.

Need for college teachers. Here we are concerned with the number of college teachers who will be available to teach these students. The Research Division of the National Education Association reported [3] that in 1960–1961, 155,823 persons were mem-

[1] *Opening (Fall) Enrollment in Higher Education, 1961: Institutional Data,* U.S. Department of Health, Education and Welfare, U.S. Government Printing Office, Washington, D.C., 1961. Data reported represent degree-credit enrollment in 1985 institutions of higher education in the aggregate United States.

[2] Seymour Harris, "College Salaries, Financing of Higher Education and Management of Institutions of Higher Learning," *A.A.U.P. Bulletin,* September, 1958, pp. 589–595.

[3] Research Division, N.E.A., *Teacher Supply and Demand in Universities, Colleges and Junior Colleges,* 1959–1960 and 1960–1961, National Education Association, Washington, D.C., May, 1961, p. 7.

bers of the resident faculty of 1,615 institutions—universities, colleges and junior colleges. In these institutions at that time there were also 69,401 part-time college teachers, 2,284,646 full-time students and 924,249 part-time students. Thus the total number of teachers available, full- and part-time, was 225,224, and the total student body to be taught, full- and part-time, was 3,208,895.[4] We can see that the ratio of full-time staff to full-time students was roughly one to fifteen. If all members of the staff and all members of the student body were counted, the ratio would drop to one staff member to fourteen students. The customary ratio in colleges over the years has been one to ten. In reference to this question Seymour Harris writes:

Improved methods of communication, larger classes, fewer courses, etc. might well make it possible to increase the ratio of students from ten to one to fifteen to one. There is nothing sacred about the ten to one ratio. In fact, when it is considered that in elementary schools the ratio is thirty to one and in secondary schools twenty-two to one, one is puzzled by the ten to one ratio in higher education. In these days of emphasis on self-education, is this ratio justified? [5]

Many educators are thinking about this problem today and are generally in agreement that this ratio will be changed. It may well be that even the suggested ratio of fifteen college students to one faculty member will prove to be too small to accommodate the exploding college population of the future unless the number of college teachers available is greatly increased.

If the estimate of six million college students by 1970 is accepted as a base, and if we assume as high a student-teacher ratio as fifteen to one, we see that 400,000 college teachers will be required by that date.[6] Since we must make allowance for

[4] This figure does not tally with the figure given in Table 1, since only 1,615 institutions replied to the *Teacher Supply and Demand* study as compared with 1985 institutions supplying data for *Opening (Fall) Enrollment in Higher Education, 1960.*

[5] Seymour Harris, *op. cit.,* pp. 594–595.

[6] Dr. Ray C. Maul, assistant director of research for the N.E.A., said in 1959 that nearly 500,000 new college teachers will be needed by 1970. He listed these needs: 35,000 new teachers of English, 32,000 teachers of education, 30,000 of engineering, 25,000 of biological sciences, 22,000 of business

retirements, this figure would mean that 15,000 college teachers should be qualified each year. The latest figures available show that in 1960–1961 a total of 10,221 persons were newly qualified for college teaching, but that only one-quarter of these have earned their doctor's degree. It is surely not an overstatement to suggest that almost twice that number must get the doctorate annually if the need is to be met. Indeed, President Pusey of Harvard has suggested that 25,000 Ph.D.'s will be needed each year.[7] When it is realized that more than 40 per cent of these scholars will not enter college teaching, but will be attracted into more remunerative work in business, industry, government or public administration of some sort, it is evident that President Pusey's figure is none too large.

Qualifications of the college teacher. The Educational Policies Commission suggests that "five groups in American society may be drawn upon for faculty service to a greater degree than at present."[8] These groups are present students, women, minority groups, older persons and specialists available on a part-time basis. (Though the masculine pronoun is used throughout this book to refer to the college professor, it is intended of course to include both men and women faculty members.) If these are the human resource pools from which our supply of college teachers must come, how may we identify them and what individual characteristics should be sought in those we choose? It goes without saying that all teachers should be in good health and be physically and mentally alert. Qualities of cooperativeness, resourcefulness and leadership are essential. All teachers should possess character, commitment and competence. Integrity is, of

and commerce, 22,000 of foreign languages, 17,000 of mathematics, 16,000 of chemistry, 15,000 of history, 12,000 of physics, 10,000 of economics, and 7,000 of political science. *Education Summary,* January 27, 1959, p. 3.

[7] Dr. Eckert of the University of Minnesota substantiated this figure when she wrote, "America's 1900 colleges and universities will need upwards of 250,000 teachers in the next decade to provide for the estimated six million students who will overflow our college campuses by 1970." Ruth E. Eckert, "When Teachers Join College Faculties," *North Central Association Quarterly,* October, 1959, p. 161.

[8] Educational Policies Commission, *Higher Education in a Decade of Decision,* Washington, D.C., 1957, p. 10.

course, basic to all citizens. Commitment to teaching, research and the scholarly life is essential as well as appreciation of the fact that college teachers are dealing with life at perhaps its most crucial point. College presidents desire to employ professors who have command of their subjects, who know how to teach and have a warm regard for students. In addition, the real college teacher is eternally asking "why?" He is a seeker after knowledge, he hopes to extend its frontier, he takes little for granted unless it is substantiated by evidence, he wants to understand the meaning of life and his part in it and he wants to understand the world in which he lives and the forces at work in it. He strives for excellence in all he does. He has a passion for freedom and for his fellows. This is the person who should choose college teaching as a profession.

Rewards of college teaching. Assuming that a young person feels himself qualified and that there are likely to be openings in his field (these are not uniform across the board), what may he expect in the way of satisfactions from college teaching? Though the greatest of these always comes from his relationships with his students, there are many ways in which conditions within the university or college contribute to the teacher's satisfactions or lack of them. The following nine of these will be briefly considered:

(1) Appointments
(2) Promotion in rank
(3) Salary schedules and merit raises
(4) Opportunities in teaching and research
(5) Tenure and retirement
(6) Fringe benefits
(7) Leaves of absence and conditions of work
(8) Staff planning and committee work
(9) Communication and staff morale

Appointments. It may be useful to indicate to prospective college teachers that, in general, positions are filled through personal contacts and through placement lists maintained by various disciplines, by the American Association of University Professors, by university placement offices and by commercial placement bureaus. Though it would be difficult to obtain accurate statistics on the percentage of appointments obtained through each of these sources, it seems safe to say that in college teaching the majority of positions are obtained through personal contacts. In the past it has not usually been necessary for a really good prospect for college teaching to register with a commercial bureau, although there are several very good agencies in the country. Candidates frequently have their credentials prepared in a university placement bureau in order not to plague their friends with requests for references. But the really good prospective college teacher has been so much in demand that even such listings are not usually necessary. A more likely procedure is that college presidents, deans and department chairmen, through their contacts with the heads of various departments in well-known colleges and universities, obtain the names of desirable candidates and approach them directly.

Persons who are asked to write recommendations for placement bureaus, from which credentials are sent to widely separated institutions of many kinds, are constrained to write very general statements, sometimes not very helpful ones. The writer may wish to recommend a candidate for one kind of situation, but not for another, and he tends to avoid saying negative things because of the damage they might do if the recommendation were sent to an institution in which the candidate would be likely to make good. Many employing officials scan credentials which they receive to discover the name of a person whom they know. If one is found and the prospective employer has confidence in the kind of recommendation this person writes, more weight will be attached to his statement than to any of the others.

The appointment of new persons to a faculty is possibly the most important task that a president, a dean or a department chairman has to undertake. Deutsch in a recent book has a chapter entitled, "The Faculty—They Really Make the Institution." [9] A

[9] Monroe E. Deutsch, *The College from Within*, The University of California Press, Berkeley, California, 1952, p. 56.

good faculty plus a carefully selected student body do indeed make an institution. Therefore, while the candidate seeks a job, the institution searches for the really fine faculty member. Many administrators have learned the hard way that it is easier to take care in employing a person than it is to get rid of an unsatisfactory one later. How then does an institution protect itself against such a risk?

Some institutions require that a national search for available talent be made. Perhaps at this point it should be reluctantly stated that members of some departments do not desire outstanding people added to their department, because such persons might become a threat to the mediocrity present. But really fine, competent college teachers want outstanding persons as colleagues, and to such a faculty the requirement of a national canvass is a sensible one. Perhaps the canvass may turn up sixty-five or seventy promising names, about each of whom information is assembled. This information, which includes age, personal qualifications, education, experience, recommendations and the salary and rank required by each candidate, is carefully studied. Through a process too varied in different departments and too involved to be described in detail here, the list may be narrowed to four or five people. These persons are then invited to visit the campus, where all members of the curriculum area may meet and talk with each candidate. Usually a group meeting is held, so that all regular staff members may hear the candidate's views at the same time. An advantage of this procedure is that such a meeting makes it impossible for the candidate to express one point of view to one staff person and an opposing view to another (though, fortunately, this does not often happen). Following the visit brief individual conferences are held by the dean or chairman with all staff members in the curriculum area to obtain their reactions to the candidate as a person and as a prospective colleague. This procedure is necessary since staff members do not always express themselves freely in front of their colleagues, and if there are reservations about a prospective staff member, they should be known. Furthermore, no person should be invited into a situation in which he will face so much hostility that he cannot function. Following these conferences a decision should be made by the dean or other administrative officer as to whether or not to recommend the candidate to the president and the governing body. Though such a screening process as has been described will not eliminate all mistakes in the making of appointments, it will greatly reduce them. Certainly it is an important step in the direction of building a faculty that will really "make the institution." The first appointment is for a probationary period of two, three or four years, depending on the candidate's previous experience, tenure and professorial rank.

Promotion in rank. When a college teacher obtains his first appointment but lacks other experience significant to his employment, he is likely to be named as an instructor. In many fields the doctorate is required for this position, and in most it is prerequisite to promotion to an assistant professorship. Some institutions have a policy of moving a staff member "up or out" after four years, which is based on the conviction that administrative officers should be able to make up their minds in four years as to whether or not the instructor should be retained or released.

It is customary in some colleges and universities to keep a faculty member in the rank of assistant professor for six years before he becomes eligible for promotion. These same institutions often have the same time lapse for the promotion of an associate professor to the rank of full professor unless a merit promotion shortens the time. Thus it would appear that the college teacher who began as an instructor might have to wait sixteen years before he could obtain a full professorship. Moreover, it should be noted that he might have to wait longer! Promotion from one rank to another is not usually automatic, and the college teacher might be forced to wait a year or two at the top of each rank before being recommended to the next. This delay may be caused by the fact that others of equal worth have more seniority, by failure of persons at the upper rank to retire or by some failure of the individual college teacher to convince his colleagues of his worthiness to be promoted.

On the other hand, the number of years which must elapse

before one reaches a full professorship may be shortened in a number of ways. Conditions at the time of hiring may enable the candidate to secure a higher rank and hence start a rung or two up on the academic ladder. Some college teachers deliberately plan to change positions every three years or so, in each instance asking for an advance in rank. While these devices are legitimate, there is also the less desirable practice of obtaining an offer from another institution and threatening to leave unless both the salary and rank offers are met.

Of more fundamental interest is promotion as a result of merit. Such promotions are usually accorded to those whose teaching is outstandingly successful or who have done significant writing or research. "Steady promotion," says Woodburne,[10] "is, as it were, a mark of academic respectability." While no promotion should be made without a salary increase, no tangible reward can be compared with the importance attached to promotion in rank.

Factors usually taken into account in deciding on promotion for any faculty member in a university are (1) research, (2) publications, (3) teaching, (4) student advising, (5) community or public service, and (6) university committee service. While the order of importance here listed may not be significant in some institutions, it will be in others. For example, some smaller colleges will place teaching first because they are primarily teaching institutions; community colleges may give high priority to public service; and "first line" universities are likely to put great emphasis on research and writing. Therefore, the college teacher needs to discover the relative weight placed on each of the factors in the institutions he is considering. Perhaps he should realize also that his own values may change from a heavy interest in teaching in his earlier years to a later interest in writing. What is needed in colleges and universities today are "triple threat" or "quadruple threat" men and women who can do three or four of the things listed above exceedingly well.

The whole subject of evaluating the services of a faculty member is discussed in Chapter 10. Some methods used are evaluations

[10] Lloyd S. Woodburne, *Faculty Personnel Policies in Higher Education,* Harper and Brothers, New York, 1950, p. 20.

by advisory committees of the faculty, ratings of students and alumni, standing in the profession as represented by professional memberships, critical reviews of their publications, and the like.

Faculty salaries. Staff salaries paid by institutions of higher education vary with (1) the type of institution, (2) the amount of its endowment, (3) the type of control, (4) the size of the institution, (5) the level of instruction and (6) the region of the country in which the institution is located.

The following table presents data [11] based on returns from 1,458 colleges and universities. Five hundred and fifty-five of these were public colleges and universities, representing 91.6 per cent of the enrollment in public institutions. Nine hundred and three were private colleges and universities having 82.3 per cent of the enrollment in private institutions.

TABLE 2

AVERAGE 9–10 MONTH FACULTY SALARIES, ALL RANKS COMBINED, BY ENROLLMENT

Data Classifications	Public and Private	Public	Private
Total—all institutions	$7,240	$7,480	$6,830
4-year total	7,330	7,570	6,960
Enrollment below 500	5,470	6,640	5,360
500–999	6,050	6,190	6,020
1,000–2,499	6,690	6,740	6,660
2,500–4,999	7,290	7,300	7,250
5,000–9,999	7,410	7,250	7,700
10,000 and more	8,260	8,230	8,370
2-year total	6,620	7,000	4,910
Enrollment below 500	5,430	6,030	4,660
500–999	5,930	6,100	5,180
1,000–2,499	6,840	7,050	5,550
2,500 and over	7,680	7,680	——

[11] U.S. Department of Health, Education and Welfare, *Higher Education Planning and Management Data,* 1960–1961, Circular #651, U.S. Government Printing Office, Washington, D.C., 1961, pp. 2–3.

From these and other data drawn from the same source [12] the following conclusions seem to be justified:

(1) In both public and private institutions the universities pay the highest salaries, followed by liberal arts colleges, teachers colleges and junior colleges.

(2) Salaries generally increase following a rise in the enrollment level.

(3) Public junior colleges, teachers colleges and technical institutes pay higher salaries than do private institutions in the same categories. But private universities pay higher salaries than public ones.

(4) Salaries from highest median to lowest are paid in the Far West, Middle West, Middle Atlantic, New England, Northwest, Southwest, Southeast.

It is evident that the prospective college staff member needs to consider the type of institution, the type of support it receives, its size and its location if salary is a dominant factor in his choice of institution.

Salary schedules. The majority of colleges have a schedule in operation. The following is a typical one:

Instructor	$4,000 to $5,800
Assistant Professor	5,800 to 7,600
Associate Professor	7,600 to 9,400
Professor	9,400 to 11,200 [13]

If an automatic increment of $300 were given each year, it would take six years for a faculty member to reach the point where he was eligible to be promoted to the next rank. In the instance given above, promotion is not automatic and must be merited for professional reasons "of substance." While most colleges and universities have some sort of schedule of salaries by rank, in only two-

[12] *Ibid.,* pp. 19–20.
[13] Compare with the figures given in Sidney G. Tickton, *Teaching Salaries Then and Now,* Fund for the Advancement of Education, New York, May, 1961, pp. 7–13; also "Annual Report by Committee Z," *A.A.U.P. Bulletin,* June, 1961, pp. 101–134.

fifths of these are the salary increments specified. According to the Research Division of the National Education Association, "With the exception of the public institutions in two states, salary schedules (as the term is generally used in public-school circles) are in operation in only a small per cent of the institutions of any type or in any region." [14]

When an institution does not have an automatic increment, recommendations for salary increases are frequently initiated by department chairmen and forwarded to the dean of the respective college. If he concurs in the recommendation, he will send it on to the vice-president, and eventually it reaches the president and the board of trustees for action. How much will this increase be? Here is the point at which inequities arise. Some chairmen recommend an increase of $1,000, others $500, and still others may recommend an increase of $250 for every one. The first chairman may be recommending the $1,000 increase for a particular college teacher because he has merited it by superior performance, or because the chairman is afraid of losing a competent man. The second chairman wishes to encourage two men and so prefers to spend $500 on each rather than give $1,000 to only one. The third chairman may be trying to keep as many persons satisfied as he can without attempting to recommend merit increases. There is perhaps no more sensitive area affecting faculty morale than the policy employed in giving salary increases. Much can be said in favor of automatic increments as a way of dealing with this problem. Some administrators have found it possible to combine automatic increments with additional merit increases where the faculty clearly recognizes the merit of the staff members who are thus recognized. To insure such recognition some administrators insist that a faculty-elected committee participate in recommending any merit increases.

Prospective college teachers should know that for faculty in certain fields higher salaries are stipulated than for the rest of

[14] Research Division, N.E.A., "Does It Pay to Teach in Colleges?" *Research Bulletin,* May, 1960, published by National Education Association, Washington, D.C., p. 36.

the college staff. These fields are medicine, law, science and engineering; and less commonly, dentistry, business, and mathematics are included. Also higher salaries are often offered in fields where the supply of college teachers is scarce. In 1959–1960 and in 1960–1961 these fields [15] were physical science, mathematics, foreign languages, engineering, biological sciences, business, education, English and psychology. In these fields salary schedules in some regions are likely to be exceeded simply because the demand for teachers is greater than the supply.

Some educational leaders are of the opinion that to attract and hold competent college teachers, faculty salaries must be increased by at least 50 per cent during the next five to ten years on the basis of present price levels. If such action is taken, the prospect for more satisfactory financial rewards for the college teacher seems fairly bright for the future.

Opportunities in teaching and research. Whether one works in a field where the supply of teachers is scarce or plentiful, there are opportunities and advantages common to all college teachers. First among these is the satisfaction obtained from maintaining contacts with generations of young people. Young people between the ages of eighteen and twenty-five are at the period of their lives when they identify and begin to develop lasting interests. It is a special opportunity and privilege to work with them during these impressionable years.

But college teaching not only affords the opportunity of influencing the interests, attitudes, values and decisions of college students; the latter reciprocate by influencing college teachers *if they are willing to listen!* It may be commonplace to say that teaching one college generation after another keeps the professors young, but it is also true. More than this, students with maturing, uninhibited minds often question the professor's thought in such a way as to cause him to see some area of his study, thought and teaching from a new angle. Most college

[15] Research Division, N.E.A., *Teacher Supply and Demand in Universities, Colleges and Junior Colleges,* 1959–1960 and 1960–1961, N.E.A., Washington, D.C., p. 23.

teachers readily acknowledge that some phases of their own teaching and writing have been stimulated by the students whom they have taught. On the other hand, one of the most satisfying rewards of college teaching comes from the opportunity to see college youth discover new avenues of thought and action. There are few things as exciting as the opportunity to see a new idea, hypothesis or attitude toward life catch and hold the young person.

Intimately related to the teaching function of the college teacher is his research. To the public, college teachers do not seem to have heavy schedules, since in most collegiate institutions the usual hours in the classroom do not exceed fifteen per week, and in the better universities they are more likely eight or ten hours. The teaching task is made more difficult if the staff person has to read and prepare for more than three different courses. Even then, he may be expected to offer three other courses the following term and must, therefore, keep up to date in his research and reading in all six fields. Further, what outsiders do not recognize is that behind each hour spent in the classroom is (or should be) at least two hours of preparation. Hence, if one teaches fifteen hours, he will spend an additional thirty hours in preparation and thus have a forty-five-hour week. One could hardly expect that a college professor on such a schedule could do much research, especially if he also advises students, serves on faculty committees and is active in the community and state.

But the teacher who has a teaching load of eight hours and spends sixteen hours in preparation has a total teaching load of only twenty-four hours, which leaves him sixteen hours of the normal forty-hour week to spend in research. In the interests of truth it must be admitted that the author does not know of any college professors really committed to their jobs who confine themselves to a forty-hour week. Probably it would be more nearly correct to say that they spend sixty hours a week at their work. Some of them get so interested in their research that at times they even work "around the clock." Nevertheless, the satisfaction which comes from an investigation, from an original contribution to knowledge, from a creative effort, or from the exploration of an "outrageous hypothesis" is one of the greatest rewards that come to the college teacher, whatever his workload may be.

Academic freedom and tenure. In academic circles the attainment of tenure, after a probationary period, is a highly prized possession. Tenure is linked with academic freedom, without which there could be no true university or college. The role of the college is not only to transmit our cultural heritage from the past, but to add to the sum total of knowledge by pushing back the walls of ignorance and extending the frontiers of learning. Indeed, each candidate for the degree of doctor of philosophy is expected to make an original contribution to knowledge. Almost by definition, therefore, the professor and his doctoral candidates are likely to affront some segment of the population for an economic, political, social or religious reason. Hence, freedom to teach and to do research are dependent on tenure in an educational institution. The issues surrounding academic freedom and tenure are discussed in Chapter 3. Suffice it to say here that if the board of trustees has an officially adopted policy on academic freedom and tenure, the college teacher has the satisfaction of knowing that within limits he has a real measure of security.

Retirement benefits. Though most young college teachers evince little interest in retirement provisions, since for them retirement age seems a long time off, it should be a matter of importance to them as well as to the older college teacher, who may have been underpaid for many years. Since the great majority of colleges are in the federal Social Security system, most college teachers have the protection that this system provides, meager though it be. With a college retirement plan in addition to social security, the professor's retirement income will be more nearly adequate. Under such a plan the college contributes from its current budget, and the professor authorizes a deduction from his annual salary. Deductions from a teacher's salary check for social security and retirement represent deferred payments on money actually earned.

Properly speaking, these payments in behalf of the college teacher should be considered a part of his annual salary, although this point is often overlooked.

There are two kinds of retirement systems—those that are completely funded and vested and those which are not. Most municipal or state retirement systems are not completely funded and thus are not actuarially sound. However, it is assumed that an entire staff of employees would never retire at one time, and so it has not seemed necessary to keep the total amount actually on hand to cover such an eventuality. The municipality or state is confident that, by having a portion of the money on hand, it will have sufficient funds to pay an annuity to the relatively small per cent of its employees who retire each year. Some municipal and state governments, when short of cash, have been tempted to borrow from retirement funds or to use them for collateral in other borrowing. This type of retirement program is clearly not funded since it does not have the money on hand to "pay out," if all persons retired simultaneously. In fact, such a contingency is guarded against by the requirement that a teacher must reach a certain age or serve a certain number of years before becoming eligible for retirement payments. Moreover, members of such retirement systems have the credit of the state or municipality back of the program, and their chances of receiving the amount expected on retirement are just as good as is the credit of the governmental institution itself.

The other type of retirement is completely funded and vested. A "funded" system is one in which 100 per cent of the money that has been paid in is on hand and can actually be paid out for any number of its members at any time. Furthermore, this money is "vested" in the names of particular persons and becomes a permanent part of their property or their estate. Perhaps the best known of the funded and vested plans for college teachers is the Teachers Insurance and Annuity Association, which is used in nearly 900 colleges and universities. Under T.I.A.A. a college may elect to pay in 10 per cent of a faculty person's salary, while the teacher also contributes 10 per cent. Thus, if his salary is $8,000, the college adds $800 for his retirement as well as the $800 deducted from his annual pay. The teacher's actual income then will consist of $7,200 in cash and $1,600 in retirement funds, or a total of $8,800. When retirement funds are wisely invested and conserved, the college teacher has reasonable assurance that the payments he receives after retirement from one of the plans described and from the federal Social Security system will provide him a respectable, albeit reduced, standard of living in his later years. The biggest threats to the achievement of this goal are the rising cost of living and the decreasing value of the dollar.

One other difference between the two kinds of retirement plans described should be mentioned. Municipal or state retirement systems often require that a college teacher remain in the system twenty-five or thirty years to become eligible for a retirement allowance. In this case, should a teacher move to an institution in another state, he can usually withdraw only the amount of his own contribution to the retirement fund and none of the money paid into the fund by the state or municipality. If he has been in an institution which uses T.I.A.A. and moves to another that also uses it, his program for retirement income is uninterrupted. If he moves to another institution not under T.I.A.A., he can sometimes maintain his retirement program simply by keeping up his own contributions and requesting that the new institution take over the contribution made by the college previously employing him. If the institution cannot do this, the college teacher can continue to pay in as much as he desires from his own funds, and thus keep his retirement fund growing. In institutions under T.I.A.A. the college teacher who decides to leave the profession can draw an annuity not only on what he paid in but also on what the college paid in for him. There is a great deal of advantage from the point of view of mobility in belonging to a retirement system that is actuarially sound—funded and vested.

Fringe benefits. Since the costs of what have been referred to as "fringe benefits" in many institutions exceed 10 per cent of total salary expenditures, they should perhaps no longer be considered as peripheral. In addition to federal Social Security and the university's retirement annuity, other specific benefits are:

(1) Group hospitalization
(2) Major medical coverage
(3) Accident insurance
(4) Health service provided by institution
(5) Life insurance
(6) Sabbatical leaves
(7) Vacations with pay
(8) Sick leaves with pay
(9) Reduction of tuition to employee's dependents
(10) Discounts on purchases
(11) Housing for some employees
(12) Loan funds for sizeable purchases
(13) Significant recreational facilities

Differences exist between public and private institutions and in various parts of the country as to the frequency with which these benefits are provided. However, vacations with pay and sick leaves with pay are provided in the majority of institutions of both types. Group hospitalization, major medical coverage, accident insurance, health service, life insurance, reduction of tuition to dependent children, discounts on purchases and loan funds were in 1957–1958 more frequently provided by private institutions than by public ones. Of the institutions that furnished college-owned housing for 5 per cent or more of their salaried employees, private institutions and public colleges of the South showed the two largest percentages, with a smaller proportion of private institutions of the Northeast third in rank. While sick pay and vacations with pay are usually provided by the institution, the costs of most other fringe benefits are divided between the individual and the institution. Three services available to employees acting as an employee group are group hospitalization, accident insurance and major medical coverage, services which are not subsidized by many institutions. More and more these so-called "fringe benefits" are being carefully considered by faculty groups interested in improving the economic status of the college teacher.

Sabbatical leaves. About 25 per cent of both public and private institutions give paid sabbatical leaves to their teachers with the cost shared by the institution and the individual. In institutions on the semester system these leaves come every seventh year or semester. Most universities on the quarter system base the teacher's salary on nine months' service but divide the pay into twelve equal monthly installments. When such teachers teach during their fourth quarter, they receive additional pay. Usually some limit is placed on the number of successive quarters that can be taught. Eligible faculty members have been in some instances permitted to take one semester or quarter off with full pay or two semesters or quarters with half pay. Because of two factors— stringent institutional budgets and the belief that the individual should invest in himself—such trend as can be discerned is toward half pay.

The workload carried by most college teachers clearly suggests that the time for investigation and writing during the collegiate year is sharply limited. At best, research projects can only be started and preliminary research done; periodically an uninterrupted time for writing and completing research should be allowed. This is the real purpose of sabbatical leaves. Indeed, some institutions have eliminated the idea that staff members have the *right* to a leave every seventh year and have made the granting of requests for leave with salary conditional upon the nature and worth of the research and writing project proposed. It seems safe to say that in the future sabbatical leaves will not be used as long vacations with a little travel, reading and investigation sandwiched in to satisfy the letter of the regulation, but that they will be utilized for self-improvement, writing and research.

The large institution or the small college? Prospective college students consider seriously the advantages of a small college as compared with a larger institution. College teachers are confronted by the same decision and may be influenced by some of the same factors. It is, of course, impossible to say that a college of a certain size is better than one that is larger or smaller—the choice is an individual matter. Yesterday when there were fewer openings for the college teacher, he had less choice in the matter, but the variety of opportunities and institutions available to most college teachers today make it necessary for a deliberate decision to be made.

The choice will not be made solely on economic grounds. Some small colleges pay as well as many larger institutions, although on the average they do not. It cannot be made solely on the assumption that in a small college the professor can know his students better than is possible in a large university, for a remarkable degree of concern for the individual student is evidenced by faculty members of some large institutions. Neither can the decision be made on the basis of the quality of intellectual climate of the campus, for there are some small colleges whose intellectual interests excel those of many universities. In every case the decision will be an individual one based on the teacher's personal predilections and a combination of many other institutional factors.

Conditions of work. The prospective teacher needs to know ahead of time what can be expected from college teaching so far as conditions of work are concerned. Unfortunately, educational institutions do not have the funds with which to provide ideal working conditions for their staff members. In most instances travel allowances, secretarial help, office space and parking space are limited. A junior staff member may expect to have his way paid to one national conference a year, to divide a secretary's time with three or four other teachers, and to share an office with at least one other person. In many instances also adequate funds for library books, audiovisual aids and other equipment are not available. If a teacher requires expensive equipment, he may have to wait three or four years before the budget can provide it.

Staff planning and committee work. While more adequate consideration will be given in Chapter 9 to the teacher's function as member of a faculty, it should be noted here that the opportunities for staff planning and committee work in any given institution, or the lack of them, are important to the prospective teacher. In some institutions faculty members have nothing to say about changes to be made in the course of study, nor even about the improvement of their working conditions. One might conclude in such instances that the institution in question is run in an authoritarian manner.

Other colleges make substantial provision for faculty members to participate in planning, department by department, division by division. Committees are often given the responsibility for planning the curriculum and for setting up admission requirements and graduation standards. They are also consulted with regard to the teaching load and other conditions of work. It may be assumed that in these colleges there is an academic democracy which, while often time-consuming, can be very satisfying to the staff and bring excellent results in the program. There are, of course, faculty members who wish to avoid such staff planning and committee work. Whatever the individual college teacher's personal view, he should discover before accepting a position what the institutional practice is in relation to the participation of college teachers in staff planning and committee work. Working with one's colleagues in a constructive and cooperative fashion can be a source of real satisfaction for the college teacher.

College teacher morale. The *esprit de corps* of the students and the faculty is central to the accomplishment of the purposes of the institution. If the morale is high, the prospects for high achievement of both groups are increased; if it is low, the reverse is true. It would seem, then, that much attention would be given to this matter, yet the fact is that good morale is too often taken for granted. One important factor in the achievement of good morale is the relatively simple matter of maintaining open avenues of communication. The "scuttle-butt" resulting from a "rumor factory" on the campus can do a great deal of harm to both students and staff. Wild reports of what has happened or is going to happen are soon scotched when a two-way communication plan has been established.

The college president who has no way to listen directly (first-hand) to the students is in danger of misunderstanding them. If he has no way to listen directly to the faculty, he is in similar danger. Some presidents make time in their schedules to meet with these groups, a far safer procedure than relying on information received from the deans, vice-presidents or other assistants. Some presidents write letters to students in the campus newspaper and to faculty members in a faculty letter regularly issued. Though this practice is helpful, perhaps a better device is a regular separate meeting with representatives of each of these groups, where the president can tell of the problems, progress and plans of the college and the students and faculty can ask questions and express their ideas of the best ways to forward the institution's welfare. In small colleges where chapel meetings or convocations are held frequently, these perhaps provide some opportunities— though not enough in themselves—to keep open the avenues of communication. In larger universities the deans of the various colleges are likely to encounter the same problem and experience the same difficulty in solving it. Whether president or dean, the administrator who operates without being informed from the grass roots may find his "house of cards" tumbling around him on some unfortunate day.

While communication is essential in maintaining morale, other factors are also important. In 1958 the American Council on Education summarized a study in college teacher morale by Hammond.[16] Fifty presidents of state universities in forty-six states were asked to rate twelve items in order of importance to the morale of the college teacher and to add any which they felt had been omitted. Twenty-six replies were received, and it will be noted that most of the items discussed in this chapter were listed, communication being placed fourth in order of importance. The morale factors reported by Hammond are as follows:

(1) Advancement in salary and position possible for those who meet published qualifications

[16] American Council on Education, Washington, D.C. *Letter,* August 12, 1958.

(2) Guarantee of academic freedom

(3) Teaching load which permits research for those so inclined

(4) Being kept informed on university policy and on other items of importance to teachers

(5) Guaranteed tenure to insure satisfactory performance

(6) Teachers allowed to teach courses they want to teach

(7) Local, state and national acceptance and recognition on a stature equal to that accorded other professions (law, medicine, etc.)

(8) A definite salary scale based on qualifications

(9) Satisfactory classrooms, equipment and plant facilities

(10) An established, liberal retirement program

(11) Granting of awards, grants, fellowships and/or scholarships for advanced degrees for those exhibiting outstanding scholarship or teaching skill

(12) Freedom from administrative duties

Beyond these tangible advantages, the college teacher has the opportunity and privilege, mentioned earlier, of working with young people. Further, he has the additional privilege of being associated with some fine colleagues. While the test screens of education through which he and they have passed do not guarantee, they do presage a high type of person. Since members of the faculty have been educated in many differing disciplines, they may not agree intellectually; indeed, it would be undesirable that they should. They should, however, have a genuine liking for one another personally. The scholarly community is made up of diverse interests and diverse minds, but in this diversity there is a fundamental unity—the desire to help the maturing student achieve for himself that inquiring mind and set of values that will push forward the central purpose of higher education—to help the new generation to think effectively and creatively and to act maturely and responsibly.

CHAPTER 2

A Brief History of Higher Education in America

LIBERTY CANNOT BE PRESERVED WITHOUT
GENERAL KNOWLEDGE AMONG THE PEOPLE.
—*John Adams*

The development of higher education in the United States reveals diversity of purpose and pattern. In the beginning the purpose was chiefly a religious one, and most of the early colleges were established by Protestant sects. Of the first nine colleges, founded between 1636 and 1769, all but one were established by churches to train ministers and to give Christian education to young people. Indeed, about two-thirds of all the 1,900 institutions of higher learning in the United States today were founded under church auspices.

EARLY DEVELOPMENTS

Purposes of early colleges. Harvard College, our first institution of higher learning, was started in 1636 with the purpose of leading students "to know God and Jesus Christ, which is life eternal." Fifty-seven years elapsed before the second college, William and Mary, was founded, "to the end that the Church of Virginia may be furnished with a seminary of ministers of the Gospel, and that the youth may be piously educated in good letters and manners." The mottoes adopted by many of the first nine colleges, listed in the table below, show the religious influence.

There was, however, a second purpose for the founding of the early colleges—that of making higher learning available in this country for the sons of the well-to-do, thus making it unnecessary for them to return to England for further learning. From almost the beginning there was a secular trend competing with the religious one. It will be noted in the above table that one of the first nine colleges, the University of Pennsylvania, was not founded by a religious denomination. This college was organized under the influence of Benjamin Franklin for a broader and more utilitarian purpose, though it undoubtedly came under some Quaker influence.

TABLE 3

FACTS CONCERNING THE FOUNDING OF THE FIRST NINE
COLLEGIATE INSTITUTIONS IN THE U.S.

Year	Institution	State	Founding Sect	Motto
1636	Harvard	Massachusetts	Puritan	"For Christ and the Church"
1693	William and Mary	Virginia	Anglican	
1701	Yale	Connecticut	Congregational	"Light and Truth"
1746	Princeton	New Jersey	Presbyterian	"Under God's Guidance It Flourishes"
1753–55	Pennsylvania	Pennsylvania	Nondenominational	
1755	King's College (now Columbia)	New York	Anglican	"In Thy Light Shall We See Light"
1764	Brown	Rhode Island	Baptist	"In God We Trust"
1766	Rutgers	New Jersey	Reformed Dutch	"Sun of Righteousness, Shine upon the West Also"
1769	Dartmouth	New Hampshire	Congregational	"Virtue Rejoices in Trial"

These first colleges followed the traditions of Oxford and Cambridge though most of them never became great collections of colleges as the English universities did. Entrance requirements demanded little more than a knowledge of Greek and Latin. Most of the faculty members were clergymen. The curriculum of the early college was usually copied from the English universities, and its central core consisted of the classical languages and literatures. The course of study was the same for all students. Bachelor's and Master's degrees were awarded from the beginning, though the requirements for the latter varied greatly in the different institutions. A century later few changes in the curriculum were found. An interesting sidelight on the method of instruction followed at this time was that courses were listed according to the name of the textbook to be studied.

Most of the early colleges had great difficulty in obtaining the necessary funds to maintain their operations. Some secured gifts from interested people in England, and there were a few grants from government. Otherwise, the chief source of income was the tuition fees. Enrollments were small. Yale, for example, had thirty-six students when it was founded in 1701 and only 338 sixty years later. Moreover, though some poor boys were given scholarships or allowed to "work their way through college," there were hundreds more who were unable either to travel the great distances to these schools or to pay the fees once they arrived.

Expansion of colleges. The religious awakening which occurred in the early part of the nineteenth century, along with the vast westward expansion of our country, had a notable effect on higher education. With a zealous missionary purpose the churches established many small colleges, which made it possible for young men who wished to study for the ministry to obtain the needed education nearer home and at a much smaller cost than if they had to attend one of the larger eastern colleges. There was considerable competition between the churches in establishing these institutions in the newly settled territory. Many of the denominations felt that they must have at least one college in every state, and because of this sense of urgency many small colleges were founded hurriedly with no plan for adequate support and little attention to a desirable location. The result of these and other errors, according to Brubacher and Rudy, was that "of five hundred colleges founded in sixteen representative states before the Civil War, only a little more than one hundred survived as permanent institutions. This was a mortality rate of 80 per cent." [1]

In spite of this fact these small colleges not only made a higher education far less costly for the young people of the frontier towns, but met their special needs in a way that the large institutions of the East would not have done. By developing purposes and methods of their own, they contributed markedly to the variety of education in the United States, and by enrolling the children of poor farmers, they also had a democratizing effect on education.

State universities. In the meantime while these small religious colleges were being established, the effect of the European Enlightenment and the ideas spread abroad following the French and American revolutions were largely responsible for the demand for public, state-supported higher institutions which would be free of sectarian control and would offer a broader curriculum, especially in the natural sciences. The University of North Carolina and the University of Georgia, which opened in 1795 and 1801 respectively, were the first state universities. However, though they received grants of land or money from the states at the outset, they did not receive regular appropriations for their operation. In fact, it was not until after the Civil War that state governments took over the full support of state universities.

Many of these so-called universities did not embody the idea of a university as it is generally regarded today—an institution of learning of the highest grade, having a college of liberal arts and a program of graduate study, together with several professional schools and faculties and authorized to confer degrees. However, one institution, the University of Virginia, which was established by Thomas Jefferson, did meet most of the qualifications and so might be considered America's first real state university. Brubacher and Rudy say,

It is an authentic example of this type for a number of reasons. First of all, it aimed from the beginning to give more advanced instruction than the existing colleges, to permit students to specialize

[1] John S. Brubacher and Willis Rudy, *Higher Education in Transition,* Harper and Brothers, New York, 1958, p. 71.

and to enjoy the privileges of election. Its course of study when it opened for instruction in 1825 was much broader than that which was customary at the time. Secondly, the University of Virginia was by the express intent of its constitution a thoroughly public enterprise, rather than a private or quasi-public one. Finally, its early orientation was distinctly and purposely secular and nondenominational. In all of this, it represented the most thorough going embodiment of the "revolutionary" spirit of the Enlightenment to be found in American higher education during the first decades of the nineteenth century.[2]

Influence of the German universities. It is impossible, even in this brief summary of the development of higher education in the United States, to pass over the influence of the German university on American higher education. Attracted by the freedom and the opportunities there, more than nine thousand Americans studied in German universities between 1815 and 1915, the greatest number of these being there from about 1880 to 1900. Schmidt explains the attraction of the German method to American youth as follows:

At the German universities Americans studied philology and comparative literature, history and philosophy, chemistry and medicine, economics and the new science of psychology. What impressed them most was the freedom of choice and of expression allowed both students and professors, the insistence on rigorous scientific method for the establishment of all facts, and the utter devotion to truth, rationally determined. . . . The lecture, the laboratory and the seminar were the new educational methods that the returning scholars brought with them from Germany and the means by which they hoped to bring American education to maturity.[3]

Many of the students returned from Germany with the Ph.D degree, and these men were in great demand by colleges and universities. By employing the methods of German higher education in their classes they exercised a direct influence on the

[2] *Ibid.,* p. 144.
[3] George P. Schmidt, *The Liberal Arts College,* Rutgers University Press, 1957, pp. 159–160.

methods of American education. Probably the largest single change was the emphasis on a new type of scientific research. Though this influence was felt in most of the larger American universities, Johns Hopkins University, founded in 1875, was based almost entirely on the German pattern, and here the combination of teaching and research was plainly evident. As Abraham Flexner pointed out, "Johns Hopkins made it possible for the first time for the scholar's life in America to be unified. Scholars could now combine teaching and creative research in their own specialized fields." [4]

WOMEN'S COLLEGES

Growth of women's colleges. The beginnings of higher education for women did not take place until nearly two centuries after the founding of Harvard. Indeed, the public tended to hold a deep-seated skepticism about the value of higher education for women. It was feared that such training would raise women above the duties of their "station" and that advanced training would have an adverse effect on their health. They were delicate creatures, so different in mental and physical make-up from men that they would not be able to survive the intellectual efforts that were demanded. Much of the opposition came from men's colleges.

All of our early colleges were men's colleges. Harvard, Yale, Princeton, Columbia, Brown, Rutgers and Dartmouth, among others, still maintain this early characteristic. However, in the intervening years some coordinate women's colleges have been established—Radcliffe at Cambridge (1894), Barnard at Columbia (1889), Pembroke at Brown (1891) and Douglass at Rutgers (1918). Though Yale, Princeton and Dartmouth maintain their male character in entirety, a few others have become coeducational, notably William and Mary and Pennsylvania.

In spite of the strong feeling on the part of many early day

[4] As quoted by Brubacher and Rudy, *op. cit.,* p. 177.

leaders that only men needed a college education, we do find some women's colleges being founded in the first half of the nineteenth century. Wesleyan Female College of Macon, Georgia, established in 1836, was the first college in the country to confer a degree on women. A similar institution, Mary Sharp College for Women in Tennessee, opened in 1852. In the North the first college for women, now known as Rockford College, was chartered in 1847 in Rockford, Illinois; though originally a seminary, it offered a strong liberal college course. The Female Normal Institute and High School in Wisconsin, now Milwaukee Downer College, was chartered in 1851 and given the right to confer degrees. Elmira College in New York, founded in 1853, was the first women's college to offer, from the beginning, a program fairly comparable to that of the men's colleges. The earlier institutions offered a liberal education to women which was quite different from that to be obtained in a men's college.

Before the Civil War the "female colleges" had a difficult time. The age of admission had to be kept low because many girls were unable to obtain secondary education. Standards were likely to be sacrificed in order to attract paying students. Endowments were almost totally lacking. Two things were necessary before colleges for women could become a reality. New and adequate high schools and seminaries were required to give better preparation so that women could actually enter advanced studies, and it was necessary to win the approval of influential people in order to obtain financial support.

The three decades following the Civil War found the argument that higher education was dangerous to women giving place to discussion regarding the kind of education they should receive and whether they should be trained coeducationally or in separate colleges. In the rich, populous northeastern states the pattern established was the superior, but separate, women's college. This pattern not only fitted in with the genteel tradition but was inevitable since the eastern colleges refused to admit women. Matthew Vassar's gift made possible the establishment of Vassar College, the first fully endowed institution for the education of women. Opening for instruction in 1865 at Poughkeepsie, New York, its ample funds helped in maintaining high standards of scholarship which previously had been largely a matter of theory. In 1875 Wellesley College, at Wellesley, Massachusetts, began its career and opened the first scientific laboratories for women. Sophia Smith's will of 1868 set aside endowments for Smith College, which opened in 1875 at Northampton, Massachusetts. Sophia Smith has the distinction of being the first woman to endow a college for her sex. From the very outset Smith provided a course of study almost identical with that of the best men's colleges. Though Wellesley did not require Greek for admission until 1881, the admission requirements of Smith College could be matched with those of Harvard or Amherst. A similar parallelism can be noted for the four years of work at Smith and also at Wellesley. In 1885 Bryn Mawr made its debut and ambitiously sought to offer women opportunities for graduate studies comparable to the best of Harvard or Johns Hopkins.

Throughout the post-Civil War era the number of America's colleges for women showed a slow increase until, by 1901, the United States Bureau of Education listed in its report a total of 119 women's colleges. The figure reached 154 by the middle of the twentieth century. After 1896 the principle of separation in higher education for women received renewed emphasis because of the entry of Roman Catholic institutions into the field of higher education.

Objectives of education for women. Always inherent in the movement for college education for women has been the problem of the proper objectives of such an education. Eighteenth-century thought held that women should be prepared primarily for home duties and should cultivate grace and gentility. With the emergence of the first women's colleges in the nineteenth century, the emphasis shifted to mental discipline and preparation for professional competence, especially teaching. A great deal of importance was placed on religious objectives.

For the most part the women's colleges slavishly followed the programs of the men's colleges. However, after women had demonstrated their ability to pursue the same curriculum as men, a movement was started to provide women's education based on their special needs as shown by follow-up studies of the activities of alumnae of women's colleges. Many persons believed that the women's colleges should attempt to establish their own distinctive type of higher education. The twentieth century brought the emergence of such experimental programs as those at Stephens, Bennington and Sarah Lawrence.[5] The experimental colleges began to formulate objectives which realistically took into account the distinctive role of women in modern American life.

Coeducation. The first American coeducational college made its appearance at Oberlin, Ohio, in 1833. Oberlin was established by a religious group which opened the college doors to women and to the colored race from the very beginning, an unprecedented procedure in the educational history of the English-speaking world. In 1844 three female graduates joined nine male graduates to receive the Bachelor of Arts degree. These were the first American women to earn the degree by the completion of a program of studies identical with that required of male candidates for the same degree.

In the western states and in the newer universities of the East, such as Cornell and Boston University, coeducation gradually became the pattern, and at least a dozen colleges and state universities were offering coeducation before 1860. Coeducation was general in the Midwest, where academic tradition was lacking and where the social influence of women was greater. Here women were active in every movement for cultural upgrading, and they were even beginning to assume political responsibilities. In the frontier areas coeducation was the only answer, and it made education financially possible for both sexes. Regardless of the many arguments against coeducation, the trend was strongly in this direction. By 1870 coeducational colleges outnumbered separate women's institutions twenty times, and by 1900 coeducation had spread to 71.6 per cent of American institutions of higher education.

[5] See Chapter 5 for an account of the programs of these colleges.

What is the future of men's and women's colleges? According to Raymond Walters' figures for 1959–1960, there were about seventy colleges which restricted admission to men and about 160 which restricted it to women. He states: "Of these separate men's and women's colleges, about 60 per cent are under the control of the Roman Catholic Church; some are related to Protestant churches, others are non-denominational colleges of historic antecedents; and a half-dozen women's colleges in the South are state-supported. Coeducation predominantly prevails in American higher education." [6]

It seems likely that if social trends continue in their present direction, most young men and women will be educated together either in coeducational institutions or in coordinate colleges where they are taught for the most part by the same college faculty. A recent newspaper article quoted the president of Vassar College as having predicted that within twenty-five years many of the independent women's colleges will become parts of universities for men, be transformed into coeducational institutions, become units of state universities or be taken over by the government.[7] It seems likely that this prediction will come true for most women's colleges, but probably not for such generously endowed "name" institutions as Mount Holyoke, Smith, Vassar and Wellesley. What is not likely to occur is the founding of a large number of new separate colleges for women, or for men either.

BROADENING THE CURRICULUM

The struggle for electives. We have already noted that there was little change in the curriculum of the American college during the first century of its existence. Much the same could be said for the second century, though during this period there were

[6] Raymond Walters, "Statistics of Attendance in American Universities and Colleges, 1959–60," *School and Society*, 88, January 2, 1960, p. 5.

[7] *The New York Times*, May 16, 1961.

rumblings of discontent about the rigid classical curriculum demanded of all students. The University of Virginia was the first to offer the privilege of election to its students from the beginning. However, in this instance the student had only the right to choose his course of study; within the course chosen all students followed a program of prescribed studies.

During the second quarter of the nineteenth century a few colleges and universities adopted courses "parallel" or optional to the traditional classic one, these consisting usually of modern languages, history and science. However, the institutions involved found that the addition of these courses, particularly those in science which required laboratories, added greatly to the cost of maintaining the colleges, and this was one reason for their lack of success. Another was the rather surprising fact that there was no rush of students to enroll in the new curriculum; rather, the majority shied away from the innovation. From the beginning the movement was strongly opposed by Yale and Princeton, and the Yale Report of 1928 had great influence on American education as a whole in its support of a single curriculum which included a core of knowledge considered essential to the educated man. Another deterrent to the adoption of the elective system was the persistent though often passive opposition of the majority of the college professors. It is difficult today to understand the amount of hostility which many educators felt toward abandoning the required traditional curriculum. According to Brubacher and Rudy, "The central educational battle of nineteenth century America was fought over the elective system. This is the question which aroused the greatest amount of controversy in the academic world, inflamed passions as no other educational issue was able to do, and most clearly reflected the impact of modern technology upon the traditional college." [8]

The most powerful proponent of the elective system and the one who probably did most to turn the tide in its favor was President Eliot of Harvard. Taking office in 1869, he remained as president for forty years, during which time he was able to defeat

[8] Brubacher and Rudy, *op. cit.*, p. 96.

the opposition of the faculty and others to the plan. The system favored by Eliot was a completely elective system with no specification other than the number of credits required for graduation. By 1886, according to Schmidt, "a Harvard undergraduate could earn the A.B. degree by passing any eighteen courses, no two of which need be related." [9] The women's colleges were usually on the side of the elective system, though most of them did not go all the way with it as Harvard did. Schmidt tells us "they were also among the first—Bryn Mawr took the lead here—to initiate the system of group majors which was to become the almost universal pattern of American colleges." [10]

With the retirement of Eliot from the Harvard presidency in 1909 and the election of President Lowell in his place, a similar plan was adopted at Harvard, with the purely elective principle giving way to a combination of required subjects and electives. Freshman and sophomore students were required to choose courses from groups of subjects so that they would know something about many areas of learning. In the junior and senior years the students picked a field of concentration in which they were expected to achieve mastery. Outside this field, however, they were allowed considerable freedom of choice of subjects.

Generally speaking, it is this combination of required and elective subjects that is characteristic of most university and college curriculums today, though there are a few, notably St. John's, which still require that all students take the same prescribed course. At any rate, the controversy which aroused so much feeling in educational circles in the latter part of the nineteenth century seems to be pretty well settled today.

The land-grant colleges. One reason for the struggle against the prescribed classical curriculum was the need felt by many for instruction in farming, manufacturing and other trades requiring training of a technical nature. Along with the demand for a broader curriculum and for some choice of subject matter on the student's part came a movement for business, technical and agri-

[9] George P. Schmidt, *op. cit.*, p. 172.
[10] *Ibid.*, p. 141.

cultural courses. Many members of farm organizations believed that the federal government should establish colleges to give training in these fields. The result of several years of pressure by different groups was the passage of the Morrill Act in 1862, which called for federal aid to agricultural and mechanical colleges. The passage of the act was facilitated by the fact that southern Congressmen, who opposed the bill, had withdrawn from Congress because of the Civil War. The act provided that every state should receive 30,000 acres of public land for each senator and representative in Congress to which it was entitled by the apportionment of 1860. In those states where sufficient public land was not available, land-scrip titles to federal land, salable to private persons, were issued and the proceeds used for educational purposes. At first no other aid was given, and some of the colleges involved found tough going, but in 1890 a second Morrill Act greatly increased federal aid to these institutions.

In addition to providing vocational training, these colleges had a strong democratizing effect on American higher education, for they made it possible for thousands of young people to attend college, who would otherwise have been unable to do so.

PROFESSIONAL EDUCATION

This type of education represented another breaking away from the rigid requirements of the first colleges, though most early education in the professions took place completely apart from them. The apprentice system was the common method of preparation for ministers, doctors and lawyers, and modifications of the apprenticeship plan are still followed in some professions. Formal professional education, which can be little more than mentioned here, began with preparations for theologians in the middle of the eighteenth century. A chair of medicine was established at the University of Pennsylvania in 1765, formal preparation for lawyers began in the post-Revolutionary period, and the first technical institute was founded in 1824. However, while some

professional education was available earlier, as late as the last half
of the nineteenth century the majority of physicians, lawyers and
ministers in the U.S. were receiving little or no formal training
in an institution of higher education.[11]

Perhaps the development of professional education in this country can be better shown by brief sketches of what happened in
four of the professions—medicine, law, engineering and teaching.

Medical education. Early medical education, like most other professional education in this country, consisted largely of apprenticeship training. A would-be doctor became associated with a physician, who gave him instruction and supervised his training in
medical practice in return for such services as cleaning bottles and
instruments, mixing drugs and even taking care of the doctor's
horse. By the middle of the eighteenth century, however, some
classes in anatomy were available. Soon after the establishment of
the first medical school at the University of Pennsylvania in 1765
there were medical schools in New York and at Harvard and
Dartmouth. According to Hofstadter, "The purpose of the early
schools was to combine the features of general education, apprenticeship in medicine and a lecture curriculum in medicine,
combined with attendance at hospital practice." [12]

In the early 1800's many less desirable small proprietary medical
schools were established by individual physicians or groups of
physicians. In these schools the course of study was of only a year's
duration, and there were no laboratory facilities. They were organized chiefly for profit, with the physicians who gave the lectures dividing the income obtained from the students. These
schools not only gave meager training to the students, but also,
because of the competition they furnished, tended to lower the
quality of work required in the better schools.

In 1859 a school in Chicago (which later became Northwestern
University's College of Medicine) introduced a three-year medi-

[11] Earl J. McGrath, *Liberal Education in the Professions,* Bureau of Publications, Teachers College, Columbia University, 1959, p. 28.
[12] Richard Hofstadter and C. De Witt Hardy, *The Development and
Scope of Higher Education in the United States,* Columbia University Press,
New York, 1952, p. 82.

cal course, and other institutions began to raise their standards of medical education. In spite of scattered improvements, however, medical education in America was the subject of intense criticism in 1910 when Dr. Abraham Flexner made a survey of medical education in this country and Canada for the Carnegie Foundation for the Advancement of Teaching. According to McGlothlin, "His scathing denunciation of the medical schools of the time grew out of his revulsion at schools whose programs were limited to transmitting skills instead of scientific knowledge, and which were incapable of attaining even these inadequate ends." [13] Dr. Flexner's report had such far-reaching effects that it is considered a turning point in the professional preparation of physicians. In fact, it caused some of the poorer schools to close up shop entirely. Others undertook to meet the criticisms by inaugurating programs of major reorganization, the result of which was that within a generation American medical schools had reached a position of leadership in the world.

McGrath [14] suggests that there have been five stages of medical education, which are summarized below. Probably most other professional education would fall into similar categories.

(1) The apprentice stage, in which the person aspiring to become a doctor indentured himself to an established practitioner. Apprenticeship was the customary training for physicians until late in the nineteenth century.

(2) The proprietary school stage, in which a number of physicians joined to form a teaching group, levying fees on the students and sharing the proceeds.

(3) The university school stage, in which the medical college was fully integrated into the life of a university, the medical curriculum was extended to four years and admission requirements were raised and standardized. During this stage and simultaneously with the issuance of the Flexner report, the Association of American Medical Colleges laid down as a pre-medic requirement one year of collegiate training.

[13] Wm. J. McGlothlin, *Patterns of Professional Education*, G. P. Putnam's Sons, New York, 1960, p. 11.

[14] Earl J. McGrath, *op. cit.*, pp. 29–33.

(4) The pre-professional requirement stage, during which the medical schools demanded three or four years of college work for admission. This action signalized the recognition among members of the profession that a broad education in the liberal arts and sciences was essential to professional competence. However, this basic education was narrowly limited to subject matter which had a clear professional value.

(5) The general education (today's) stage, in which it is recognized that premedical instruction ought to include subjects not directly related to practice. The prevailing philosophy of medical educators is that the student should gain as broad and liberal an education as possible during the undergraduate years and leave specialization in the scientific fields until he enters medicine.

Law schools. As with medicine and the other professions, the apprenticeship system was used in the training of lawyers up to almost the time of the Civil War. In return for clerical services a student had the opportunity to read the law books in a lawyer's office and to receive guidance from him. After his training was considered to be complete, he took a brief informal examination before being admitted to the bar. This type of training was expanded in some cases into schools of law conducted privately by individual lawyers. Of these the most noted was the law school of Judge Tapping Reeves in Connecticut, which lasted from 1784 to 1833. At the time that this school closed, there were seven law schools in universities, boasting in all about 150 students. The method used was mainly that of studying textbooks on legal principles.

The most important change in the teaching of law occurred at Harvard with the election in 1870 of Christopher Langdell as dean of the law faculty. He believed that the study of law should consist of a careful analysis of leading cases. In 1871 he wrote:

Law, considered as a science, consists of certain principles or doctrines. To have such a mastery of these as to be able to apply them with constant facility and certainty to the ever-tangled skein of human affairs, is what constitutes a true lawyer; and hence to acquire that mastery should be the business of every earnest student of law.

Each of these doctrines has arrived at its present state by slow degrees; in other words, it is a growth, extending in many cases through centuries. This growth is to be traced in the main through a series of cases; and much the shortest and best, if not the only way of mastering the doctrine effectually is by studying the cases in which it is embodied.[15]

The influence of this change in the method of teaching law at Harvard was so marked that it was adopted by an increasing number of schools until, by about 1920, the majority of American law schools were employing the case method of teaching.

In law as in medicine the need for broad, liberal preprofessional training is now being generally recognized, though law schools still receive considerable criticism for the narrow specialization of the prescribed law curriculum. Because of the indispensability of lawyers in government, business men's organizations, labor unions and many other associations, it is necessary that they not only be broadly trained for policy making, but also that they accept a high degree of social responsibility.

Engineering. Prior to the second quarter of the nineteenth century, there was almost no formal training available to engineers. The turning point in this profession came in 1824 when S. V. Rensselaer of northern New York State provided the funds for the Rensselaer Polytechnic Institute, the first genuine technical institute in America. According to Brubacher and Rudy, the founding of this school "signaled the fact that American life was becoming increasingly complex. No longer would simple empirical techniques be sufficient to meet the intricacies propounded by the growing industrialization of the country. The application of science, not just to medicine, but to all phases of life, began to make demands on occupations which could only be met by more formal schooling." [16]

Up until about 1850 Rensselaer and the United States Military Academy at West Point were the only institutions which pro-

---

[15] From "A Selection of Cases on the Law of Contracts," 1871, as quoted by Hofstadter and Hardy, *op. cit.,* p. 74.
[16] Brubacher and Rudy, *op. cit.,* p. 206.

vided graduate engineers. By this time the need for trained men to help in the expansion of railroads and canals intensified the need for more colleges of engineering, as did also the urgency of the need for technically trained men in the armies of the Civil War. Some universities added separate schools of science. The Lawrence Scientific School instituted by Harvard in 1847 was one of these, and Yale's Sheffield Scientific School was begun in the same year. In 1865 one of the most famous technical schools, Massachusetts Institute of Technology, was founded. And in all of the land-grant colleges, up to the beginning of the twentieth century, many more students were enrolled in the mechanical arts and engineering courses than in agriculture.

The proliferation of schools of engineering in this century is still not great enough to provide the trained men required for the complexities of our modern industrial and scientific civilization. Moreover, engineering has been called the most backward of the professions in doing away with narrow specialization and adding liberalizing and socializing courses. M.I.T. is probably leading the way in this movement. According to Hofstadter, "Its administrators have discovered, among other things, that it will be in a better position to hold and invigorate its most distinguished scholars in the physical and mathematical sciences if it builds around them an atmosphere of liberal culture." [17] In 1951 *The New York Times* said in this connection:

Along with this [training for versatility] the university will try to give the engineer more effective means of applying science to the needs of mankind in a practical and economical manner. . . . The object should be to train men who will become leaders in the university, industry or government. These leaders must be able to operate successfully in a society—rendered complex by science—by reason of their sound grasp of scientific subjects; their ability to apply these well; their understanding of the framework of society within which the applications will be made, and their worth as educated men.[18]

[17] Hofstadter and Hardy, *op. cit.,* p. 99.
[18] *The New York Times,* November 4, 1951.

In line with these ideas Harvard, Carnegie Tech and many other colleges of engineering are strengthening their humanistic offerings, but there probably remains a longer way to go in the profession as a whole than in most of the other professions.

Another development which will probably become increasingly important is a shift from an emphasis on detailed techniques to a broad training in principles and methods of applying them to the constantly changing conditions of present-day life. This development is perhaps most marked in engineering, but it is also being noted in other professional fields.

Teaching. The education of teachers, unlike that of physicians and lawyers, did not begin with an apprentice system. It seemed to be assumed that anyone with a smattering of education could teach. In the early days the work was singularly uninviting with poor working conditions, very low salaries, a short term of work, brief teacher tenure and little or no prestige. When the need for courses in pedagogy became generally felt, the subject was studied in the secondary schools and the academies.

The normal school, which came into being largely through the work of Horace Mann and Henry Barnard, was the first great agency for the education of teachers. The first private normal school was established in Concord, Vermont, in 1823, and the first state-supported one in Lexington, Massachusetts, in 1839. However, though the normal schools largely took over the training of teachers, the greater part of their work was still not properly at the level of higher education. Indeed, in Pennsylvania the normal schools often served as the high schools of their communities.

It is interesting to note that the practice of giving teachers intensive training during the summer months began in 1839, when Henry Barnard brought together twenty-six young men and gave them professional instruction for six weeks. He also made it possible for them to observe in the Hartford public schools. There is also the record of a summer school in the 1870's for teachers in Martha's Vineyard, at which Francis W. Parker developed the lectures that were later published as "Talks on Teaching." [19] Another interesting point is that the State of Rhode Island considered teacher training so important that its normal school students were admitted without tuition, and those who lived at some distance from the school were given mileage payments. By 1900 the state-supported normal school had spread into nearly every state.

Departments of education added in colleges and universities were the second development in this country in the preparation of teachers. Indiana University opened a "Normal Department" in 1852, the University of Iowa in 1855 and the University of Wisconsin in 1863. Most of these departments gave training only in elementary education. By 1880 this "Normal Department" phase had largely run its course, and colleges and universities devoted their attention to the professional education of secondary teachers, leaving the preparation of elementary teachers largely to the normal schools.

Gradually the independent normal schools have given way to the teachers' college, generally a four-year college granting degrees, and the university college or school of education. The reasons for the latter, according to the *Encyclopedia of Educational Research,* were that "the University departments needed more freedom than departmental status would permit to determine their curriculums and requirements and especially their practice and experimental facilities." [20]

In the last twenty years large numbers of teachers colleges have become state colleges, and university schools and colleges of education are tending toward becoming graduate schools of education. Thus the education of teachers has progressed from one or two years of normal school education to four years in a college or university, in which on the average approximately 80 per cent of the future teachers' courses are taken in general or liberal education. This phase of the teacher's preparation is larger than many

[19] Walter S. Monroe, Editor, *Encyclopedia of Educational Research,* The Macmillan Company, New York, 1941, p. 1200.
[20] *Ibid.,* p. 1202.

persons suppose. As knowledge continues to explode, teachers need to know more and more in order to teach adequately. In fact, it is probable that four years of liberal education will soon be a requirement for all teachers, though the program of studies may include some pre-teaching courses. Independent liberal arts colleges have always prepared many classroom teachers, and this trend seems likely to continue. Advanced preparation of teachers, including both liberal and professional aspects, is likely to be done at the graduate level.

Professional aspects of liberal education. A point which is frequently overlooked is that the liberal arts themselves frequently serve a professional purpose. In this connection McGrath says,

For all intents and purposes the majors in the several academic departments with their increasingly high degree of concentration within a single discipline, or, more commonly, a narrow subdivision thereof, are professional programs. No less than the programs in engineering, pharmacy and education, they are highly specialized, they stress professional skills, and generally they lead directly to related advanced education or to employment in a specific type of occupation. The majority of students in liberal arts colleges, by the time they choose their major, have as clear a vocational goal as their fellow students in professional schools.[21]

What seems to be developing is a pattern in which liberal arts colleges provide some professional training and the professional schools encourage or require students to take liberal arts courses along with those which develop professional skills.

THE CHURCH-RELATED COLLEGE

As a result of several factors, many colleges which originated under church auspices became independent and prided themselves on being non-sectarian. At present 745 colleges and universities (about 39 per cent) in the United States are still church-related; 490 (about 26 per cent) are independent; and 675 (about 35 per

[21] Earl J. McGrath, *op. cit.,* p. 57.

cent) are tax-supported. The public-supported institutions tend to have larger student bodies, however, with the result that about 58 per cent of the student population in the United States is to be found in colleges and universities under public auspices.[22]

Relationships between colleges and churches. In spite of the fact that a smaller percentage of American young people today attend a church-related college than formerly, this type of school still plays an important role in American higher education. "Church-related" is, however, a somewhat indefinite term which indicates a variety of relationships between churches and colleges. Generally speaking, these schools receive substantial financial support from religious denominations and are in turn partially controlled by them. Sometimes the college is owned outright by a religious body. In many cases the institution is required to have on its governing board some who are members of the religious denomination that furnishes the support. A different sort of tie-up is indicated in the following set of standards for an institution's affiliation with a church which was adopted by the Board of Christian Education of the United Presbyterian Church, U.S.A.:

(1) The college shall adopt a statement of purpose clearly defining its status as a Christian college. The statement of purpose shall be included in the statement of institutional purpose in the official catalog and should furthermore indicate that the college is affiliated with the United Presbyterian Church, U.S.A.

(2) It shall be the declared policy of the college to employ as regular members of the faculty only men and women who are active members in good standing of some evangelical Christian church which affirms its loyalty to Jesus Christ as the divine Lord and Savior. The Board does not rule that this action is to affect faculty members already employed.

(3) The college shall provide courses in Biblical studies and shall require at least one such course for graduation.

[22] These figures were derived from U.S. Department of Health, Education and Welfare, *Higher Education Planning and Management Data,* 1959–1960, Circular #614, U.S. Government Printing Office, Washington, D.C., 1960, p. 4.

(4) The college shall submit annually to the Board of Christian Education complete financial information for the year on forms supplied by the Board and shall have an audit made by a certified public accountant. It is further recommended that the statements contained in the accountant's report shall conform with the accounting principles applicable to institutions of higher education.

(5) The college shall be officially and fully accredited by the regional accrediting agency. If not so accredited, it shall be specifically approved by the Board of Christian Education upon recommendation of an examining committee consisting of the Presbyterian College Union, two other members of the Presbyterian College Union elected by the Nexus Committee of that body, three members of the Board of Christian Education and the Director of the Department of Colleges.[23]

Other protestant denominations have different sets of standards. Roman Catholic colleges are often, if not usually, controlled by the various orders of priests and sisterhoods.

If the college professor cannot subscribe to whatever standards a church-related college requires, he should not accept employment in it. In addition, if he is expected to perform some specific duties related to the church with which the college has a connection, such as leading a young people's group, he should be told of this expectation. Indeed, all terms of employment of this sort should be in writing so that there can be no misunderstanding about them.

Objectives. Those who believe strongly in the blending of religion with higher education feel that these two forces, working together, can help young people achieve integrated personalities in this difficult time, that education helps them to understand the many and diverse forces in American life today and to see where they can best fit into the complicated pattern, while religion provides a set of values with which to measure all experience. To many educators the Christian college is the institution most ideally suited to helping young people achieve this unity and

[23] Adopted by the Board of Christian Education, Presbyterian Church, U.S.A., April 28, 1943.

integration of personality. It should be recognized, however, that many church-related colleges do not accomplish this aim.

Reasons for separation. As has been said, many church-related colleges became independent, non-sectarian institutions. Sometimes this break occurred because the church was too restrictive. It is not uncommon to hear staff members say that the church wants a hundred thousand dollars worth of control while giving only five thousand dollars worth of support. Sometimes it was thought better to cut all denominational ties in order to receive financial support from sources that could not or would not support a specific religious group.[24] Others broke with the church on purely intellectual grounds, among which was the traditional American view that church and state should be kept separate. Obviously, state-controlled institutions in a country that has no state religion have no choice other than to adopt this position. Our country owes much to the religious groups that founded so many institutions of higher learning. However, it seems clear that, since church-related colleges are likely to have a smaller and smaller percentage of the college student population, they must, if they are to be influential in the years to come, be quality institutions in all respects.

THE JUNIOR COLLEGE

Authorities have pointed out that American higher education has created three innovations not found in the institutions of Western Europe. They are the four-year liberal arts college, the two-year community college and the board of control associated with each. Our concern here is with the two-year junior college, which is probably the most robust and rapidly growing development in higher education in America today. In 1947 the Com-

[24] In 1905 the Carnegie Foundation was established "to provide retiring pensions for the teachers of Universities, Colleges and Technical Schools" in the U.S., Canada and Newfoundland. Sectarian colleges were excluded, and a number of them abandoned that status in order to become eligible for the benefits provided.

mission on Higher Education appointed by President Truman estimated that at least 49 per cent of the population had the mental ability to complete fourteen years of schooling with a curriculum that should lead either to gainful employment or to further study.[25] Before many years have passed, the goal of a high school education for every young person will be substantially achieved in all parts of the United States. The objective just cited states a goal for education beyond the secondary period, and if this goal is to be even partially achieved, many young people will need to obtain the first two years of their college work in a junior or community college.

Enrollment. Reliable figures showing enrollments in public and private junior colleges prior to 1915 do not exist, but Bogue stated that in 1914–1915 there were seventy-four such colleges with a total enrollment of 2,363.[26] This figure may be compared with that of 1960–1961, at which time there were 631 institutions, 530 of which reported a combined enrollment of 567,478.[27] Any prospective college teacher who overlooks these institutions may miss a very fine opportunity for employment.

Control of junior colleges. Junior colleges are controlled either by private or public bodies. About three out of five are under public control, and the bulk of the enrollment is in public institutions, with a ratio of eight to one. The private institutions are either church-related or independent colleges. Public junior or community colleges may be controlled by a local school system or by an authority derived from a larger taxing base, such as combined school districts which together control a single community college. Financial aid is provided in a variety of ways. Some colleges are supported by direct state appropriations, some receive

[25] *Higher Education for American Democracy: A Report of the President's Commission on Higher Education,* Vol. I., Harper and Brothers, New York, 1948, p. 67.

[26] Jesse P. Bogue, Editor, *American Junior Colleges,* 3rd ed., American Council on Education, Washington, D.C., 1952, p. 10.

[27] N.E.A. Research Report, *Teacher Supply and Demand in Universities, Colleges and Junior Colleges,* 1959–1960 and 1960–1961, National Education Association, Washington, D.C., May, 1961, p. 7.

state assistance based on average daily attendance and local taxes and some depend wholly on income from local tax sources and from tuition payments.

Early purposes. It is believed that the first junior college was organized in 1902 in Joliet, Illinois. The reasons given for its origin are interesting because they differ in some respects from those ordinarily advanced today. These early reasons were:

(1) The four-year college covered too long a period of a student's life.

(2) Students were graduating from the four-year college at too advanced an age.

(3) There was too much overlapping and duplication between high school and college.

(4) Much of the work of the freshman and sophomore years of college was purely secondary in character.

(5) The reorganization would eliminate duplication and shorten the four-year college course by combining its junior and senior years with those of the graduate school.

The first two of these reasons are not usually mentioned today, and the last three, though still germane, are not stressed.

Functions. The functions of the junior college that are generally recognized today were probably first given in detail by Koos, as follows:

(1) Provision of college credit courses of a kind usually given in the freshman and sophomore years of degree-granting institutions. These programs are sometimes referred to as "transfer-credit" courses because many of the students taking them will expect to enroll for further study in some degree-granting institution after finishing their two years in a community college.

(2) Provision of so-called "terminal" courses for students who do not expect to continue their education more than two years beyond the high school.

(3) Maintenance of a program of adult education, usually on a non-credit basis.

(4) Community services, through staff members with specialized talents.

(5) Guidance services, not only for the person intending to transfer to another college, but also for those intending to enter occupational life immediately, as well as for the adult population interested in the adult education program.[28]

These five functions differ in considerable degree from the original purposes previously cited, and they indicate a wide field of needed service in which a college teacher might well be interested.

The figures given above indicate that the junior college is already absorbing some of the increase in college attendance. However, it seems clear, that as Medsker says, "No unit of American higher education is expected to serve such a diversity of purposes, to provide such a variety of educational instruments, or to distribute students among so many types of educational programs as the junior college." [29]

Problems of the junior college. The junior college has many problems which remain to be solved, some of which will be discussed more adequately in Chapter 3, but which will be only mentioned here.

(1) Who should go to the two-year college? Should the doors be open to all high school graduates, or will there be a means of selective admission?

(2) If all high school graduates are accepted, how can the courses offered be made flexible enough to challenge the student with superior ability without discouraging the person who is ambitious for an education but less able scholastically?

(3) While the terms "junior college" and "community college" have been used interchangeably, which if either term should be

---

[28] Leonard V. Koos, *The Junior College,* University of Minnesota Press, Minneapolis, Minnesota, 1924, pp. 23–24. See also Tyrus Hillway, *The American Two-Year College,* Harper and Brothers, New York, 1958, Chapter 3.

[29] Leland L. Medsker, *The Junior College—Progress and Prospect,* McGraw-Hill Book Company, Inc., New York, 1960, p. 4.

accepted? The designation "terminal" sometimes applied seems unfortunate since many good students are well prepared for further study after completing a "terminal" curriculum.

(4) Is the junior college really a part of secondary education or of higher education?

(5) What can be done to offset the disadvantages resulting from the two-year period of time, which seems to some to be too short to build either adequate traditions or excellence?

(6) How shall the community college be financed? Will the American people be willing to make the community college an extension of the system of tax-free public education, or will the student be expected to bear at least a share of the cost?

(7) Is the junior college plan a better one than increasing the number of extension centers of established universities?

(8) Should the community colleges be part of a state-wide system controlled by the state, or should they remain under local control?

(9) What kind of people are needed as faculty members?

Advantages of the junior college. Despite all these unresolved questions, the public community colleges have a number of advantages. They are economical to attend; tuition fees are usually low or non-existent. They are close to the homes of their students, providing both social and economic values. They are responsive to local needs. Their programs are flexible. Through their adult programs they provide opportunities to older people for continuing education. They are able very quickly to achieve full stature and prestige, as compared with the much longer period necessary for such attainment by a four-year, degree-granting institution.

In the future, the number of places where higher education is available to young people can probably be increased most advantageously by increasing the number of public community colleges. If this proves to be true, these institutions will render an increasingly important service in the development of opportunities for education beyond the high school in the United States.

CHAPTER 3

Issues in
Higher Education

... IF THERE ARE NOT MAJOR CONTROVERSIES GRIPPING
THE ATTENTION OF A SCHOOL, A COLLEGE, OR A BUSI-
NESS, THEN THAT INSTITUTION IS DYING—TRAINING FOR
THE PAST, NOT EDUCATING FOR THE FUTURE.

—*Edgar Dale*

In the brief résumé of the history of higher education
in America given in the previous chapter there were evidences of
difference of opinion concerning some of the issues which arose.
Many of these issues in education are still alive today and will be
discussed in this chapter.

A dual system? The first of these issues relates to the matter of
maintaining a dual system of private and public colleges and
universities. It is generally agreed that, while the individual
college teacher may have good reasons for preferring to work
in one system rather than the other, there is great strength to
education in the United States as a whole in having both kinds.
It was pointed out in the previous chapter that private colleges
were founded as much as 150 years before the first state university
received a charter, and to some extent this priority in founding is
symbolic of what has been a desirable relationship between these
two systems. Partly because they had a head start, but also because private auspices often utilize more imagination and have
greater freedom of operation, the best private colleges have given
others a "bench-mark" against which to measure their efforts.

There is little doubt that such institutions as Harvard University, Columbia, the University of Chicago and Stanford University have provided such a "bench-mark" in each of their respective regions. In the smaller college arena Davidson, Reed, Oberlin,
Lawrence, Swarthmore and Occidental colleges, among others,
have performed a similar service. This is not to deny the fact
that there are many weak small colleges. Indeed, a few are so
weak that they solicit students who have been denied admittance
by state-supported universities. Many of these small colleges have

poorly paid faculties, some of whom are poorly trained. But the important functions of good private colleges are to serve good students who thrive better on a small college campus and to provide such a high quality of instruction that state institutions find it necessary to keep up their standards. Indeed, there has been a widely held belief, if not actual evidence, that small colleges turn out proportionately more excellent scholars than do the larger institutions. It is perhaps difficult to explain why this situation may exist. Are more fine students admitted to the private college? Is the latter able to give the "under achiever" or the "late bloomer" a better chance at a college education? Does the more intimate relationship between student and professor make the difference? Or does the greater freedom of operation in the small college engender greater initiative and maturity in the student?

Let us suppose for a moment that there was only one system of higher education in the United States. If it were publicly supported, might it become politically dominated? Would the scholars be told what they could and could not teach? Certain universities here and abroad had devastating experiences of this sort during the Nazi and McCarthy eras. Would this system of publicly supported higher education be given adequate financing? Under present circumstances public universities compete for funds before legislative bodies with road builders, mental hospitals, welfare agencies and others which also legitimately seek support. Would a single system of higher education intensify this competition because of the greater number of institutions involved?

Or suppose that the single system of higher education was entirely privately supported. Would the cost to the student be so high that many who could profit from higher education could not afford it? Would such a system result in some institutions being fanatically religious and others fanatically dedicated to some particular economic, political or social doctrine? Since an informed citizenry is the *sine qua non* of democracy, can a free country permit all of its higher education to be carried on by private institutions no matter how good they may be? Most educators believe that the dual system now in existence provides checks and balances which benefit both types of institution, and society as well.

Right or privilege? A second issue may be stated in the form of a question: Is college education a right or a privilege? The U.S. Office of Education estimates that, if present predictions come true, 4,360,000 students will be in public colleges by 1970 and 2,236,000 will be in private colleges. Should college doors be open wide to every high school graduate, or should a college education be considered a privilege to be earned, open only to those young people who can benefit themselves and society by advanced study? Most people would probably agree that everyone has the right to pursue education to the full extent of his capabilities. Thus the right to a college education is conditioned, not by purchasing power nor by social class, race or religion, but only by demonstrated ability. The following statement relates this question to the interests of the country: "The ideal goal of a democracy is that every individual realize his full potentialities and live a meaningful and satisfying life." [1]

That this issue is not confined to the United States is shown by information coming from England. There three new universities have been established at Brighton, Norwich and York; three more are to be built at Canterbury, Colchester and Coventry; and another whose location was still being considered at the time of writing will soon be under construction. These new universities have been recommended in England as "the best means of providing places for some of the increased number of students who will be coming forward." [2] Thus Britain seems to have modified a previous long-standing practice of admitting to British universities only those able students for whom there were a limited number of "places"; it will now provide more "places."

We may well ask why a good many young people want to go to college. Some are looking for prestige and status; others to in-

[1] "Is College Education a Right or a Privilege?" a forum discussion conducted by the editors of *Ladies' Home Journal*, October, 1959, Reprint, p. 2.
[2] *Manchester Guardian Weekly*, May 25, 1961, p. 2.

crease their lifetime earnings. Too often such reasons seem to reflect what students believe they see in the attitudes of adults. If they go to college for some other reason than primarily for an intellectual experience, it may be because they fail to see that their elders value such experience. Perhaps also in mass education we have lost much of the significance of what intellect is and what thinking is. Parents and teachers sometimes fail to create in youth the desire to seek knowledge of their own accord or to become independent thinkers instead of mere "repeaters" of the ideas of others.

Who, then, should go to college? Will there be room in our colleges and universities for all normal young people who desire to attend? Is it the place for all who may wish to attend? Should the college be a dumping ground for those who wish to avoid going to work? Should the "lunkheads" be thrown out of colleges? Each of these questions deserves careful consideration.

There are many arguments for providing a college education for all normal young people who wish to attend. (1) This policy would keep young people out of the crowded labor market for a few years; (2) it would provide a measure of social control of young people for four more years; (3) it would help meet the need for more educated people at a time when knowledge is exploding; (4) it would provide more intelligent voters; and (5) it would help in developing human abilities to the highest capacity in our increasingly complex society. It is difficult also to argue that children of some taxpayers may have a college education, while the children of others may not.

We also hear arguments against the policy of a higher education for all who wish it. (1) The shortening of the life "work span" of young people makes it necessary for parents to carry a heavy financial load for a longer time; (2) the nation does not have the facilities or the college teachers to educate all young people through four years of college; (3) such numbers would be involved that a college education would almost inevitably be lowered in quality just when we need to increase its quality to match our competitors in other parts of the world; and (4) continuing adult education after high school is more desirable and practical for some students than a four-year college education.

The telling arguments on both sides of this question may point up the need to establish some priorities. If there are insufficient funds for education at all levels, it would seem that priority should be given to the education of younger children, since so much of one's later achievement depends on the early formative years. Similarly, if there are insufficient funds for all levels of education, adult education must yield to college education. The American people can afford and will pay for whatever quantity and quality of education they believe to be desirable. It should be remembered that in a democracy we have a continuing obligation to upgrade and improve intellectual achievement—not just of the few but of all at every level of ability, since all people eventually share in basic policy-making decisions.

How meet costs? A third issue relates to ways in which the cost of a college education should be met. Should the student pay the full cost, part of it or none of it? Should the public pay the full cost? If not, what part of it? [3] The answers to these questions will vary somewhat depending on whether the student chooses to attend a private or a public college. There have been a number of instances in which the public has paid the expenses of the student, allowing him to attend the college of his choice. The National Youth Administration in the 1930's provided money for a work program in recognized colleges.[4] The G.I. Bill at the end of World War II provided tuition and maintenance for veterans to attend either private or public institutions. New York State has designated public funds to enable winners in state-wide scholarship examinations to go to any college. These funds usually cover tuition and fees only. Also in New York State a bill has been passed appropriating $100 to $800 annually (depending

[3] This issue is fully discussed by John Millett in his chapter on "The Role of Student Charges" in *Financing Higher Education, 1960–70*, McGraw-Hill Book Company, Inc., New York, 1959.

[4] *Recognized* usually meant accredited by a regional accrediting association or licensed by a State Education Department.

on the need) for every young person in the state who attends an institution of higher education in New York State, the money to be paid to him through the college of his choice. In Britain local municipalities set aside a portion of their budgets to enable outstanding local youth to attend a British university. However, though we see that public money has been spent for young people to attend private colleges, the proportion of the expenses provided from some governmental source has been lower in cases of attendance at private colleges than for young people attending public institutions. Part of the reason for this, of course, is the belief in the traditional American doctrine of separation of church and state, since many private colleges are church-related.

But if the student chooses to attend a publicly supported college, what portion of the cost should the public bear? It may be helpful here to review the experience of the lower public schools. It is a little difficult today to realize that the public schools which undergird all higher education have had their struggles. Cubberley [5] designated the seven strategic points in the struggle for free, tax-supported, non-sectarian, state-controlled schools as follows:

(1) The battle for tax support
(2) The battle to eliminate the pauper school idea
(3) The battle to make schools entirely free
(4) The battle to establish state supervision
(5) The battle to eliminate sectarianism
(6) The battle to extend the system upward
(7) Addition of the state university to crown the system

It appears to be agreed in this country that the universal education of youth is essential to the well-being of the state, and to this end school attendance is made compulsory in most states, at least to age sixteen. A second proposition that is generally agreed to is that public elementary and secondary schools shall be free. Public money raised by a general tax may be used to provide education

[5] Ellwood P. Cubberley, *Public Education in the United States*, Rev. ed., Houghton Mifflin Company, Boston, Massachusetts, 1934, pp. 176–177.

as the state requires, and the tax may be general though the school attendance is not. Early legislation on the subject may be found in the Massachusetts Laws of 1642 and 1647 and the Connecticut Law of 1650. While in the northern states final acceptance came by 1850, it was delayed in the southern states by the Civil War and the reconstruction period. The first time that the right of all children to free public education has been challenged in recent times was when the Supreme Court decision of 1954 caused some southern states to threaten to abolish their public school systems.

Thus in the lower schools the battle for tax support and the battle to make elementary and secondary schools entirely free have been won, although in some states parents must pay for textbooks and supplies. What might be the argument for entirely free, tax-supported higher education? (1) One of these is that since human factors are the most important resource the nation has, they should be developed to the fullest capacity. (2) Such an investment would be in the interests of the safety of our country as well as the development of its productivity. Thomas Jefferson once said, "Liberty and learning must each lean on the other for their mutual and surest support." (3) A third argument is that to force the college student to bear the full cost of his education discriminates against the able student with low economic resources. Ability comes from every segment of our society regardless of social class, race, color, creed or economic status, and qualified students should be able to go to college regardless of their ability to pay. (4) Because of endowment funds, scholarship grants and other resources of the private colleges, their students rarely pay the full cost of their college education. Therefore, those who attend public colleges should not be asked to do so.

Some of the arguments against payment of the full cost of higher education by the public are: (1) Except for the amount spent for past and future wars, education costs are already the biggest drain on the tax dollar, and to increase this amount by paying the full cost of a college education for all youth who wish to attend would endanger continued public support for all education. (2) Since the individual will reap a large personal and financial reward from his college work (perhaps as much as $200,000 in a lifetime), he should be willing to pay for it. (3) If the students are required to pay the major share of the cost, the number of those attending college would be reduced and it would be easier to maintain high quality in higher education. (4) Provisions for scholarships and loans to able but needy students would enable them to attend college without saddling the public with the full cost for all students.

There will probably be a great deal of discussion and controversy before this question is finally resolved. It might be more appropriate to state the question this way: How *much* of the cost of a college education should the student pay and how much should the public pay? Probably each should pay something. In public institutions today the student pays roughly one-third of the cost of his education. What is needed is a realistic appraisal of the portion each can and should pay to secure the largest development of the nation's human resources for the good of the person and of society.

What shall constitute the college curriculum? This important issue has many parts to it. There are three substantive parts in a college—the students, the faculty and the program. Although buildings and administration, including finances, are important, these factors cannot assure excellence unless there is high quality in the other three. Thus the following discussion of some of the factors involved in formulating the curriculum points up some of the most crucial issues facing the American college today.

Liberal education a preparation for advanced studies? The first of these relates to whether American college education should be primarily directed toward preparation for advanced studies or chiefly concerned with the value of its own courses regardless of the future academic career of the student. In the first years of this century it may have been less difficult to answer this question when, out of 5,900,000 college-age students, only 237,600 went to college, 27,400 obtained the bachelor's degree and 5,800 attended graduate school, of whom 1,600 obtained the master's degree and 250 the doctorate.[6] A determination to serve the majority would have caused the American college at that time to be primarily concerned with the value of its own courses without reference to advanced work in the fields covered. Berelson says, however, "Since 1950 graduate enrollment has grown faster than the undergraduate, and doctoral enrollment has grown faster than total graduate enrollment at all types of institutions." [7] In spite of this great increase in numbers, however, as late as 1958 only a relatively small percentage of our young people were taking graduate work in universities. At that time only 7.2 per cent of the 22–24 age group were enrolled in graduate courses and only 3.2 per cent of the 25–34 age group.

Some of those who feel that the aim of all liberal arts education in the early college years should be preparation for advanced work argue (1) that the people of the United States are living in an age of specialization; (2) that our country is engaged in a contest with a considerable portion of the world for the solution of scientific, military, agricultural, political, economic, racial and other problems; and (3) that the nation with the best developed specialized knowledge in these fields will be able to do the most to keep the peace of the world and bring the comforts and security of life, including education, to all people. Hence the goal of the American college should be, it is argued, not the intrinsic value of courses but preparation for advanced studies.

Nevertheless, a realistic assessment of the trends suggests that, even though the number of young people who pursue advanced degrees is growing, the percentage is still relatively small, and college courses, therefore, must have intrinsic values of their own, apart from preparation for specialization. It may be, as will be noted later, that these two purposes of the college curriculum are not necessarily antithetical.

Academic specialization or liberal education? Another curriculum issue which is somewhat similar to the one just considered

---

[6] Bernard Berelson, *Graduate Education in the United States,* McGraw-Hill Book Company, Inc., New York, 1960, p. 26.
[7] *Ibid.,* p. 101.

raises the question of whether college education should be oriented primarily to academic specialization or be restricted to liberal education. This issue is probably one of the most controversial in liberal arts colleges at the present time. The young college professor, fresh from his highly specialized doctoral program, quite naturally desires as quickly as possible to teach his specialty, and if he does not wish to do this, he should not have been employed. But if he insists on teaching only in his narrow special field to the exclusion of some of the beginning courses which contribute most to liberal education, he has lost his perspective. This narrow interest is the effect of too much of advanced work in both English and American education.

Indeed, it has been charged that highly trained specialists in the humanities are often unable even to discuss their ideas with highly trained scientists. Their vocabularies and interests are so different as to make communication impossible. A talented electrical engineer and inventor was once asked his idea of a liberal education. His answer was, "It's what I haven't got." C. P. Snow, noted English novelist, discusses this situation in his little volume, *The Two Cultures and the Scientific Revolution*. He says, "Constantly I felt I was moving among two groups [scientists and writers] comparable in intelligence, identical in race, not grossly different in social origin, earning about the same incomes, who had almost ceased to communicate at all." [8] Is there not the possibility of real danger in a democratic society when free men who must decide important issues are unable to understand or even to converse with one another?

Moreover, it is the product of our graduate schools who teach in the American college, and it is not always clear that they apprehend their special field in perspective. Indeed, it is not uncommon for professors in the natural and physical sciences to fail to appreciate the work of their colleagues in the humanities and the arts and vice versa. Social scientists, too, preoccupied with their own fields, frequently fail to perceive the contributions of

[8] C. P. Snow, *The Two Cultures and the Scientific Revolution,* Cambridge University Press, New York, 1959, p. 2.

their associates in the sciences and the humanities. This situation is not likely to be corrected until a continuing strand of liberal education is found in every program of advanced study, thus keeping specialism constantly in touch with it. This remedy may not assure that specialized knowledge will be seen in its appropriate relationship to all knowledge, but it will at least afford the opportunity for some integration of knowledge. Many years ago when Woodrow Wilson was a college professor, he wrote:

The separation of general and special training is an acute sympton of the disease by which we are now so sorely afflicted. . . . Knowledge must be kept together. . . . The liberal education that our professional men get must not only be antecedent to their technical training; it must also be concurrent with it. No more serious mistake was ever made than the divorce of technical or practical education from theoretical.[9]

A study published in 1959 seems to indicate that representatives of professional and technical faculties react favorably toward the general views expressed so long ago by Wilson, but that when these same individuals were questioned specifically about the matter, "they showed a strong inclination toward requiring those courses [in liberal arts and sciences] which have a direct relevance for the vocational field." [10]

If Virgil Hancher's idea could be carried out, this issue could be more easily resolved. He says:

We forget that it is possible to become liberally educated by the teaching and the study of professional or specialized subjects in a liberal manner. It is nearer the truth to say that there is no subject matter worthy of a place in the curriculum of a modern Land-Grant

[9] Woodrow Wilson, "Should an Antecedent Liberal Education Be Required of Students in Law, Medicine and Theology?" *Proceedings* of the International Congress of Education, 2nd ed., World's Columbian Exposition, Chicago, 1893, pp. 116–117.

[10] Paul L. Dressel, Lewis B. Mayhew and Earl J. McGrath, *The Liberal Arts as Viewed by Faculty Members in Professional Schools,* Bureau of Publications, Teachers College, Columbia University, New York, 1959, p. 39.

college or state university which cannot be taught either as a professional specialty or as a liberal subject.[11]

However, since most professional courses are not taught in a liberal manner, this point of view is probably not too helpful at the present time. Probably, as suggested in Chapter 2, the solution lies in the inclusion of truly liberalizing courses in all technical and professional education.

A common curriculum or differentiated offerings? In the light of these considerations another question presents itself. Should collegiate education provide a common curriculum for all or differentiated offerings? The struggle to make part of the curriculum elective was discussed in Chapter 2. There are, however, some good arguments for the common curriculum. Society has a stake in making certain not only that good citizenship is cultivated, but that leadership is developed. In today's world, people need to know something about science, our cultural heritage and effective use of the English language. Only by requiring that all students follow the same curriculum can we be sure that no important understandings and skills are neglected. Moreover, many fields of learning are so technically specialized that students who devote themselves exclusively to them not only miss out on the general background we expect of all educated people, but, as previously indicated, actually find it difficult to communicate with one another.

The most telling argument against the fixed course of study is that it ignores the facts about individual differences of students in interests, attitudes, aptitudes, abilities and goals. With the larger college enrollments, it seems likely that the range of differences among students will widen. If the quality of instruction in higher education is not to deteriorate, provision must be made for this enlarged range of interests and abilities. We must

[11] Virgil M. Hancher, "Liberal Education in a Professional Curricula," *Proceedings* of the 67th Annual Convention of the American Association of Land Grant Colleges and State Universities, Columbus, Ohio, November 10–12, 1953, p. 50.

remember also that there are objectives which rank higher in importance than those to be achieved by the common curriculum. The fundamental outcomes to be sought are that students (1) learn to draw conclusions only from sufficient facts and after weighing the evidence, (2) develop a sound set of values against which to judge the work of a project or an idea and (3) learn to think and act creatively.

Perhaps a satisfactory compromise between the common curriculum and the elective system could be reached if during the first two years of their college work students were required to take about two-thirds of their courses in a common curriculum designed for the purpose of general education, leaving them free to choose, under some guidance, one-third of their work. The last two years might well contain a continuing strand of general education with the major portion devoted to major and minor fields of concentration.

Vocational training or general education? Closely related to the previous discussion is the question of giving technical and vocational training in college. It must be recognized that the majority of college students wish to study something "practical" as early as possible, something related to their proposed work in life. Indeed, students are often heard to ask, "What good will this course do me?" Many face the predicament of the student who was heard to remark shortly after graduation from a liberal arts college that he had been prepared "to do nothing." It was probably as a result of the situation illustrated by this statement that since about 1875 the four-year, independent liberal arts colleges have included in their curricula an increasing number of professional courses.

The answer to the question of whether or not to include vocational training in a college course probably depends on the answer to one which has already been discussed, "Who should go to college?" One important factor must be taken into account in deciding this issue. It is said that 60 per cent of the population is not equipped to deal with abstract ideas, that 25 per cent can deal with the abstract only if ample illustrations are offered and only 15 per cent with abstract ideas as such.[12] Since true liberal arts courses deal mainly with ideas, vocational training would need to be a part of the curriculum if all or even the majority of young people are to have a higher education. Then, too, while general education for becoming a good citizen, neighbor and parent is important, everyone ultimately must earn a living. This requirement involves vocational training from the semitechnical and technical to the achievement of the highest competence in a profession. However, with the complexity and constant change in business and industry today, it is frequently found that apprenticeship, internship and on-the-job training are more effective in many fields of work than is vocational training in college.

Many educators are opposed to vocational training in college because they believe that it is dangerous to study to be a specialist before one has become a generalist. This view is based essentially on the belief that any specialization must be seen in a larger setting lest it get out of perspective or balance. Moreover, many argue that colleges should not teach what can be learned elsewhere. It is extremely important for collegiate institutions to devote themselves to the extension of knowledge, to its dissemination, and to insuring the effective utilization of it. Perhaps the most important and, in the long run, the most practical thing of all that a college can do, next to helping the student develop the ability to think, is to develop new theories.

It seems certain that some liberal arts colleges, in their desire to attract students, have yielded too much to the pressure to install skill courses in such subjects as secretarial studies, commercial or business studies, laboratory techniques and occupational therapy. On the other hand, to say that nothing of practical value should be offered in college would be going too far in the other direction. The important thing is to make certain that every college student receives a foundation in the liberalizing,

[12] See chart and discussion in James W. Thornton, Jr., *The Community Junior College,* John Wiley and Sons, Inc., New York, 1960, pp. 11–14.

general education courses before going on to specialization in either the academic or vocational fields.

Role of the federal government. A fifth issue relates to the role to be played by the federal government in providing financial support for American colleges and universities. Many people are not aware that the government has been giving support to institutions of higher education in one form or another since 1787. This was the date of the Northwest Ordinance which declared, "Religion, morality and knowledge being necessary to good government and the happiness of mankind, schools and the means of education shall forever be encouraged." One of the early grants of money for higher education was made in 1802 to the newly admitted state of Ohio, which received a very large amount of land to be sold for this purpose. A similar grant was made to each new state as it joined the Union. Since 1862 and 1890, the dates of the Morrill Acts, the federal government has supplied large sums for the purpose of improving agricultural and mechanical products and processes. It has given direct financial support and exercised substantial control over schools for the Indians. Howard University, a Negro institution in Washington, D.C., is also included in the federal budget. Perhaps the largest single involvement of the federal government in higher education was the payment of the educational expenses for a vast number of veterans after World War II and the Korean War. The question, therefore, is not whether we should have federal aid to higher education—we have it. The question is whether such aid should be extended.

Those who believe that it should be extended argue that since the federal government collects most of the taxes, it is the governmental body most able to pay the bills. When the amount required for all educational expenses—local, state and national—exceeds all other costs of government except the amount required for past and future wars, perhaps the case for financial support by the federal government is a strong one. Another argument is that because states vary in their financial capacity to pay for higher education, the federal government must serve as an equalizing agent. It is well known that the State of Mississippi, for example, is less able to pay for higher education than California or New York, even though the citizens of Mississippi are putting forth greater effort financially than any of the richer states. Should the young people of any state be denied an adequate higher education because of their place of birth? Besides, the increasing mobility of the population means that many such young people will move to another part of the country, where they will be handicapped because of having received a less adequate education than the native residents. Even if they do not move, their vote in national elections counts just as much as that of the best educated citizens.

The matter of whether or not there should be federal aid to higher education is immensely complicated by the question, should federal aid be given to private institutions? As was indicated earlier in the chapter, the Legislature of the State of New York has approved a recommendation that Empire State funds, at the rate of $100 to $800 per student, be given to the students through the colleges chosen by those applying at and admitted to accredited collegiate institutions in New York State. However, New York State is a special case because private colleges in that state took care of most of the need for higher education for many years, and only in the last fifteen years has there been a state university system. Therefore, such a precedent will have little influence on the rest of the nation.

Those who favor federal financial aid for private, independent and church-related colleges believe that since parents pay taxes to the federal government, their children should share in any benefits and not be penalized if they choose to attend a sectarian institution.

The opponents to federal aid for higher education oppose giving any funds, some of which will ultimately wind up in private or church-related institutions. They believe that this action would violate the traditional and widespread belief in separation of church and state in this country. Next they argue that federal aid to education will lead to federal control, and they cite the disastrous examples of Fascist Italy, Nazi Germany and Communist Russia, whose governments controlled all of education and the truth was often not allowed either to be known or taught. Some educators who fear federal control favor federal aid for construction of college dormitories and classrooms but not for teachers' salaries, while others insist that any federal aid of whatever sort would open the door to the total control of the colleges and universities in this country by the national government.

If the dangers are as great as some opponents insist, federal aid should indeed be resisted. However, in view of the history of the federal government's participation in higher education, which has extended over a century, they do not seem to many educators to be as great as the danger of failing to develop a high quality system of higher education in this country. Local communities, the states and the federal government must work together in this enterprise. Also there is a safeguard which a democratic people have, a safeguard which was not possessed by the people in Nazi Germany and Fascist Italy. This is the secret ballot by which those in power may be "kicked out" if the citizens do not like what is being done.

The American college an instrument of public policy? A sixth issue concerns the extent to which American collegiate institutions should be used as instruments of public policy. A few examples will illustrate this issue. In the 1860's the Union forces were in need of armaments for prosecuting the war and of agricultural products to feed the troops. One of the purposes of the Agricultural and Mechanical Arts institutions established under the Morrill Act was to provide trained personnel which would assist in meeting these urgent needs of the federal government.

After World War II it was necessary to demobilize a vast army slowly enough to prevent the necessity for veterans to engage in such activities as selling apples on the Main Streets of our cities, as they were forced to do after World War I. This desire to slow the return of veterans to civilian employment was one of the reasons for the passage of GI Bill number 346 and of a similar bill following the Korean War. In these instances the federal government made use of institutions of higher education to implement national policy. The success of the G.I. Bill made new allies for education and thus was partly responsible for some of our current college problems. Fathers and mothers, having attended college and enjoyed and profited by it (their records were better than those of the average student) naturally wanted their children to have the same experience, and as these veterans produced the birth rate bulge, the number of students wishing to attend college was greatly increased. More than this, higher education is now frequently thought of as a means of recruiting personnel for government, research and science. It also helps in the achievement of a high level of business efficiency by providing educated personnel.

The real question here is how far education can be used as an instrument of national policy and still remain primarily an educational system. Is there any doubt that for the past three decades Russian education has been a direct instrument of national policy? Has it not had a heavy overlay of Marxist indoctrination, and has not the general independence of judgment encouraged in other European countries been stifled? In such a system educators are not observers—they are participants. If higher education becomes almost solely an instrument of national policy, what will be the effect upon the freedom of the mind?

The resolution of this question is not easy. Certainly in times of emergency all social institutions must aid the government in whatever ways they can, but we might ask whether higher educational institutions should continue to be used beyond the period of the emergency. This is a question which will probably be of increasing importance in the years ahead.

Academic freedom and tenure. Academic freedom, the seventh issue, will be discussed at some length because of its tremendous importance for the college teacher and his students. In January, 1915, a few months after the beginning of World War I, an organizational meeting was held to form the American Association of University Professors. At this time a Committee on Academic Freedom and Tenure was appointed, which included members of a joint committee, previously appointed, representing the American Economic Association, the American Political Science Association and the American Sociological Society. The committee made a study of the problems of academic freedom as a whole and prepared a general report which was adopted and became known as the 1915 Declaration of Principles. During the first year eleven cases of alleged infringement of academic freedom and tenure were considered. These included the dismissal of individual professors, the dismissal or resignation of groups of professors, the dismissal of a university president, and the complaint of a university president against the board of trustees.

The 1915 statement named three goals to be accomplished: (1) to safeguard freedom of inquiry and teaching, (2) to protect college executives and governing boards, and (3) to render the profession more attractive by insuring its dignity, independence and security of tenure. To achieve these goals the 1915 statement proposed four courses of action: (1) action by faculty committees on reappointments, (2) definition of tenure for each rank, (3) formulation of grounds for dismissal and (4) a provision for a judicial hearing before dismissal.

This 1915 statement was superseded by a 1925 Statement of Principles resulting from a conference called by the American Council on Education. The 1925 Conference Statement on Academic Freedom and Tenure, later endorsed by the Association of American Colleges and the American Association of University Professors, was more precise than the previous one, but it stated its points negatively—"a university may not" or "a college professor may not." While the earlier statement had listed freedom of inquiry and research as an essential element of academic freedom, it had included the statement that this freedom "is almost everywhere so safeguarded that the dangers of its infringement are slight." By 1925, however, it had become clear that freedom of inquiry must be dealt with. Consequently the 1925 Conference Statement contained the following negatively stated principle: "A university or college may not place any restraint upon the teacher's freedom in investigation, unless restriction upon the

amount of time devoted to it becomes necessary in order to prevent undue interference with teaching duties."

In 1940 a third Statement of Principles [13] was agreed upon and
endorsed by the American Association of Colleges, the American
Association of University Professors and the Association of American Law Schools. In this statement, which is currently in force,
principles are stated positively. It includes an item on freedom
in publication of results of research and adds a provision relating
to research for pecuniary returns. The probationary period for
academic tenure is reduced from ten to seven years, and there is
a provision for a carry-over in case of a change of positions. More
precise provisions for a judicial hearing are spelled out, including
the right of the college teacher, against whom charges have been
filed, to have an adviser or counsel and to have a full stenographic
record of the hearing.

The preamble to the 1940 statement contains the following two
paragraphs:

The purpose of this statement is to promote public understanding
and support of academic freedom and tenure and agreement upon
procedures to assure them in colleges and universities. Institutions of
higher education are conducted for the common good and not to
further the interests of either the individual teacher [14] or the institution as a whole. The common good depends upon the free search for
truth and its free exposition.

Academic freedom is essential to these purposes and applies to both
teaching and research. Freedom in research is fundamental to the
advancement of truth. Academic freedom in its teaching aspect is
fundamental for the protection of the rights of the teacher in teaching
and of the student to freedom in learning. It carries with it duties
correlative with rights.[15]

[13] A shortened version of this statement is printed in the *Appendix*.
[14] The word "teacher" as used in this document is understood to include
the investigator who is attached to an academic institution without teaching duties.
[15] "Academic Freedom and Tenure," *A.A.U.P. Bulletin*, Vol. 33, Spring,
1947, p. 74.

However clear it may seem to the academic profession, academic freedom is not understood completely by the general public. American education has been criticized in certain quarters because captured American soldiers have been "brain washed" and have, it is alleged, admitted certain weaknesses in American democracy and later espoused Russian communism. Yet during the late forties and early fifties American teachers in their classrooms did not feel free to examine critically and dispassionately the merits and weaknesses of both systems. They did not feel free to do so because certain senators and congressmen intimidated witnesses before their committees. Such tactics tended to curtail the full pursuit of freedom to learn and freedom to teach. At an earlier period two professors were dismissed from a university because they reported an investigation, the results of which were critical of the economic interests represented on the Board of Trustees.

These are only two of many instances of the failure on the part of the public to understand that academic freedom to teach and to investigate is central to the purpose of all higher education. If the college teachers in the iron curtain countries had true academic freedom, it is unlikely that the iron and bamboo curtains would exist many more years.

Correlative with academic freedom is academic tenure, and each is dependent on the other. There is no freedom for a college teacher if after he earnestly teaches what he believes to be true, he is dismissed from his post because the administration, represented either by the president or the board of trustees, disagrees with him. Yet there are board members who say, "Tenure! why, I don't have any tenure. Why should faculty members have it?" Tenure not only supports academic freedom; it is a bulwark against political influences. Without it, theoretically at least, many faculty members could be displaced at each election time. Insecurity of tenure causes bad morale and is detrimental both to the educational institution and to the students who attend it. Granted that some persons achieve tenure who should not do so, abolishing tenure is not the remedy. Rather, the remedy lies in careful selection at appointment time and careful evaluation during the probationary period. If these two screens are not effective, the A.A.U.P. Statement of Principles contains provisions for filing charges against and dismissing the offending or incompetent party.

If education is one of the cornerstones of the structure of a democratic society, if progress in human relations, in science, in literature and in the professions is essential to civilization, then men and women of the highest ability, of broad and deep learning, and of strong character and independent spirit should be attracted to the profession. Since salaries alone are not sufficient to accomplish this aim, an honorable, secure position and freedom to perform their functions honestly are important to such men and women.

Accreditation. Should American colleges be evaluated by accrediting processes? This final issue is one which concerns educators today. There are three types of accrediting of colleges and universities: accrediting by the state, accrediting by regional associations and accrediting by professional associations.

State accrediting. The charters granted by the state to colleges and universities are in themselves a form of accreditation. Such charters grant the legal authority to institutions to offer collegiate instruction leading to qualification for degrees.

Accrediting by regional associations. An excellent treatment of the struggle for control over standards is given by Selden in his book, *Accreditation*,[16] in which he explains the historical antecedents leading up to the present situation. In the 1870's, 1880's and 1890's the lack of any agreement among colleges concerning their entrance requirements made it necessary for high schools to prepare their students for many separate college examinations, no two of which were likely to be based on the same syllabus. The resultant confusion led to the formation of the New England Association of Colleges and Secondary Schools in 1884 and the

[16] William K. Selden, *Accreditation*, Harper and Brothers, New York, 1960.

North Central Association of Colleges and Secondary Schools in 1895. Later the Middle States Association, the Southern Association, the Northwest Association and the Western College Association, all now known as regional associations, were formed. Though the original reason for their founding was to obtain agreement on college admission standards, their function has been broadened and one of their main purposes today is the accreditation of high schools and colleges.

When it is time for a college to be accredited or to have its accreditation renewed, a team or committee of visitors, consisting usually of educators from several accredited institutions, visits the college, usually for a two- or three-day period, depending on the size of the institution. In former times such teams applied standards to the institutions which were largely quantitative. Such questions would be asked as: what are the standards for admission? how many volumes are there in the library? how many Ph.D.'s are on the faculty? how much endowment has the college? what is the value of the physical plant of the college? Today in one of the largest regional associations, the North Central Association of Colleges and Secondary Schools, the procedure is quite different. Visiting teams inquire into the institution's own goals and relate the accrediting process to them. Answers are sought to such questions as the following:

(1) Is the educational task of the institution clearly defined?

(2) Are the necessary resources available for carrying out the educational task of the institution—financial resources, physical plant, faculty resources, library resources?

(3) Is the institution well organized for carrying out its educational task—board of trustees, president, dean and faculty?

(4) Are the curriculum and instructional programs adapted to the goals of the institution?

(5) Are conditions of faculty service likely to promote high morale—faculty offices, fringe benefits, tenure, salaries, teaching loads (including the number of preparations, the number of hours of teaching and the size of classes)?

(6) Is student life on the campus well balanced and educationally meaningful? Is there a student personnel program which includes freshman orientation, health service, loan funds, placement office and extracurricular activities, including athletics?

(7) Is the level of achievement of students consistent with the goals of the institution? Is there academic testing of freshmen and sophomores? What is the drop-out rate? How do students rate on the Graduate Record Examination?

In small institutions visiting committees are likely to explore these questions as a total team, but in larger ones the team is divided into smaller groups, each of which agrees to explore one or two of the questions. The final report, however, is agreed upon by all. Most visiting teams are careful to check with the institution regarding the factual part of their report before it is submitted to the accrediting association. This practice tends to insure that any recommendations made by the team have a sound basis in fact. The trend in such accreditation today seems to be in the direction of stimulating boards, administrators and faculties to improve what they are doing.

Accrediting by professional associations. While the regional associations were developing patterns for institutional accreditation, associations of schools giving professional training began developing patterns for accrediting such schools as colleges of commerce, schools of music and teachers' colleges. This type of accrediting was either supplanted or followed by professional associations setting up such agencies as the Council on Medical Education, Council on Dental Education, Council on Nursing Education, Engineering Council on Professional Development and the National Council on Accreditation in Teacher Education, to name only a few of the many councils of this kind.

The multiplication of these external agencies operating on individual institutions began to bring protests. C. H. Marvin wrote, "Colleges and universities cannot function as trusted, free institutions of higher learning unless their faculties and administrations representing them are kept from interference by standardizing organizations." [17] And a few years earlier Capen had laid down an outright challenge to accrediting agencies:

The issue is plain. Is the American university system to be dominated by competitive blackmail, or is it to be conducted in accordance with the best judgment of the boards and administrative officers charged with this responsibility through charters and through legislative enactments? The American universities gave the standardizing agencies license to live. Whenever the leaders of the universities are ready to unite in the decision that these agencies shall live no longer, they will disappear. I think that day approaches.[18]

The National Commission on Accrediting. In 1949 the National Commission on Accrediting was formed by the presidents of the land-grant colleges, the liberal arts colleges, state universities, private universities and urban universities. Chairman Reuben G. Gustavson of this National Commission explained that the reason for the formation of the Commission was to find ways and means of dealing with a large number of accrediting agencies which were having a powerful impact on educational policies.[19] Five years later Ewald B. Nyquist, Deputy Commissioner of Education for New York State, reported on the achievements of this National Commission on Accrediting.

It has stimulated all accrediting agencies to examine their purposes and objectives. It certainly has reduced abuses in accrediting. It has contained accreditation and confined it to certain limits and agencies. It has provided accrediting at large with a definite purpose and objec-

[17] C. H. Marvin, "National Commission on Accrediting," *Bulletin*, Association of American Colleges, No. 36, March, 1950, pp. 53–54.

[18] Samuel P. Capen, "Seven Devils in Exchange for One," *Coordination of Accrediting Activities*, American Council on Education Studies, Series 1, Vol. 3, No. 9, American Council on Education, Washington, D.C., 1939, pp. 16–17.

[19] Reuben G. Gustavson, "An Introduction and a History of the Relationship of University and College Organizations to Accrediting Agencies," *Excerpts from Addresses*, National Commission on Accrediting, Washington, D.C., January 8, 1952.

tives which accrediting did not have before. It has, in effect, provided a firm basis for the national development of accrediting activity.[20]

No college teacher can afford to be unaware of the possibilities of accrediting, for good or ill. The showdown predicted by Capen has been either postponed or eliminated, but will accrediting, in fact, interfere with the free functioning of institutions of higher learning? Will standards of collegiate work be better maintained and raised to a higher level with regional accrediting or without it, with accrediting by profession or by discipline or without it? In the light of a rising college population which may increase both the number and size of institutions, is accrediting a necessary safeguard of quality? In the face of exploding knowledge and a new technology to facilitate learning, will the instrument of accreditation be more helpful than harmful?

Summary. These then are the issues which confront higher education today: Shall there be a dual system of public and private colleges and universities? Is college education a right or a privilege, and who should go to college? How shall the costs of college education be met? Shall there be a common curriculum or differentiated offerings? Shall college education include vocational training or be restricted to general education? Shall it be oriented to specialization or restricted to liberal education? Shall it be primarily directed toward preparation for advanced studies or concerned primarily with the inherent value of its own courses? What role should be played by the federal government in financing higher education? To what extent should the American college be used as an instrument of public policy? Why are academic freedom and tenure so important to the college professor? Should American colleges be evaluated by accrediting processes?

Each of these is a vital issue on which the college teacher must make up his mind. On many of them he can probably take no firm stand until he has added experience to his thinking; others will be more easily resolved. The important thing is that he come

[20] Ewald B. Nyquist, "National and Regional Development in Cooperative Evaluation and Accrediting Activity," *Journal of Engineering Education,* 44, May, 1954, pp. 533–538.

to his own decision on each issue. The way in which these issues are finally resolved will play a large part in the direction of his profession, higher education, in the future. They are worthy of his best thought. There will be additional discussion on some of these issues in the chapters that follow.

CHAPTER 4

The
Academic Program
of the College

I THEREFORE CALL THAT A COMPLETE AND GENEROUS
EDUCATION WHICH FITS A MAN TO PERFORM JUSTLY
AND MAGNANIMOUSLY ALL OF THE DUTIES, BOTH
PUBLIC AND PRIVATE, OF PEACE AND WAR.
—*John Milton*

The American college has many facets. It is a community in itself, with campus and grounds, classroom buildings and dormitories, library, power and heating units, food service, laundry and book store. Then, too, it has a recruiting staff, an admissions office and a personal counseling staff, an academic staff, secretaries, building engineers, grounds keepers, dietitians, chefs, gardeners, coaches, trainers and the like. A college has an extracurricular program which may consist of intramural sports, clubs, dramatic organizations, band, orchestra, a capella choir and men's and women's glee clubs. There is also intercollegiate competition in such major sports as football and basketball and in the minor sports of baseball, track, swimming, golf, tennis, hockey, fencing and lacrosse. Intercollegiate competition is found also in intellectual activities, such as oratorical and extemporaneous speaking contests and in debating, to say nothing of college quiz bowls and talent competitions. But the heart of the collegiate institution consists of the students, the faculty and the academic program. Furthermore, it is the faculty that in the last analysis controls the curriculum of the college, and it is for this reason that the curriculum is to be considered here.

PURPOSES

In midyear 1960 a national magazine printed an advertisement which asked the question. "Where do great ideas come from?" It answered its own question as follows:

89

From its beginnings this nation has been guided by great ideas. The men who hammered out the Constitution and the Bill of Rights were thinkers—men of vision—the best educated men of their day. And every major advance in our civilization since that time has come from minds equipped by education to create great ideas and put them into action.

So, at the very core of our progress is the college classroom. It is there that the imagination of young men and women gains the intellectual discipline that turns it to useful thinking. It is there that the great ideas of the future will be born.[1]

This is a good statement of the importance of the central task of a collegiate institution. In a previous chapter it was noted that the aim of the early colonial colleges was to educate ministers and some of the well-to-do. This aim, though not antithetical to the ones stated in the advertisement, has been greatly broadened, and the ways in which the aims of higher education are achieved today differ quite sharply from those of a century or more ago.

If someone who was quite unfamiliar with today's colleges were to survey the present collegiate scene, what might he deduce to be the purpose of those who attend colleges today? If he were to make a judgment on the occasion of a football or basketball game in a stadium or field house, might he not conclude that one purpose of the existence of a college is to entertain twenty thousand or more alumni, students and citizens at an athletic event? If he visited the plush dormitories and houses on many of our university campuses, might he decide that colleges exist to provide a sort of club for sophisticated young people who live an easy life sprayed with a veneer of so-called education? If he mixed with young people on some campuses, he would find that a respectable class grade was "the gentleman's C," and that if a mark of "A" were to have been received, this would be all right providing the student had not made an obvious effort to achieve it. Of course, such small aims are fortunately not truly representative of American college students. What are the real purposes of a college?

General aims of a college. In general, these may be said today

[1] *The Saturday Review*, July 16, 1960, p. 85.

to be three. A college exists to serve society, to perpetuate itself and to serve the individual. The advertisement cited at the beginning of this chapter indicated that colleges exist to serve the nation. They do this in many ways, both directly and indirectly. Their service to individuals helps the individual to serve society better; but they also serve the larger whole directly. In addition to their regular teaching function, scientific departments take on government projects. Medical schools constantly engage in research to conquer man's physical ailments, to improve physical and mental health and to lengthen the span of life. Colleges of education conduct research to improve man's basic abilities to learn to handle increasingly complex matters involving basic life decisions, as well as to survey local educational systems to aid in improving them. Schools of social work study the problems of families, of group life, of the unfortunate who may be dependent because of age, physical handicaps or loss of parents. Colleges of commerce study the rate of economic growth, the causes of business failures, recessions, depressions and business cycles, and problems of costs in production and in marketing. Colleges of business assist local businesses. Society's interest is more than the sum of the interests of the individuals of which the college is composed. Nations dedicated to the preservation of freedom, justice, self-government and world peace and the amelioration of suffering, want, hunger and disease need to be served by men and women who emerge from colleges with the determination and the skills to tackle and solve these immense problems. Colleges do indeed exist to serve society.

It is a rare institution that does not seek to perpetuate itself. Business organizations certainly do, as well as social agencies, hospitals, legal agencies, churches and character-building agencies. However, it is particularly important in a democratic society that schools and colleges, at least the better ones, be perpetuated. In governments where the people make many of the decisions, they must be informed. It might be argued that such mass media as the press, radio and television could and do inform the citizens, and there are some newspapers and some radio and television programs where mass media have proved to be immensely informative. Unfortunately, such examples are all too few, and they do not reach all the people. Only the educational system reaches nearly everyone and is relatively unbiased, impartial and non-political. These are sound reasons for perpetuating the American college. Moreover, the college is devoted to the transmission of our cultural heritage, to its extension and to the discovery of new knowledge. Less desirable motives for the survival of colleges could no doubt be found, but they are not the important ones.

There are several ways in which the college aims to serve the individual; for example, a college exists to teach facts, to prepare young people to earn a living, to teach them how to think, how to assume leadership in intellectual matters and how to develop their total personalities so that they may live socially, responsibly, unselfishly, honestly, intelligently, alertly.

Another way of stating the purposes of the college in serving the individual is that it exists to help the student become a better worker, a better homemaker and a better citizen. While this statement is a comprehensive one, it offers little help in aiding the institution to know *how* to make a better worker, citizen and homemaker. A third statement of aims might be to help the student grow mentally, spiritually, physically and socially and to help him discover his interests and aptitudes. All of these statements are both useful and inadequate. They emphasize desirable goals, but do not reveal which are the most important nor how they are to be achieved.

The goals we select for our educational program are of tremendous importance, for as Justman and Mais say, "The educated person today needs powers surpassing those of any previous age. There is more to be learned, yet to be a learned person is not enough: one must be right thinking, right feeling, right doing. If our educated person lacks the erudition of the Renaissance scholar or the urbanity of the Victorian gentleman, that is no cause for discouragement. He is probably better balanced, and balance is what we urgently require." [2]

---

[2] Joseph Justman and Walter H. Mais, *College Teaching,* Harper and Brothers, New York, 1956, pp. 21–22.

General objectives of liberal arts. Two broadly conceived objectives of any academic program are liberation [3] and discipline. The first occurs with the opening up to the individual of new fields of knowledge. Two remarkable science phenomena of the last quarter century illustrate this point. The first of these was the splitting of the atom. This discovery liberated man in the sense that it has put at his disposal power and energy undreamed of by the ordinary person prior to World War II. The second phenomenon was the freeing of man from this planet with its promise of the coming exploration of outer space and probable interplanetary visitation. These are dramatic examples, but even the smallest bit of new knowledge has its liberating effect, whether it be in archaeology, biochemistry, microbiology, history, literature or the arts. One whole purpose of the liberal arts is to set men free.

The second objective, as indicated, is discipline. The constant struggle of all men is to be able to take charge of themselves intelligently and to be accountable for their freedom of behavior. Discipline comes, in part, in mastering new knowledge, but such learning must have both purpose and real substance. There is no purpose or substance in the memorization of a series of nonsense syllables, but students of mathematics are expected to master substantial concepts and skills which can eventually be put to use. Discipline also comes from the reactions of one's peers. Physicians, psychologists, writers and investigators of many kinds covet the respect of their contemporaries and discipline themselves to be worthy of it.

CURRICULAR OFFERINGS

Classification of college offerings. The aims of any given American college, though not specifically labeled as such in the catalog,

[3] An elaboration of this objective is to be found in Algo D. Henderson, *Policies and Practices in Higher Education,* Harper and Brothers, New York, 1960, pp. 24–28.

are often better revealed by an examination of the academic menu put before the student. What is he expected to learn and what, in addition, is he given the opportunity to learn? In the American liberal arts college, studies commonly found in the curriculum, not including basic skill courses such as those ordinarily required in English and mathematics, are grouped in three categories: the humanities, the social sciences and the natural and physical sciences.

In a recent address Frederic Heimberger, of Ohio State University, analyzed the objectives of these three classes of studies in a general way as follows:

The objectives [of the humanities] are to introduce the student to his possibilities for continuing growth as a thoughtful and reasoning person, sensitive to the aspirations and attainments of others; to acquaint him to at least some degree with the treasures of human thought and expression at his command; and to develop in him a continuing desire to have his full share of the legacy of all creative efforts. . . .

The objectives [of social science] are to make sure that the student has at least a basic understanding of the fundamental ideas upon which our society has been built, the social institutions through which these ideas have been given effective meaning, and the never-ending process of development through free choices limited only by concern for the rights and well being of others. Emphasis should be put upon the values of a free society and the responsibility of the individual for participating actively in the issues and decisions of the day. . . .

The objectives [of science] are to acquaint the student with the kinds of problems which lend themselves to possible solutions through the use of science, to introduce him to differing scientific techniques through significant illustrative experiences, to give him a sense of perspective in the development of science, and to develop in him an understanding of the basic community of all scientific disciplines.[4]

---

[4] Frederic Heimberger, "An Approach to General Education in a Large and Complex University," unpublished address before the American Anthropological Association, June, 1960.

These comprehensive paragraphs give us a good overview of the objectives of general education in the collegiate institution. Dressel, Mayhew and McGrath list the liberal arts subjects as follows: "art, biology, chemistry, economics, English composition, foreign language, history, literature, mathematics, music, philosophy, physics, physiology, political science, psychology, religion, sociology and speech." [5] Each of these has its own peculiar and often separate value.

Broad-field courses. Broad-field courses, now offered in many colleges, are designed to give the student an over-all view of a large area of subject matter. They bear such inclusive titles as Man and Society, Our Physical World, Theories of International Power, Ideas and Institutions in European Civilization, and History of Ideas. A course entitled American Studies, for example, might cover American history, American literature, American politics, American economics and American education, all of which are considered in their relationship to one another. Against the criticism that such courses are necessarily superficial must be weighed the value of understanding the relationship between ideas from interdependent fields.

During World War II teams of civilian administrators were trained to be ready to organize civilian life in Germany and in Japan after invasion. In the Civilian Administrators Training Schools (CATS) a region of Germany was studied, perhaps Bavaria. Here these teams studied the language, agriculture, industry, banking, schools, police and fire protection, family life, religion and other facets of Bavarian life with a view to helping in the re-establishment of normal civilian activities. This experience caused many faculty members who were involved in these courses to realize how closely their field of interest and study was related to that of many of their colleagues. The less specifically oriented broad-field course in the college has a similar effect. The introduction of such courses involved a major curriculum re-

[5] Paul Dressel, Lewis B. Mayhew and Earl J. McGrath, *The Liberal Arts as Viewed by Faculty Members in Professional Schools,* Bureau of Publications, Teachers College, Columbia University, New York, 1959, p. 35.

organization, the purpose of which was to reconcile the conflict between specialization and general education.

An example of one such offering—a Course in Contemporary Developments in the Sciences and Mathematics—is listed below:

I. Introduction
   A. Aims and purposes of science
   B. Organization of the natural sciences
   C. Scientific research
   D. Scientific manpower (science and scientists)
II. The course
   A. Earth
      1. Dating and age
      2. Geophysics
      3. Meteorology and climatology
      4. International geophysical year
   B. Life
      1. Origin
      2. Photosynthesis
      3. Food and health
   C. Raw materials
      1. Metals and corrosion
      2. Rare earths and artificially prepared elements
      3. Polymers
   D. Energy resources—current and future
      1. Fossil fuels
      2. Nuclear
      3. Solar
   E. Universe
      1. Cosmology
      2. Radio astronomy
   F. Electronics and automation
   G. Mathematics
      1. Binary number system and its use
      2. Use of statistics
      3. Topology

The author of this course writes:

> Actually, this course by its very nature does not have a body of well-defined course content considered requisite to any other subject area, but is almost the scientist's last opportunity, not only to acquaint the students with contemporary developments in the natural sciences, but also to interpret science itself to prospective laymen; laymen whose functions and views as workers with students and teachers can be of considerable importance to the future of science itself.[6]

Thus this faculty member has cast his lot in this course with the general education needs of the student. This kind of education has been defined as that part of the total education of the student which deals primarily with common persistent problems of the individual and of society (as they interact) and which gives meaning and commonness of purpose to life.

There are six types of broad-field courses. First, there is the chronological course which considers various fields of study century by century. Second, there is the mosaic course, in which various interrelated problems are considered. Third is the aesthetic principles course which considers such factors as rhythm, balance and color in a variety of fields. Fourth, there is the theme-centered course, based on such subjects as classicism, romanticism, realism or the spread of the scientific view, the relation between freedom and authority in many fields, the rise of the common man. Fifth is the functional course, illustrated by the Civilian Administrators Training Schools briefly described above. And, sixth, there is the organization by correlation courses which attempts to give a total view of life problems; for example, a course in Social Implications of Modern Science. It is hoped that such correlation courses taken together will help the student:

(1) to understand and be able to manipulate the physical world
(2) to understand, defend and extend our cultural heritage
(3) to understand himself in his relations to other people

[6] Anton Postl, "A Course in Contemporary Developments in the Sciences and Mathematics," unpublished hectographed material, Oregon College of Education, Monmouth, Oregon.

(4) to understand the contemporary scene and deal effectively with it

(5) to understand mass media of communication and their effects on society, and

(6) to understand and participate in the creative arts

Opinion with regard to the desirability of correlations courses is divided. Some faculty members believe that it is unrealistic to expect the immature student by himself to correlate the knowledge acquired in his various fields of study. Indeed, they assert, if professors are unable or unwilling to accomplish this aim in their teaching, how can the younger, less sophisticated student be expected to do it? Other professors stress the interrelationship of knowledge and the necessity for this kind of awareness in the solution of many problems which are interdisciplinary in character. On the other hand, there are faculty members who assert that no one can integrate knowledge for someone else and that correlation and integration must occur in the mind of the student. Further, they believe that by their very nature, correlation courses must be "thin," that they lack depth, thoroughness and discipline. The young college teacher will encounter these different views on any faculty of which he is a member, and he must decide which he will support. Presumably he will make his judgment in accordance with what he considers to be valid aims of the college as expressed through the organization of the curriculum.

Vocational subjects. Another point which must be considered is that, as we noted earlier, nearly all liberal arts colleges have gradually been including in their educational programs subjects which are mainly vocational in their objectives. Most frequently included are elementary and secondary education, home economics, music education, business courses, retailing, merchandising and secretarial work, as well as preparatory courses for medicine, dentistry, law, engineering, theology, social work, library science and physical therapy. It may be observed in passing that when many of the liberal arts colleges added these vocational subjects, they urgently needed to attract students. Today it does not appear that in the foreseeable future colleges will have much difficulty in enrolling qualified students, and it remains to be seen what the institutions will do under these circumstances with these more recent additions to their programs. In this connection, Deutsch says, "There are fields which are perfectly worthy to be taught, and yet not in a true college. . . . Perhaps one way to answer the question in the large is to ask oneself whether the field to be taught is a profession. If it is not, then the presumption is that it should be taught in a trade school, not in a college or university." [7]

Specialism. Coincidental with the inclusion of vocational subjects was the development of specialism, which was mentioned in Chapter 3. According to McGrath and Russell, the average number of departments in liberal arts colleges had risen from fifteen to twenty-nine by 1957, and in many departments of small liberal arts colleges (those with enrollments of under one thousand) the total number of hours of instruction in any one field exceeded by four or five times the hours required for a major in the field! [8] The emphasis on graduate education with its stress on specialization and ofttimes narrow research, through which training practically all college teachers go, almost inevitably leads to more courses, since each new professor with a recent doctor's degree has a specialty he desires to teach. Unfortunately, in many colleges the advanced studies of some professors have caused them to lose sight of the aims of their colleagues on the staff. Laudable as is his dedication to his own field of study, the professor needs to see it in relation to the total curriculum and to its effect upon the maturing college student. Each area of study is important to the well-rounded life of the student.

Subjects to be required. Amid the increasing number of

[7] Monroe E. Deutsch, *The College from Within,* University of California Press, Berkeley, 1952, p. 187.

[8] Earl J. McGrath and Charles H. Russell, *Are Liberal Arts Colleges Becoming Professional Schools?* Bureau of Publications, Teachers College, Columbia University, New York, pp. 5–6.

courses listed in the average college catalog today, how can one choose those which make an indispensable contribution to a liberal education, giving the student the abilities and the common intellectual body of knowledge previously referred to? A recent study revealed that more than two-thirds of the combined professional faculties in 182 professional and technical schools favored either encouraging or requiring students to take the following specific subjects, given here in order of their rating: English composition, history, mathematics, speech, literature, psychology, physics, chemistry and philosophy. Rated close to this first group were foreign language, political science, biology and sociology. These ratings represent the judgments of 3,400 individuals in the selected technical or professional schools.[9]

The college faculty must ultimately decide what shall be the requirements for graduation. Suppose, for example, that an institution requires for a bachelor's degree the following semester hours of credit: English, 10; social science, 18; laboratory science, 8; speech, 3; psychology, 3; physical education and hygiene, 2; major, 30; two minors, 20 each; electives, 14; or a total of 128 semester hours. In contrast to the combined judgments of the faculties reported above, this faculty has apparently decided that the aims to be gained by the study of mathematics and philosophy either are not as important as the aims of the areas included as required subjects, or can be achieved through the study of those subjects as electives. Of course, these areas could be included in the fourteen hours of electives allowed, but the elective subjects chosen must include also whatever the student wishes to study in art and music, logic, ethics, religion and foreign languages. How does a faculty determine what should be required and what should be elective? Presumably, required areas of study are those without which a college graduate would not be considered an educated person. We should recognize the fact, however, that full agreement as to the characteristic ingredients of a college education is not likely to be achieved.

In the illustration given the reader may observe that more of

[9] Dressel, Mayhew and McGrath, *op. cit.*, p. 35.

the areas left to be studied as electives could be included in the required program if the number of hours allocated to social science, English and the majors and minors were reduced. This suggestion brings us to the problem of breadth and depth of study. It would indeed be possible, in the course of a college education, for the student to obtain a smattering of all areas with little or no mastery of any. Usually college faculties have favored the dual aim of providing the student the opportunity to become conversant with broad fields as well as to specialize in one or two.

A sample program of liberal education. A sample program directed to a liberal education is depicted in the following chart:

A PROGRAM OF LIBERAL EDUCATION

First Year	The English Language	Modern Foreign or Classical Language ——— The Nature of Language	Introduction to Science ——— Mathematics	The Bases of Human Social Life
Second Year	World Literature	Modern Foreign or Classical Language, continued	A Physical or Biological Science or Mathematics	The Modern World
Third Year	Music Graphic and Plastic Arts	Work in a Special Field of Interest	Course outside of Field of Interest	Social Science or Philosophy
Fourth Year	Tutorial, Correlative Reading	Work in a Special Field of Interest	Work in a Special Field of Interest	Special Problem or Area Study

Comprehensive Examination

This chart depicts a well-planned program of liberal education. The first column shows the humanities in each of the four years; the second, modern foreign or classical language, together with a major field of interest; the third column shows science and mathematics, along with a major and minor field of interest; and the fourth column is devoted largely to the social sciences. The uninitiated college professor will wish to compare and contrast this four-year program with the "subjects to be required" and the suggested requirements for the bachelor's degree, given earlier in this chapter.

TRENDS

Independent study. One trend in the academic program of the American college is toward putting the junior or senior student on his own in some plan of independent study. Honors courses now provided in many colleges permit the student, under the guidance of a professor, to work on his own at his own rate of speed. Tutorial systems which provide a student with a tutor with whom he has a weekly conference are now found more frequently. Even colleges that continue the customary class instruction often declare "reading periods" for a week or two, during which the students devote themselves to reading, free from the interruption of classes. Many institutions provide for a program of individual study, worked out by student and professor together, which the student carries out, checking in occasionally with the professor and checking out with him at the evaluation period. Most of these plans for independent study are elaborated in Chapter 5 in which the academic programs of eight colleges are described.

Curriculum revision. With the explosion of knowledge, college professors and administrators are of necessity engaging in the revision of curriculum. In the fields of mathematics and science in particular, courses which had very satisfactory and worthwhile content prior to 1940 are now likely to be out of date. That this is true in other fields as well is indicated by the dean of a well-known College of Medicine, who said recently, "90 per cent of the prescriptions written today could not have been written ten years ago." Revision, however, does not mean the mere adding of new courses to the curriculum. Already the proliferation of courses in many of our colleges and universities is alarming.[10]

Justman and Mais have written an interesting section on techniques of curriculum revision from which the following questions are derived: What educational purpose is meant to be served by the revision? Is a change in curriculum really needed? How is the proposed change to be developed? Do the new courses proposed meet the purposes avowed for them? Do they meet the specifications of a good "learning experience for students?" What provision is made for the evaluation of a single course or a comprehensive curriculum? [11] If satisfactory answers can be found to such questions, it would seem that curriculum revision, when it occurs, is likely to be accomplished on a sound basis. However, someone has said that it is harder to change a college curriculum than to move a cemetery! Knowledge itself or the interpretation of it has changed, and college students are entitled to the latest and best information we possess. This is the basic reason for curriculum revision.

Academic organization. There are two patterns of organizing the curriculum now being utilized in colleges. The traditional plan is the departmental one, with departments of history, economics, sociology, political science, English, foreign language, physics, chemistry, biology, geology, speech, journalism and the like. There seems to be something of a trend today toward organizing the curriculum on the divisional plan, in which all subjects are included under such broad categories as the humanities, the social sciences and the natural sciences. There are three advantages of the latter plan: (1) it provides for greater coordination of curriculum content among departments; (2) it provides for the elimination of duplicate courses; and (3) it helps students solve problems which cut across departmental lines.

[10] For a discussion of the great increase in the number of courses, see Monroe Deutsch, *op. cit.*, p. 190.

[11] Joseph Justman and Walter H. Mais, *op. cit.*, pp. 156–165.

Outcomes

The academic program is not designed to make students "serve time" nor to give them degrees. Someone has quite properly said that education does not come by degrees. The purpose of the program is to produce a cultivated person, one who has knowledge and appreciation of great literature, art, music and science, who has some knowledge of how to live with others and some insight into world affairs. Certainly he should have an understanding of the democratic way of life and of democratic values as well as an appreciation of the sacrifices that have been made by others to achieve and sustain them. A good college program should enable graduates to do difficult things well and should make them eternally curious about life—its opportunities, challenges and meanings. Perhaps Lessing, the great German critic and dramatist, summed it all up in the statement, "The end of all education is to make men see things that are big as big and things that are small as small."

CHAPTER 5

Colleges with
Special
Programs

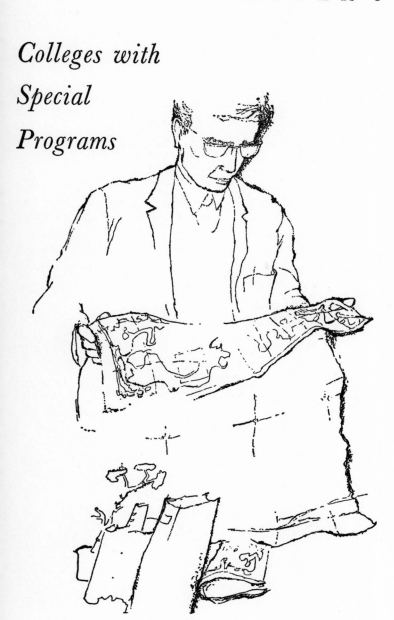

THE ULTIMATE PURPOSE OF ALL EDUCATION IS WISDOM
AND UNDERSTANDING, EVEN MORE THAN KNOWLEDGE,
THOUGH UNDERSTANDING IS IMPOSSIBLE WITHOUT
KNOWLEDGE.
—*Carl F. Wittke*

Curricular revision goes on in all good colleges. It occurs in a department of psychology in which the staff determines to overhaul its offerings. It occurs when a single professor determines to revise the contents of even one of his courses. Valuable as are these efforts, they are sometimes defeated by other segments of the program or factions of a faculty. If the projected change threatens long-established tradition or someone's vested interest, often there is a sufficient number of opponents (usually opposing for different reasons) to throttle the proposed change before it starts, or to insure its failure if the innovation actually gets under way. Resistance to change appears to be a characteristic of higher educational institutions; hence experimentation and change within a long-established collegiate structure are difficult. For this reason many scholars have sought employment in institutions where there is hospitality to new educational ideas. Sometimes these may be additions to the traditional curriculum. In other colleges scholars have found a haven in which to escape the drag of tradition and thus to establish a new order of education without the conflicting demands made on the student when a curricular innovation seeks to thrive in the setting of a traditional college curriculum.

Most of the special programs described in this chapter were started as experiments, and they attracted the faculty members and the students who believed in the kind of program posited. Since they were also supported by the respective boards of trustees, the optimum possibilities for engaging in new practices were believed to be present.

All college teachers should be familiar with programs of this sort, not only because they have implications for the future of higher education as a whole, but also because they may suggest to the enterprising professor ways of improving his own course offerings or of being an effective member of a college curriculum committee.

ANTIOCH COLLEGE
YELLOW SPRINGS, OHIO

Founded in 1855 by Horace Mann, who was also its first president, Antioch was one of the most progressive colleges of its day. From the beginning it accepted women students as well as those of every color and creed. What was perhaps even more unusual was its lack of stress on grades and the fact that it permitted some electives.

The "cooperative plan" for which Antioch is famous was instituted during the presidency of Arthur E. Morgan, who assumed the office in 1920. An insistence upon education being related to what is real is found in every phase of the college program.

Antioch's program consists of four parts, the first of which is the academic program. The aim of this program is to develop the whole person and, to this end, to help each student to develop the following goals (a list which merits careful reading):

An adequate philosophy and a way of life consistent with it

Appreciation and understanding of oneself

Orientation to the physical universe and human society

Ability to choose and progress in a useful and satisfying career

More effective human relationships in family life, career and civic life

Appreciation of the fine arts, of life and participation in creative activity

Good management of one's resources and ability to keep expectations and achievement reasonably related

Self-directed and continued educational growth during and beyond college

Skill in changing habits or attitudes that limit achievement of these objectives

All students begin with a program of general education in the humanities, the physical sciences and the social sciences before going on into their fields of concentration. According to a table published in a recent Antioch catalog, the seniors score considerably above the norm in their respective fields. In a study financed by the Fund for the Advancement of Education of the Ford Foundation, Antioch is ranked ninth among colleges in producing male scholars in the natural sciences, social sciences and humanities.

At the beginning of the senior year the program provides for an independent study period, during which the student engages in autonomous study or scholarly research, usually off campus.

Work periods. The second and most distinguishing part of the Antioch program is the plan of alternating study and work periods. The list of nearly 350 cooperating employers, or "field faculty," includes business and publishing firms, radio and TV stations, social and professional agencies, manufacturing concerns, retail stores, utility companies, government agencies, hospitals, libraries and museums, public and private schools, social service organizations and summer camps. Some of the employers are located in foreign countries. There are two work periods each year, and while one student is working, his counterpart is on the campus studying. All freshmen begin their college careers with a three-month study period.

Each student has a personnel adviser who helps him decide on a job after discussing the student's interests, educational needs and future plans. Work appointments are made by the college, but the cooperating employer is free to dismiss any student who fails to do the job well. At the end of each work period the employer rates the student's performance, and this rating becomes part of his permanent record. Antioch students are in demand because of the high caliber of work such college-trained students can perform. They receive the regular remuneration usually paid to employees of their ability and experience. Because of the extended time given to the work periods, the normal time required for graduation is five years. Six periods of remunerative employment plus ten quarters of regular classroom work are required for a Bachelor's degree from Antioch.

The "community program." The third part of the Antioch program is called the "community program," the purpose of which is to provide a laboratory in democracy. It covers all campus activity not directly planned as academic work. Three student representatives serve on the Administrative Council, which not only advises the President on college policy, but participates with him in important administrative decisions. The Community Council, consisting of six students and three faculty members, has authority in the area of community life. The Council and its committees

provide such basic community services as the college bookstore, voluntary fire squad and student bank. They see that student automobiles are in good condition and properly insured, and establish standards of safe driving; they conduct elections and help new students adjust to college. They are responsible for many social, cultural and recreational activities.[1]

Students are expected to assume adult responsibility for the well-being of the Antioch community and to act always with moderation, good taste and respect for the views of others. Students are on their honor to adhere to college standards and examinations are unproctored. There are no intercollegiate athletics but a rich program of sports for everyone, including basketball, softball, tennis, badminton and golf—the sports activities in which they will be most likely to participate after college. Though there are a great many social events in the college, there are no exclusive social organizations. There are rich opportunities, and a good deal of encouragement, for student participation in dramatics, music, the arts, radio (students manage and operate an educational FM radio station) and writing for the college newspaper, magazine, radio station or theater workshop.

[1] *Antioch College Bulletin,* 1959–1960 and 1960–1961, p. 25.

Students prepare for and participate in social action by organizing religious and welfare activities, leading discussion groups on civil liberties, minority group relations and other social issues, and forming independent political organizations.

Study abroad. The opportunity for a year of Antioch study abroad constitutes the fourth and last part of Antioch's program. The purpose of this part of the program is not just to furnish the student with the opportunity for travel, but rather that

with the U.S. in a position of world leadership, we must be prepared for world responsibilities, based upon knowledge and understanding of many peoples of the world. And in college, what better preparation is there than living with other peoples, knowing them as friends and neighbors and fellow-workers, being closely and sensitively aware of their cultures, sympathetic to what makes them similar and dissimilar to us? [2]

The same pattern of alternating work and study is followed in the study abroad, and the year's work earns regular credit toward a degree. To enroll in a foreign university a student must have completed two years of college work with a cumulative grade point average of at least 2.5 and must have developed skill in the language of the country in which he chooses to study. For the work program abroad the student must have had at least twenty-six weeks of satisfactory work experience and must have necessary work skills. The university has established three Antioch centers of University Studies to help the student become oriented to work and study abroad—one at the University of Besançon in France, another at the University of Tübingen in Germany and one at Guanajuato, Mexico.

BENNINGTON COLLEGE
BENNINGTON, VERMONT

Bennington College, an undergraduate women's college, opened in September, 1932, after seven years devoted to study and prep-

[2] *Ibid.,* p. 30.

aration. The college is located four miles from the village of Bennington and 150 miles west of Boston. Enrollment is limited to 350 students, and the following factors are taken into account in admission:

The amount and kind of ability the candidate possesses; the way she has used that ability; the scholastic standards she has had to meet; the scope of her secondary program, especially where the choice has been open to her; her drive, sustaining power, and independence; her attitudes toward herself and other people; the genuineness of her interest in college; and the validity of her interest in Bennington.[3]

The applicant is expected to take the Scholastic Aptitude Test of the College Entrance Examination Board and the C.E.E.B. achievement tests if these are necessary to the understanding of her scholastic record.

Bennington tends to attract women who either have or wish to develop particular talents and skills. However, such interests are not permitted to substitute for the necessary qualifications required for college work.

The college year consists of three terms, two of which are spent in residence and one in non-resident work. The latter term begins after New Year's Day and lasts for nine weeks. The spring term ends in mid-June.

Bennington's program. The first step in planning the student's work is taken with a member of the faculty selected as her counselor. There is no uniformly prescribed freshman curriculum, so that counselor and student draw up a first-term program which provides for exploration and is in accord with the student's capabilities. This joint counseling continues throughout the four years of the student's college life. During the first two years the student takes introductory and when appropriate, advanced courses, each taking up about one-fourth of her time. Thus she seeks both to obtain a solid general foundation and to try herself out in several fields. This experience helps her to choose a major field of interest or specialization.

[3] *Bennington College Bulletin,* 1960, p. 10.

Course offerings are grouped under natural science and mathematics, social science, literature and languages, dance, drama, music and visual arts. Supplementing these offerings are individual and group tutorials, which encourage the student to develop the habit of learning on her own.

The Bennington Bachelor of Arts degree is usually obtained in four years. Usually, in addition to courses and non-resident work, the student presents a piece of independent work as a senior project in her major field. No final comprehensive examinations are given, and the degree is not awarded on the basis of purely formal requirements. It is rather in recognition of the student's whole achievement and is a testimony to her readiness to continue her own education.

The non-resident term. There are two features of the Bennington program which differ from that of most colleges. The first, previously mentioned, is the Non-Resident Term. During the periods on the campus the student is busy with books, classes and ideas and lives in a small, relatively homogeneous community. During the Non-Resident Term she goes as a worker for nine weeks into a situation in which she must make her own way. Students work in factories, stores, government or social agencies, research laboratories, hospitals, museums, schools and offices. While a current list of possible jobs is available to the student and considerable help is given her, she must take the initiative, make her plan and carry it out. In so doing she gains self-confidence, maturity and a broader view of the practical world. A usual outcome also is the development of her vocational aims, skills and interests. The student herself reports in detail on her experience, as does the employer to whom she is responsible. These experiences are considered to be a serious and systematic part of a student's whole college program and constitute a part of her record which, along with the more formal course work taken on campus, determines whether or not the degree is to be awarded.

Program in the arts. Bennington's outstanding program in the arts is the second unusual feature of the college program. A quick scanning of the faculty in 1960–1961 showed twenty-seven members listed in the following areas: dance, drama, architecture, graphic arts, music, painting, ceramics and sculpture. This is a remarkable spread of interest and size of staff for a college enrolling only 350 students. Bennington has been known for many years for its interest in modern dance, but it now has a well-rounded curriculum in most of the artistic fields which extends well beyond the offerings in most liberal arts colleges.

The two distinctive features cited, together with the solid academic program, provide for the American college woman an opportunity not frequently found elsewhere.

BLACKBURN COLLEGE
CARLINVILLE, ILLINOIS

Located half way between Springfield, Illinois and St. Louis, Missouri, Blackburn College derived its name from that of a minister who was interested in the establishment of an institution to provide education for young people and to train young men for the ministry. Money for the purchase of eighty acres of land for the site of the college was raised by Mr. Blackburn, and by 1837 the land was deeded to the twelve trustees of the college. In 1857 a charter was obtained from the state legislature, which gave the college permanent tax-exempt status and permitted the trustees to name their successors. Its first presidents were Presbyterian ministers.

By 1864 a full college course of study was under way. Like many other colleges of its time, it had limited resources and financial difficulties. In 1913, with a student enrollment of thirty-five, a work-study program was instituted. Since that time the enrollment has increased steadily until the college now has about four hundred students. A new student center, residence hall and science building have been occupied. The most notable feature of the physical plant lies in the fact that the entire construction and maintenance program is carried out with student labor. There is abundant evidence of pride in workmanship, and obviously many students had to master a variety of skills in order to produce a finished product of such a high order of excellence.

The student council. The college has two expressed purposes— to provide education for use and to prepare students for responsible living in a democratic society. Students are required to become participating members of the community under the discipline of the college administration, but they are responsible also for formulating and enforcing rules of conduct and for social and recreational activity. This responsibility is administered through the Blackburn Student Council, an elected body of twelve members which makes the week-by-week decisions. Members of the men's and women's house councils are responsible for student life in the residence halls.

The academic program. The academic program is organized around the main areas of the humanities, the natural sciences and the social sciences. Following an early emphasis on general education, the student may major in one of the following eleven areas of concentration: art, biology, chemistry, economics, elementary education, English, history, mathematics, music, social science and sociology. One of the main purposes of the program is to provide high quality liberal arts education at moderate cost to the student. Every effort is made, through the work program, scholarships or grants, to assist students who need financial help. Students are admitted who give promise of being able to do the academic work, who are willing to participate in the work-study program and who indicate their intention of completing the full collegiate course.

The work program. The work program is the most unusual feature of Blackburn and is designed to assist in the educational program, build and maintain the physical plant and provide the services necessary for comfortable study and living in the college community. While the advantage of the work program to the students in the reduction of operating and maintenance costs is considerable, the educational value of the work program, though less tangible, may be equally important.

Each student at Blackburn performs fifteen hours of work per week. When these hours are assigned to the student, the academic schedule receives priority and the work schedule is built around the class assignments. The program is administered by the Work Committee, which consists of the men's work manager, the women's work manager and ten assistant work managers, who are responsible for the various departments. Job training programs are provided and senior or experienced students take responsibility for the newer members of the community. The division of authority between the Student Council and the Work Committee is quite sharp. In fact, the constitution of the Student Association forbids the Student Council to interfere in the work program. All job assignments are made by the Work Committee, which is also charged with management, supervision and grading of all student work. The students assume responsibility for all the construction and maintenance work as well as the custodial care of the institution. Work assignments are carried out by individuals or groups, depending upon the nature of the task. Faculty advisers are available for counseling services regarding both the work program and the student government.

Before the beginning of each semester the student fills out a Work Preference Blank, on which he indicates his choices for assignments. He selects from a wide range of jobs, which include kitchen and dining-hall duty, laundry work, construction work, janitor service, bookstore clerk, student center work or work as a faculty assistant.

Construction work is under the supervision of an experienced construction superintendent. His job involves the supervision of willing, but often untrained and unskilled student workmen. An elaborate set of Standing Work Rules has been developed. Through their experience in the work program students learn cooperation, reliability and responsibility. Since the student is graded on his work as well as on his studies, he may fail to graduate through failure in either area.

The foundations of Blackburn rest on Christian ideals, and Presbyterian ministers dominated its first century of growth. In Carlinville there is an admirable opportunity for the healthy development of religious, intellectual and work interests and for relating them to small-community life. It is not possible for the visitor to tell whether there are planned relationships between study and work programs, or between these two and the community, all of which might help the individual to develop a sound system of moral and spiritual values; but the opportunity for such integration is present at Blackburn College.

MONTEITH COLLEGE
DETROIT, MICHIGAN

Monteith College, an autonomous unit of Wayne State University in Detroit, opened in September, 1959, with 314 freshman students. The college was the outcome of the work of a Wayne committee on ways to achieve a closer integration between liberal and professional education. Though probably no one feature on the Monteith plan is completely novel, the combination of features is unique. Its curriculum is designed to provide the essential general education which every educated man should possess and to afford sound general education as a basis for professional study in medicine, engineering, education, law and business administration. Its organization is that of the small college which fosters the development of a sense of intellectual community.

Because Monteith is part of Wayne State University, its students have the dual advantage of being part of a small college while at the same time being able to take advantage of the great number of opportunities offered by the university, of which Monteith students represent a cross section. The requirements for admission to the college are the same as those for the university as a whole, but the total number of students admitted is limited in order to provide the values to be derived in the intimate climate of a small college. Monteith admits 320 students every fall, 160 each spring and plans eventually to have a total enrollment of about 1,200 students.

The sense of community. The aim of developing a sense of

community within the college is fostered in several ways. The required basic courses provide a unifying experience for all students. The small discussion sessions encourage interchange of ideas among students and faculty, and, according to the catalog, "The skills of analysis acquired in the discussion of a wide variety of selected readings stimulate the development of a common spirit of inquiry, a spirit which often extends beyond the classroom into research projects and which permeates the 'continual conversation' carried on in the Monteith Center." [4] The Center is located in a large house taken over by the college to provide facilities where students and faculty can meet informally for reading, conversation, social affairs and listening to lectures and good music.

The basic courses. The basic courses required of all students consist of a four-semester sequence in natural science, a three-semester sequence in the science of society, a three-semester sequence in humanistic studies and a two-semester senior colloquium, in which students read and discuss critically a series of books interpretive of the fields covered in the other three basic courses.

Perhaps, as an example, a brief explanation of the sequence in natural science will be informative. The first-semester course is devoted to logic and mathematics. The initial phase, concerned with numbers, starts with certain simple, purely logical constructs, and from these numbers the students fashion successively other kinds of numbers of ever greater complexity. The number systems thus created, with the addition of other purely logical concepts, such as set, relation and function, form the foundation for what mathematicians call "Analysis." The second part of the first semester's work consists of the study of deductive systems, such as those that must be constructed by physicists, biologists and economists.

The second semester of the natural science sequence contains four vertical threads. The first, called Cosmology, deals with the

---

[4] Monteith College, *Wayne State University Bulletin,* 1960–1961, p. 6.

solar and stellar universe. The views of Aristotle, Ptolemy, Galileo, Kepler, Brake and Newton are considered, but this thread is not solely a consideration of the history of science, but rather of man's changing view of it. The second vertical thread in the course deals with Atomism, i.e., the development of man's understanding of the chemical nature of matter. The third thread deals with the theory of the evolution of biological science, and the fourth with important problems related to the nature of science and its methodologies.

The course of the third semester includes two broad topics. The first, biological science, is concerned with cell theory, genetics and the evolution of species. The second topic deals with important aspects of physics, beginning with mass and energy and going on through field theory, relativity and quantum mechanics.

In the fourth-semester course, entitled "Abstraction and Indeterminacy," twentieth-century revolutions in physical theory, changing views on causality and the trend toward abstraction are considered.

The titles of the courses in the three-semester sequence in the science of society are suggestive of their content: Culture and Personality, Group Processes and Institutional Stability, and Decision Making and Social Control in Complex Societies.

The three-semester sequence in humanistic studies includes Man as Symbol Maker, Change in the Arts, and Experimentation and Revolt.

The remainder of the student's program is taken in professional or subject specialization in other colleges of the university or in advanced general courses either within the college or in other Wayne schools.

Students in the basic courses meet twice a week in large lecture sessions and twice a week in small discussion groups of twelve to sixteen students in the freshman year and somewhat larger groups in the other three years. The senior colloquium is divided into three sections each semester, of which the student takes only two. The senior is thrown to a considerable extent upon his own resources, for although he is required to cover the assigned reading in both sections, he need attend the meetings of only one, and these occur only once in two weeks.

During the senior year also a student seeking a degree from Monteith enrolls each semester for a course called Senior Essay. The student may choose the division of the college in which he wishes to write his essay. Though he works with the advice of a faculty member, he explores in an essentially independent fashion some limited field of intellectual interest. His study culminates in the writing of a fairly elaborate essay, in which he is expected to demonstrate a capacity for independent and mature study.

Degree requirements. Monteith grants the degree of Bachelor of Philosophy to the student who masters the basic courses and in addition completes either an individualized program of general studies or an approved program of specialized or professional education.

St. John's College
Annapolis, Maryland

The Great Books program of St. John's, supplemented by its language and mathematics tutorials and laboratory exercises in science, is a far different one from that of the other so-called experimental colleges discussed in this chapter. Two ways in which this program differs markedly from the usual liberal arts program are (1) it has a single required curriculum which all students take throughout the four years of their college life and (2) it has no departments and no conventional subject-matter courses.

St. John's claims to be the third oldest American college since in 1786 the "property, funds, masters and students" of King Williams School, which received a royal charter in 1696, were conveyed by an Act of the General Assembly of Maryland to the newly established St. John's College. In the 1920's and 1930's it followed the conventional pattern of the small American college, but in 1937 severe financial and academic difficulties caused the college to make a marked change in its program and organization. It was at this time that, under the guidance and direction of Stringfellow Barr and Scott Buchanan, the new course of study was set up designed to provide a modern equivalent of the traditional liberal arts curriculum. In 1951 the college became co-educational.

Seminars. The core of the program is the bi-weekly evening seminars at which two or three faculty members and fifteen to twenty students discuss the Great Books of the world. There are some 125 of these books, the list beginning with Homer, carrying through the Greek, Roman and Medieval periods, and continuing through Renaissance and modern writings up to the present day. The books on this list have been chosen because they

raise the persistent and humanly unanswerable questions of human existence; because they lend themselves to different interpretations and bring to light a variety of independent and yet complementary meanings; because they are works of fine art, the clarity and beauty of which reflect their intrinsic intelligibility; and finally because they are masterpieces in the liberal arts, seeking truth with adequate means. All this justifies their being called great, be they books on mathematics or books of poetry, be their subject matter scientific, ethical, metaphysical or theological. All the great books are linked together: each one of them is introduced, supported and criticized by all the others. They converse with each other, and the students find themselves taking part, within the limits of their ability, in this great and never ending conversation.[5]

A random sampling of the list includes the following, some of which are read only in part:

Iliad and Odyssey by Homer
Four of Aeschylus' dramas
Republic by Plato and seven of Plato's Dialogues
Euclid's Elements
Augustine's Confessions
On the Revolution of the Spheres by Copernicus

[5] Bulletin of St. John's College, 1960–1962, p. 7.

Eleven of Shakespeare's plays
Cervantes' *Don Quixote*
La Fontaine's *Fables*
Locke's *Essay Concerning Human Understanding*
Adam Smith's *Wealth of Nations*
Hegel's *Philosophy of History*
Faraday's *Experimental Research in Electricity*
Flaubert's *Madame Bovary*
Darwin's *Origin of Species*
Marx' *Communist Manifesto*
Thomas Mann's *Death in Venice*
Einstein's *The Theory of Relativity*

St. John's considers the authors of these great books to be the real teachers in the curriculum, for they present to the student "the substance of human experience, the elements out of which it is built, the whole range of questions that have to be raised and of answers that can be given." [6]

The average preparation for each seminar meeting amounts to about a hundred pages of reading. The method used in the seminar is discussion, with the greatest possible freedom allowed. There are only two rules in force at these sessions: (1) politeness toward all members of the group so that everybody's opinion can be heard, however sharp the clash of opinions may be, and (2) the supporting of every opinion by argument. The progress of the seminar is not necessarily smooth, and the discussion rarely leads to the solution of a problem. The aim is to develop the student's powers of reasoning and understanding and to help him arrive at intelligent opinions of his own. The ultimate aim is that the process of thought and discussion will continue with the student throughout his life.

In addition to the seminars there are five divisions of the program—the language tutorial, the mathematics tutorial, the music tutorial, the laboratory and the formal lecture.

The tutorials. All faculty members are designated by the term *tutor,* and there are no divisions of rank. Each of the tutorial

[6] *Ibid.,* p. 6.

classes meets for one hour four days a week except in the senior year, when they meet three days a week. Though a mastery of foreign languages is not the primary aim of the language tutorials, Greek and French are studied for two years each, and every student must pass a reading knowledge examination in both as a requirement for graduation. The main objective is to learn something about the nature of language in general and the English language in particular in order to develop the ability to express thoughts clearly and precisely and to study and analyze a few great models of prose and poetry. The achievement of these two aims helps in the seminars by encouraging precision of expression and by bringing issues from the literature selections analyzed into the discussions.

The chief aim of the mathematics tutorial is to give insight into the nature and practice of abstract thinking and of reasoning that proceeds from definitions and principles to necessary conclusions. According to President Weigle of St. John's,

The first year of study deals with Euclid's *Elements* and Ptolemy's *Almagest*. The second year begins with the study of the transition from Ptolemaic to Copernican astronomy, and then goes on to Appolonius' *Conics* and to the modern treatment of conic sections in analytic geometry. The third year covers differential and integral calculus, then mechanics as developed by Galileo and Newton. The fourth year deals with differential equations, modern algebraic theory, non-Euclidean geometry, and the mathematics of the special theory of relativity.[7]

The music tutorial classes meet only in the freshman and sophomore years. Their aim is not music appreciation, the development of technical skills, nor the emotional development of the student, but rather the confrontation of the student with the theory and construction of music—fundamentals of melody, form, meter, rhythm, and polyphony—and the relation of music to mathematics, physics and literature.

The laboratory. Laboratory work consists of two three-hour

[7] From a personal letter to the author.

laboratory sessions weekly throughout the four years, devoted to the theory of measurement, biology, chemistry, optics, mechanics, electromagnetism and atomic physics. Every senior works on a laboratory project of his own choosing. The aim of the laboratory work is to provide a matrix of experimentation and discussion within which a liberal understanding of science will become possible. In its description of the laboratory work the catalog contains the following statement:

> The scientific laboratory may well be the most characteristic institution of the modern world. It should be recalled that it was for the purpose of introducing and assimilating the laboratory sciences that Eliot of Harvard opened the liberal college to the elective system. The hope was that the college would provide the conditions and the techniques for the liberalizing and humanizing of science. The present disorganization of our colleges is evidence that the problem is not yet solved. It is of utmost importance that it be solved. St. John's College is making the attempt.[8]

The formal lecture. The lecture period which comes on Friday evenings is the occasion upon which the student must listen attentively. The lectures are given either by a guest speaker or a faculty member and are on a wide variety of subjects which may or may not bear upon some part of the college program. Some of the subjects covered recently are "Spiritual Isolation in the Novels of Faulkner and Hemingway," "The Political Philosophy of the Constitution," "The Three Patterns of Western Civilization," "Rousseau's Defense of Freedom," "Some Observations on the Future of Democracy in Southeast Asia," "James Joyce's *Ulysses*" and "The Definition of Kinesis in Aristotle's *Physics*." Each lecture is followed by extensive discussion on the subject, in which both faculty and students participate.

In a speech in 1959 President Weigle of St. John's assessed the weaknesses and strengths of the college as follows:

> First, one might comment on the intensely demanding nature of the program. On the positive side, students find immense personal challenge and interest in their reading and their classroom sessions.

[8] *Bulletin of St. John's College,* 1960–1962, p. 19.

This carries over into dining hall, dormitory, and coffee shop conversations and marks the atmosphere of the college as intellectually stimulating and vigorous. On the other hand, some students with inadequate academic preparation or with poorly developed work habits find the program too difficult or the curriculum not suited to their special interests and are forced to drop out. An additional hazard which some students face is heavy personal involvement with the searching questions discussed in seminar, particularly those having to do with religion.[9]

One of the weaknesses of the program mentioned by Dr. Weigle is that seniors evidence too little concern about their future careers and frequently find it difficult to make a decision about them. Many—nearly 55 per cent—continue their school work in graduate study. Some of the St. John's graduates report that they find themselves at an initial disadvantage in graduate work because of their lack of specialized subject matter, but that later their breadth of knowledge, perspective and training in the liberal arts more than compensate. About half the graduates enter the professions—teaching, writing, law, social and welfare work, medicine, engineering and the ministry, in that order. Many of the others enter business, and a substantial number go into government service.

There are three points at which President Weigle feels the liberal arts appear to have achieved at least a measure of success under the St. John's approach:

First, the emphasis upon the professions, particularly teaching, is evidence of an objective of service to society. This reflects the continuing student concern with philosophy, the why of his life and actions. Secondly, regardless of career, there seems to be an ability to bring a broad range of skills to bear on any kind of program, coupled with concern for wider philosophic problems than those confronted on the job. Finally, there seems to be a desire to go on learning—a realization that learning continues throughout life.[10]

[9] Richard D. Weigle, "The Concept of the Liberal Arts College," a lecture delivered at the University of Kansas City on March 12, 1959 as part of the program for the Second Quarter Century Year, p. 16.
[10] Ibid., p. 17.

In constantly relating the different elements of the program to one another and thus stressing the unity of knowledge, St. John's program attempts to help each student achieve true liberation.

SARAH LAWRENCE COLLEGE
BRONXVILLE, NEW YORK

Sarah Lawrence, a women's college, opened in 1928 under President Marion Coates. The first catalog said that the purpose of the college was to organize its curriculum along the lines of progressive education. Constance Warren, who became president a year later and remained in this position until 1945, described the fundamental approach as follows:

It is individualized education adapted to the different capacities, interests and objectives of individual students, to the best of the faculty's ability to understand, recognize and satisfy such differing needs. The curriculum must be flexible to serve individual ends, and cannot be considered an end in itself, or a straitjacket to fit all alike. We are convinced that the student's desire to learn is fully as important as her innate ability; one with ordinary ability and strong motivation will often accomplish more than another with superior talent who lacks that vital spark. . . .

Few of us are born with a spontaneous interest in Euripides, but all of us have a spontaneous, indeed an unquenchable interest in ourselves and from that point of view will, in time, reach the stage when Euripides is an unforgettable experience, not just another classic. Thus at Sarah Lawrence College the point at which the student starts her quest for higher learning is not the Age of Pericles but her own orbit of experiences and interests. The overwhelmingly important thing, we have found, is that the point of departure be familiar ground, so that the student experiences the development of her subject matter and is able at every point to see its relation to her long-range goals.[11]

[11] As quoted by Benjamin Fine, *Democratic Education,* Thomas Y. Crowell Company, New York, 1945, p. 115.

Individualized program of studies. This insistence upon individualized education adapted to the talents and abilities of different students has been a continuing one, and is perhaps the core of the Sarah Lawrence educational plan. In order to carry out this idea, Sarah Lawrence has no required courses, but instead the faculty plan with each student a program of studies appropriate to her particular abilities and needs. Programs are planned in only three general areas or courses in order to give the students time for concentrated study in each field and for wider reading. In the freshman year these courses are selected in separate fields in order to give the new students the opportunity to become familiar with a range of ideas and materials and with a variety of experiences in library, studio, field and laboratory. Since there are no required courses, particular attention is given to providing an intelligent sequence of studies taken from year to year. For some students the four-year program shows increasing specialization; for others who may have begun with highly specialized interests, the program is likely to be one of broadening interests and developing new ones.

The principal responsibility for helping the student plan her college life rests with her faculty adviser, called a *don*. Dons are consulted on all decisions of major importance affecting the students. They help to plan programs of study, being responsible not only for planning with the student a single year's program but also for the sequence of courses throughout her college years. They are consulted by faculty members when difficulties arise, or when important changes in plan are under way. Some students continue with the same don for four years while others select different ones each year.

The majority of the classes are small enough (eight to fifteen students) to make discussion and the interchange of ideas possible between teachers and students and among the students themselves. An individual conference, held with each student weekly or bi-weekly, supplements the work of the class. In a few courses in the sophomore and junior years the lecture method is employed, but the lectures are followed by group conferences which give opportunity for the exchange of ideas on the subject of the lectures.

The creative arts—painting, sculpture, design, theater, dance, music and writing—are included as integral parts of the academic curriculum.

Evaluation of students' work. Students' work is evaluated not by conventional grades but by reports written by the faculty and sent to the students two or three times a year. In these reports a student is judged on academic achievement, attitude toward work, study habits, ability to learn and to form judgments and use what is learned and ability to work independently.

Community activities. Students use the resources of the community widely for both exploratory field trips and for field work. During the past few years Sarah Lawrence students have conducted housing and public opinion surveys, have participated in local meetings and worked with organizations of many kinds in Westchester County, where the college is located. A program of teacher preparation with practical experience in teaching is a part of the liberal arts curriculum.

Study abroad. A year of study in France is designed for the comparatively few junior students for whom such study seems particularly appropriate and who are prepared to make the best use of it in the light of their academic interests and plans, their previous study and their knowledge of the language. Students study in France under a member of the Sarah Lawrence faculty who lives in Paris and helps each student work out a plan of study. She arranges for the registration of students at appropriate academic institutions in Paris, where the group has its headquarters. She provides tutors and special lecturers, arranges field trips and other activities related to the student's program of studies, and conducts a seminar in French Civilization which all students take in addition to their other studies. The French junior year program is open to a few students of other colleges. An opportunity is also offered for students proficient in Italian to spend the junior year in Rome. During the spring vacation there is a carefully planned field trip to Puerto Rico.

Student self-government. There is a complete system of student self-government, which with the organization of dormitory life and a large degree of personal freedom helps the student to learn how to live as a member of the community. Students share in the total planning of the college including the development of the curriculum.

Requirements for graduation. The requirements for graduation from the four-year course bring into sharp focus the purposes of the college. The Bachelor of Arts degree is awarded to students "(1) whose achievements in acquiring knowledge meets the standards set by the faculty; (2) who have learned to think intelligently about what they know; (3) who are able to consider fairly the ideas and attitudes of other people; (4) who can discipline themselves; and (5) whose education has helped them to meet more effectively their responsibilities as members of their family and social groups, as members of the college community and as citizens." [12]

Preparation for after-college life. One of the purposes of the college is to help students discover uses for their abilities in their after-college life, and those who wish to undertake graduate study in special fields are helped to plan their programs so that they may be prepared for graduate or professional study. Almost one-third of the graduating class of June, 1960, undertook advanced work of some kind. The college itself offers a program of graduate studies in the liberal arts, leading to the degree of Master of Arts, to a few holders of the Bachelor of Arts degree. The graduate, like the undergraduate program is determined by the needs of the individual student and by the facilities for instruction available at the college. There is also a Director of Vocational Planning and Placement who is in charge of the student employment program, gives students advice and information about jobs on or off campus, and works with alumnae interested in finding new employment.

[12] *Bulletin,* Sarah Lawrence College, 1960–1961, p. 10.

STEPHENS COLLEGE
COLUMBIA, MISSOURI

From the beginning Stephens College has been devoted exclusively to the education of women. It was founded in 1833 as the Columbia Female Academy by citizens of Columbia, Missouri, to provide education for their daughters. In 1856 the name was changed to the Baptist Female Academy, in 1870 as the result of an endowment gift from the Hon. J. L. Stephens it became Stephens Female College, and in 1917 it adopted the present name of Stephens College. The modern era of the college began in 1911 when the school was reorganized to provide two years of college education for women. Thus Stephens was one of the earliest pioneers in the junior college movement.

The Charters Study. James Madison Wood, who became president in 1912, was charged by the trustees with the responsibility of developing a program really suited to the needs of women students. To this end he engaged Dr. W. W. Charters to make a study of the needs and interests of women college graduates, which would lead to the building of a new curriculum.

In making this study Dr. Charters asked one thousand college alumnae to keep a record for an entire year of the ways in which they spent their time, and it was on the basis of the findings of this research that the Stephens program was built. Stephens is one of the very few colleges in America whose program has been developed as the result of such a study. Numerous studies have been made since the original one, and these have contributed facts and techniques for changing the curriculum as the lives of women alumnae have changed. The college considers attention to the unique problems of educating women to be of the greatest importance, as indicated in the following paragraph from the current catalog:

Women are traditionally the carriers of culture, the conservers of value, the arbiters of taste. In contemporary society the influence of women is not limited to the home, husband and children. The modern woman must be able to understand and to participate in national and international affairs, business, and the problems of human welfare. The responsibilities which a woman has to herself, her family and society are many and complex. If she is to be successful—if she is to become the person she wants to be—education must prepare her for the complex life ahead and for change at different stages of her life.[13]

Such education would prepare her for the three periods of her life—the period of working life, following graduation from college; the years of wifehood and motherhood; and the period which begins when her children are educated and gone from the home and she has the time to pursue her own interests and make new contributions to society.

The program. Such courses as Consumer Problems, Child Study, Personal Appearance, Fashion Design, and Marriage and the Family reflect the concern of the college with education in subjects of peculiar interest to women. There is wide latitude in course electives, each student's program being carefully considered with her adviser. The program of individual guidance begins with counseling with each girl in her home with her parents, and the adviser aids the student in assessing her own interests, abilities, needs and goals and in selecting the courses which will be of greatest help to her own individual development.

All students, however, are urged to include in their program of studies as many as possible of the basic courses in Communication, Beginning Psychology, Consumer Problems and Family Investments, Basic Beliefs in Human Experience, General Biology, General Humanities, Marriage and the Family, and Contemporary Social Issues. In all courses the relationship of knowledge to present-day issues and problems is emphasized. The student-faculty ratio is kept low.

The major program of the college is the two-year program leading to the degree of Associate in Arts. Recently a program has been inaugurated in which a student may obtain a Bachelor

[13] *Stephens College Bulletin,* 1961–1962, p. 11.

of Fine Arts degree in music, theater arts, fashion or dance. Those who pursue this program attend three yearly and two summer sessions and thus are able to complete the program in three calendar years. The college has national advisory committees which meet on campus to give critical and objective appraisals of specialized departments. For example, the Fashion Advisory Board, consisting of leading designers in the fashion industry, gives helpful suggestions for the application of instruction in fashion to the demands of the fashion industry.

Research program. One of the distinctive characteristics of Stephens is the continuous research carried on by the individual faculty member with the purpose of improving his own teaching and counseling and the program of the college. These individual and group research projects are under the charge of a trained director of research. Every phase of the program is always subject to evaluation.

The Stephens College House Plan. In 1960 a new program called the Stephens College House Plan was put into operation with one hundred first-year students who wished to concentrate on a basic core of five general education courses—Communication, General Humanities, Ideas and Living Today, Contemporary Social Issues and Beginning Psychology. Offices for the five teachers of the courses are located in the residence hall and some classes are held there. In addition to the basic courses the students may choose from one to three additional courses from the general curriculum of the college. According to the catalog, "the experiment is aimed at providing an integrated and balanced approach to liberal studies, encouraging independent learning, and fostering creative intellectual interaction of faculty and students." [14]

Out-of-class activities. The college provides the student with rich opportunities for learning in out-of-class activities. The maintenance of a cosmopolitan student body is a definite aim, and students are selected from all sections of the United States and

[14] *Stephens College Bulletin,* 1961–1962, p. 24.

from foreign countries. A fine program of cultural events brings outstanding speakers and artists to the campus. Classes are taken on trips to major cities during the year, and foreign tours during the summer are conducted by faculty members.

Religious life. It is one of the larger aims of the college to encourage the spiritual growth of students. A non-denominational Christian service is held on the campus on Sunday, and students are expected to attend this service or one of the churches in the city. Attendance at a Vesper service held in midweek is required. There is an extensive program of community service in which the girls serve in hospitals, assist in Sunday School work in churches, assist in local kindergartens and playgrounds, work with Girl Scouts and Campfire Girls and give service to elderly and needy persons.

The "Stephens Ideals," which are a college tradition, constitute a "design for living" for a Stephens girl. These are appreciation of the beautiful, cheerfulness, courtesy, forcefulness, health, honesty, love of scholarship, self-discipline, service and reverence toward the spiritual.

SWARTHMORE COLLEGE
SWARTHMORE, PENNSYLVANIA

Swarthmore College, a coeducational institution with an enrollment of about 900, was founded in 1864 by members of the Religious Society of Friends. In accordance with its Quaker background, its highly qualified students are expected to prepare themselves as well-rounded persons to become responsible citizens through exacting intellectual study. The college campus of about 300 acres is semirural and is located in a small residential suburb within a half hour's commuting distance of Philadelphia.

The stated purpose of the college is "to make its students more valuable human beings and more useful members of society." Its catalog indicates also the belief that, since democracy demands a broad base of intelligent understanding of issues and requires a high order of excellence in its leaders, Swarthmore can best serve our society by the maintenance of high standards.

The college program. The curriculum of the first two years is designed primarily to contribute to the student's general education by giving him an introduction to the content of knowledge and the methods of thinking in a variety of fields important to a liberal education. These are:

(1) The traditional humanistic studies, through which man learns to understand himself and his relationship to his fellows and the enduring values in human experience.

(2) The social sciences through which man learns to understand the nature of organized society, past and present, and his relationship to it.

(3) The natural sciences through which man learns to understand his physical environment, both organic and inorganic, outside of his own individual and social being.

By the end of the sophomore year students are expected to have made two decisions: first, what their field of concentration will be for the last two years, and second, whether they prefer to take "honors work" or continue their work in regular courses. The Honors program and the Course program are parallel systems of instruction for junior and senior students. Both are designed to evoke the student's maximum effort and development.

Work in Course. The work of juniors and seniors in Course includes some intensive, specialized study within a general area of interest. This comprises enough work in a single department to make an equivalent of four full courses. Before graduation the student must pass a comprehensive examination in his major subject. The completion of eighteen full courses, or their equivalent, with a minimum average of "C" normally constitutes the course requirement for a degree.

Work in Honors. The Honors program and seminar method was begun in 1922 under President Aydelotte and met with such success that it has been widely imitated in other institutions. It seeks to free from the exactions of classroom routine those students whose maturity, interest and capacity qualify them for independent work. The program has been characterized from the beginning by three basic elements:

(1) Honors work involves a concentration of the student's attention during his last two years upon a limited and integrated field of studies. He pursues only two subjects during a semester, thereby avoiding the fragmentation of interest that may result from a program of four or more courses. The content of the subject-matter field is correspondingly broader and demands of the student correlations of an independent and searching nature.

(2) Honors work frees the student from periodic examinations, since his thinking is under the combined scrutiny of his classmates and instructors. In electing the program he undertakes to subject himself at the end of the two years of Honors work to examinations in all of the eight fields studied. These examinations, requiring about three hours each, are prepared by examiners from other institutions, who also read the papers. They then come to the campus to conduct an oral examination of each student, in order to clarify and enlarge the bases of their judgment of his competence in a particular field of knowledge.

(3) Honors work is customarily carried on in seminars of seven students or less, or in independent projects leading to a thesis. Seminars meet once a week, in many cases in the home of the instructor, for sessions lasting three hours or more. Each student has an equal responsibility for the mastery of the whole of the material and is correspondingly searching in his scrutiny of ideas presented by his fellows or by his instructors.

At the end of the junior year Honors students are required to take the Honors examinations in the fields in which they have studied. These trial papers, however, are read by their instructors, not by visiting examiners. On the basis of the showing made in these examinations, the student may be advised or even required to return to Course, or may be warned that he continues in Honors at his own risk.

Preparation for professional work. For students who are looking forward to professional work in medicine, law, etc., the college provides a special adviser to help them arrange their programs to meet the professional school requirements. It has a special program for students who wish to major in civil, electrical or mechanical engineering leading both to the bachelor's and master's degrees in these fields.

The college catalog sums up the college purpose in these words: "A college is never static. Its purposes and policies are always changing to meet new demands and new conditions. . . . The goal is to achieve for each generation, by means appropriate to the times, the unique contribution and that standard of excellence which have been the guiding ideals of Swarthmore from its founding." [15]

TRENDS IN SPECIAL PROGRAMS

The eight colleges whose programs have been discussed in this chapter do not, of course, constitute all of the whole-college experimental or special programs that have been or are being tried in the United States. Other significant examples were the University of Wisconsin Experimental College, the General College of the University of Minnesota and the University of Chicago Plan. The programs of such small colleges as Black Mountain College in North Carolina and Goddard College in Vermont are worthy of study, but space is not available here to include these and some others not mentioned.

Are there any trends revealed in those that have been presented, perhaps too briefly to do justice to them? There seem to be

(1) a trend away from attending courses, gaining grades and college credits

(2) a trend toward inducing the student to become a self-

[15] *Swarthmore College Bulletin,* 1960–1961, p. 29.

starter and a self-disciplined person with the instructor as a guide

(3) a trend toward associating some realities—field, vocational, laboratory or community work—with the academic program

(4) a slight trend toward broad fields of concentration as opposed to narrow specialization

(5) a trend toward tailoring the program to fit the individual's needs, capacities and present interests

(6) a trend toward democratic sharing of the responsibility for campus life among administration, students and faculty

(7) a trend toward the use of seminars, honors plans and conferences in the instructional program

(8) a trend toward substituting proved competence in the student's area of study for the amassing of course credits

(9) a trend toward the dual goal of achieving some measure of vocational direction while becoming a thoroughly liberally educated person.

CHAPTER 6

The Teaching Function
of the College Professor

THE MORE A PROFESSOR KNOWS, THE MORE HE KNOWS
WHAT HE DOES NOT KNOW. IN A PROPERLY CONDUCTED
COLLEGE, THE FACULTY ARE SIMPLY THE MORE MATURE
STUDENTS WITH A SPECIAL RESPONSIBILITY FOR KEEPING
THE CONVERSATION GOING.
—*Lynn White, Jr.*

As has been said before, the excellence of an institution is determined by the quality of the student body and of its instructional staff. The quality of the staff is conditioned by the training, experience, scholarly activity and personal traits of its members. The effectiveness of the college teacher, so far as his teaching function is concerned, is dependent upon his scholarship and his ability to communicate his own enthusiasm for his field of learning and his lively interest in his students.

Certain it is that if a college instructor does not know his subject, he cannot teach it adequately. Unfortunately, a quite complete knowledge of a subject is not in itself a guarantee that a teacher can either teach it or help a student learn it. College presidents want to engage teachers who, in addition to having a thorough knowledge of their subjects, know how to teach and have a warm interest in young people.[1]

NEED FOR IMPROVEMENT
IN COLLEGE TEACHING

A point on which there is little dispute today is that there is need for great improvement in college teaching. An important measuring stick of the effectiveness of any education is its effect on the future lives of its students. In this connection Pace made a study of 951 former University of Minnesota students fifteen

[1] See Bernard Berelson, *Graduate Education in the U.S.*, McGraw-Hill Book Company, Inc., New York, 1960, p. 57.

years after they left college. In a foreword to this study Malcolm S. MacLean wrote:

We need desperately to know why there appears to be little or no difference between graduates and non-graduates, between high-ranking students and low-ranking students, after they have been a decade away from the campus. Why most of them appear to want security and contentment instead of taking a vigorous delight in "looking upon the bright face of danger" and welcoming blood-stirring change. Why, if we have taught them—far above their fellows—to think critically, they are in after-college years so obviously uncritical and inconsistent in their thinking. Why, if we have taught them to read good books, most of them read only "slick" magazines of huge circulation, newspapers, a few books of a standard below that of the freshman English class. Why, in a democracy, the most highly educated people we have, have failed so miserably to engage in community political activities; talk about broad national problems but take little interest in the methods and common thinking and planning necessary to solve these problems, and hardly any at all in local matters. Why are these alumni largely apathetic and complacent, self-centered, inconsistent? And, finally, what can the colleges do to change their processes so that future graduates may be better served, better trained, better educated? [2]

Pace's report was made in 1941. In 1952 Baker Brownell began a book with a chapter entitled "The College—a Report on a Failure," in which he listed four failures. These were (1) the inability to relate the college functionally to life as the students know it, or should know it, (2) the lack of respect for and trust in the conventional college system, (3) the use of the college as an escape from the home community and (4) the failure to train students for a community-centered or family-centered career.[3] If these indictments and Pace's findings portray a true picture of the product of our colleges, it seems evident that the college must

[2] C. Robert Pace, *They Went to College,* University of Minnesota Press, Minneapolis, Minnesota, 1941, pp. xi and xii.
[3] Baker Brownell, *The College and the Community,* Harper and Brothers, New York, 1952, pp. 3, 5, 7, 8, 10.

improve its work, especially in its most important aspect—college teaching.

Factors in College Teaching

The first factor in teaching: image of a good teacher. It is customary to say that the teacher must keep in mind two factors— the student and the subject. There is another factor which is perhaps even more important than these two—this is the college teacher's image of himself and of what a college professor is or ought to be. On several occasions the writer has asked his students to describe the best college teacher each has had. From their descriptions it seems evident that either students do not have a clear image of what a good college teacher is or that they are not in agreement about the matter. Some described professors who had warm personalities, even some who were "ham" actors. Some preferred men and women who were less dramatic but lucid and stimulating in their ideas. Grade conscious students preferred professors who were definite in assignments and precise in the delineation of all requirements. Differing personalities react differently to the personality of any teacher.

It seems important, therefore, to raise the question, What kind of image of a college teacher does the person who is preparing for college teaching carry in his mind? Is it one of a person who is strict, authoritarian, demanding, oblivious to contemporary matters, impersonal, interested only in subject matter and not in people? Or is it the image of a college teacher who is sympathetic to the student, reasonably warm in personality, enthusiastic about ideas, infectious in his own eagerness to know more and to help students learn more and to obtain high achievement?

There is no single right answer to these questions. Each person has a different heredity and has had a different environmental experience from every other and hence will react differently. The college teacher should remember that the students who are enrolled in his classes have also had varied experiences and will react differently to him as a person and to what he tries to teach them.

Quite apart from imparting information, the college teacher needs to think of the effect he, as a person, has on students in his classroom. Does he have a fundamentally optimistic outlook on life, or a pessimistic one? Though all of us experience frustration—on some days more than on others—can the college teacher avoid projecting his own frustrations on the students in his classes? Can he remember that the students, too, are trying to cope with their own frustrations, some of which lie outside the classroom, while others may be related to the subject that the college teacher enjoys teaching? The subject may indeed be a difficult hurdle for many students. Does the teacher engage in taking "pot shots" at what other members of the faculty are doing or saying, thus being an irritant whose function seems to be that of belittling the efforts of his colleagues? And will he recognize students in his classes who exhibit the same kind of behavior? What will be the effect of a frustrated college professor on a frustrated college student? Though this is probably a rare situation, the first step in becoming a good college teacher is to realize and accept one's own variability and one's own limitations. Along with such acceptance should come an appreciation of one's own strengths and abilities. A college dean was asked what he would change if he had the opportunity to change only one thing in college teaching. He replied that the factor which would lead to the greatest improvement would be a change in attitude on the part of the teachers. This is more important than a change of content or change of method. However, such a change is likely to occur only when the college professor has an adequate concept of himself as a person and an appropriate image of what constitutes a really fine college teacher.

The second factor in teaching: knowing the student. College teachers have many ways of becoming acquainted with their students. The obvious first step is to learn the students' names. One professor has candid camera shots taken at the first class session so that he can quickly associate names and faces. Another seats students alphabetically and asks them to take the same seats regularly. A third asks each student to fill out a one-page questionnaire telling about his work experience, his education up to the present time, and his goals for the future. Another instructor has a personal conference with each student as early in the term as possible so as to get to know him as a person. Still another teacher invites students to his home for an evening where he can become acquainted with them in a less formal situation. All of these methods or some combination of them will provide the opportunity to become acquainted.

A matter to which the college teacher should give some attention early in the course is the identification of gifted students. In these times with the emphasis on making the maximum use of our best talents, thoughtful provision should be made for such students. They have I.Q.'s of 130 or better, are able to learn in many fields by themselves, and should be permitted to proceed as rapidly as they can. A Nobel Prize winner once said in the writer's hearing that it is foolish to urge everyone into the study of mathematics and science; that what is needed is rather a real search for and identification and cultivation of a few persons with great talent in these fields. But talent should be cultivated to its utmost in whatever field it may be found. The college teacher, particularly the teacher of freshmen, should seek to identify, encourage, challenge and develop the gifted student, be it in human relations, the social sciences, the arts, the humanities or the natural sciences. The nation's greatest natural resource is its human resources, and the chief potential among these is the gifted college student.

It is also of importance for the teacher to know the point which each of his students has reached in his learning. This information is particularly important in studies that are cumulative in nature, such as mathematics, foreign languages, the sciences and English composition. It is widely known that secondary school preparation differs sharply from region to region, from school to school, and even from teacher to teacher within the same school. Therefore, the college teacher cannot possibly assume that all students registered in his class have the same educational background. Even when prerequisites for a course are carefully set forth, the differences, though less marked, will still be great. As a result some college teachers often ask students early in the semester to do a sample piece of work during the class period so that they may know where they can begin their teaching with some confidence that it will be apprehended. Certainly all college teachers, except those who are teaching introductory courses with which students are not expected to be familiar, should begin with some sort of review of the essential processes and content that students should have mastered in their previous learning experience.

A number of eminent laymen as well as educators have frequently ventured to prescribe for the ills of the higher educational institution without giving much, if any, evidence that they are aware of the importance of a sound knowledge of the psychology of learning and of human nature. The college teacher not only should have taken courses in psychology, but he should consider whether he has been taught only the psychology of the senses, or theories based on the learning of mice or rats, rather than the psychology of human learning and behaving. Because some college teachers have had little or no exposure to such psychology, their success in teaching is likely to be less marked than it otherwise would be. Since many volumes have been written on this subject, what is stated here is a greatly compressed version of a considerable body of scholarship.[4]

Concepts related to learning. There are five concepts related to learning which the college teacher needs to keep in mind. First, students differ tremendously in interest, in personality, in rate of maturing, in rate of learning, in past experience. No college teacher should treat his students as though they were all quite

---

[4] It is hoped that the reader will delve into this field much more deeply in such books as Lee J. Cronbach, *Educational Psychology,* Harcourt, Brace and Company, New York, 1954, and Charles Skinner, *Elementary Educational Psychology,* Prentice-Hall, New York, 1945.

alike. Second, students differ in their readiness to learn. Some students were sent to college. Some were required to take the course against their wills, while others elected it. Some were adequately prepared; others were not. Third, all students need to be motivated frequently to learn. The best motivation is not fear or threat of failure, but an enthusiasm to learn new ideas and grapple with new techniques. Fourth, young people are more able to accomplish difficult tasks than most adults believe. And, fifth, the whole goal of learning is to promote self-education, self-discipline and the ability to take intelligent charge of oneself. The real test of the effectiveness of teaching is whether learning continues long after college days are over. One way to accomplish this aim is illustrated by Barzun:

. . . the teaching impulse goes something like this. A fellow human being is puzzled or stymied. He wants to open a door or spell "accommodate." The would-be helper has two choices. He can open the door, spell the word; or he can show his pupil how to do it for himself. The second way is harder and takes more time, but a strong instinct in the born teacher makes him prefer it. It seems somehow to turn an accident into an opportunity for permanent creation.[5]

Extending this view, one can agree with Dashiell that "Education is guided learning. Learning, in turn, is habit-forming, if taken generally enough."[6]

Theory of transfer of training. A point which needs some elaboration here is the assumption made by many teachers at every educational level that training, of whatever sort, will automatically be transferred to other areas by the student; i.e., if he can apply a process of step-by-step reasoning in explaining a geometric theorem, he will apply similar reasoning to the analysis of a poem or to a problem on the football field or in a game of chess. Or these teachers believe that if a student has been taught

[5] Jacques Barzun, *The Teacher in America,* Little, Brown and Company, 1945, pp. 17–18.
[6] J. F. Dashiell, "Contributions of Scientific Knowledge about the Psychology of Learning," *37th Yearbook,* N.S.S.E., Part II, Public School Publishing Company, Bloomington, Illinois, 1938, p. 293.

to see the relationship between cause and effect in chemistry, he will then automatically see the relationship between cause and effect in human relations. However, it has been learned that such transfer occurs only when the teacher teaches for transfer—that is, when he shows the relationship between cause and effect in fields other than chemistry—and also when there exists a similarity in the two situations. College teachers will find, moreover, that the ability to cause transfer of learning to take place varies with the intelligence of the student—the greater the scholastic aptitude, the greater the likelihood that the student will make a transfer of an intellectual learning to a similar intellectual situation.

This first type of transfer is what Bruner calls "specific transfer." He also speaks of a second type—the transfer of principles and attitudes, which he explains as follows: "In essence it consists of learning initially not a skill but a general idea, which can then be used as a basis for recognizing subsequent problems as special cases of the idea originally mastered. This type of transfer is at the heart of the educational process—the continual broadening and deepening of knowledge in terms of basic and general ideas." [7]

Interested college teachers will wish to read Bruner as well as the psychological findings by Tilton with regard to this point and also (1) the trial-and-error principle in learning, (2) the principle of insight, (3) the principle of conditioned responses, (4) the role of reward and punishment, (5) the importance of the goal-seeking attitude, (6) principles of economy in learning and (7) neural bases of learning. From this reading one will probably conclude with Tilton, "that the educational task is psychologically very complex, involving to an important degree the development of memory, perception, meaning, understanding, intelligence, transfer, problem solving, interests, attitudes, appreciations, values and ideals, as well as the development of habits and skills." [8]

[7] Jerome S. Bruner, *The Process of Education,* Harvard University Press, Cambridge, Massachusetts, 1960, p. 17.

[8] J. W. Tilton, "A Psychological Basis for Learning," in *Foundations of Education,* F. C. Gruber, editor, University of Pennsylvania Press, Philadelphia, 1957, p. 39.

The more one studies the problems of teaching, the more likely he is to conclude that one cannot "teach" a person anything but can only help him to learn. Essentially, this involves complex problems of motivation and stimulation. The good college teacher seeks for signs in his students that zest, enthusiasm, curiosity and inquiry have been aroused. Only then can he have some confidence that learning for the student will be self-starting, self-directed and lifelong.

Rote learning. Few college courses depend entirely on the memorization of material, yet this is an expected exercise in many of them. As long ago as 1885 a pioneer German investigator, Hermann Ebbinghaus, described some experimental procedures on the subject of learning. He considered, and almost all psychologists today agree with him, that repetition is basic to rote learning, and he was able to plot the first "curve of forgetting." Since Ebbinghaus made his experiments, other investigators have found that if interference is kept to a minimum, less repetition will be needed. "Interference" might be illustrated by someone coming into a room where there is a group of people. If in the group there is only one person he does not know, it is comparatively easy for him to remember this person's name. But if instead of one, there are five or eight or twelve people he does not know, the "interference" caused by his attempt to remember several names instead of just one will probably prevent his remembering any of them for any length of time. Cut down the interference and rote learning speeds up. They also have proved that "overlearning"—the repetition of already-learned material—minimizes forgetting.

Yet, however effective repetition, elimination of interference, and overlearning may be in rote learning, they do not explain the learning that results from what Gestalt psychologists call insight —the sudden flash of understanding that results from a single, vivid experience. The relationship of learning by understanding and by problem solving to repetition and associative learning is still far from clear.

How large a portion of memorized learning persists is suggested by Cronbach, who tells of a college course in which students were required to name the structures of mammals before and after the course and again fifteen months later. Before the course the average score was 22; immediately following it the score rose to 62; and fifteen months later the average had dropped to 31, only nine points better than the score achieved by the students before taking the course! Thus during the period in which they were not studying zoology they forgot three-fourths of the factual knowledge they had acquired.[9] Ruth H. Thomson in testing for retention found that immediately following a psychology lecture students knew 62 per cent of the basic ideas in the lecture. A half week later they knew 50 per cent; one week later, 37 per cent; two weeks later, 30 per cent; and eight weeks later only 23 per cent.[10]

These two pieces of research do not suggest that everything learned is forgotten, nor that the mastery of subject matter is not important. They infer, however, that some skills in addition to memory need to be acquired, perhaps those recommended by the Committee on Pre-Legal Education listed later in this chapter. A zoology professor had good reason to take satisfaction in the fact that an independent investigation of the ability of members of his zoology class to draw conclusions from experiments not previously studied revealed that some time after the course had been completed, this ability had become further developed, and this occurred during the year when zoology had not been studied. College teachers need to cultivate reasoning power and critical analysis leading to sound judgments that persist long after the subject matter on which the students' wits were sharpened has faded into comparative insignificance.

Practical experience. Most advisers of doctoral candidates tend to suggest to advanced students that they write dissertations in areas in which they have had some experience. Such counsel is

[9] Lee J. Cronbach, *op. cit.,* pp. 391–392.
[10] Ruth H. Thomson, "An Experimental Study of Memory as Influenced by Feeling Tone," *Journal of Experimental Psychology,* 13, 1930, pp. 462–467.

based, of course, on the assumption that practical experience will keep the writer from making inane or impossible statements. If this is a valid criterion for research, it is even more valid for teaching. The story is told of a school psychologist who, after examining a child, recommended to the teacher that the child be given one hour of "special help" a day. If this psychologist had ever been a classroom teacher, for even a few months, he would have known that a teacher could not possibly carry out his prescription.

What is true of psychologists is equally true in other fields. Teachers of English composition will become better teachers if they have written for newspapers or periodicals. Teachers of business subjects will find that their teaching is far more vital if based on business experience. Political scientists will be more effective teachers if they are working or have worked as advisers to a small town government, a state commission or a national agency. Teachers of music who play in good orchestras will be better teachers of their particular instruments for this experience. A well-known painter teaches painting to students by working at his own easel alongside of theirs. Sociologists who are interested in juvenile delinquency, in family life, in depressed areas in large cities have many opportunities to be in touch with the realities of life, and their teaching is made more vital on this account. Furthermore, all teachers are likely to find that successful work in a practical field connected with their teaching will increase their students' respect for them as well as their readiness to accept the teaching as valid. Thus it increases the effectiveness of the teaching. In the years ahead it seems likely that some reality experience prior to advanced study and along with it will be required and will produce a better research worker and a better teacher. Such a combination has also been found to be an important factor in the employment opportunities open to new as well as experienced college teachers.

The third factor in teaching: knowledge of subject matter. The third factor in college teaching is knowledge of what is to be learned—the content, the subject matter of one's teaching. It is assumed that those who read this book will already be fairly well along on this road. Over the doors of many school and college libraries is the saying, "Knowledge is power." Many would be inclined to agree with Garrison, who calls this idea "nonsense unless it is qualified to read 'Knowledge put to use is power'." [11] A college teacher puts his knowledge to use in his teaching, as well as in his research and writing. His knowledge must be both broad and deep, and it must have meanings for students. The teacher must realize also that in most fields it gets out of date. The constantly increasing contributions to the field of literature require reading and study to keep the teacher up to date. New interpretations of history, new theories of international relations, new findings regarding our own culture and other cultures are continually being made. At the college level there is no field of teaching in which study by the professor is not steadily required. A former department head who was asked why he had accepted a deanship replied that as chairman of a large department he had been unable to keep up with the developments in his own scientific field, so he had decided that he might as well devote more time to college administration. If one desires to be an effective college teacher, he must have time to devote to keeping up to date in his field of competence.

There are other facets of subject matter which need mentioning. It should have perspective and be subjected to criticism. Criticism is one of the elements of scholarly work. Literature, drama, music and economic, social and political theories are all improved when subjected to searching criticism. To analyze and study proposals, to evaluate, synthesize and integrate—all may result in constructive thought and action. Then, too, all teaching of subject matter contains, knowingly or unknowingly, some value system. While some college teachers disclaim any concern for values in their teaching, what they do in the classroom often reveals them. The poems selected or omitted for study by an English teacher involve the application of some value system.

[11] Roger H. Garrison, *The Adventure of Learning in College*, Harper and Brothers, New York, 1959, p. 133.

For political scientists belief in the freedom of the individual represents a value. For economists the consideration of the problems of poverty and wealth, distribution and exchange, control or increase of production and consumption involves values inherent in these topics. The argument here is not in behalf of any particular value system, but rather to indicate that underlying the teaching of almost all subject matter are some value assumptions.[12] A third facet of subject matter relates to derivative skills. For example, students need to write and speak well in their own tongue as well as in foreign languages, no matter what the subject matter may be. Again from the study of subject matter students need to learn the skill of thinking critically and clearly. Two statements regarding critical thinking, one negative and one affirmative, will be illustrative. Garrison says students do not think clearly because:

(1) They either do not see a problem realistically . . . or they do not discern valid relationships among superficially unrelated events or objects.

(2) They are apt to draw hasty or unwarranted conclusions— sometimes because their data are irrelevant or missing, but more often because a "black or white" answer seems to satisfy an apparent compulsion for certainty, for being right.

(3) They often accept uncritically the assertions of authority, whether it be a textbook, a teacher, an expert or the apparent testimony of experience.

(4) Alternately, they sometimes show a stubborn unwillingness to accept a conclusion dictated by strong evidence, usually because the evidence is emotionally upsetting or unsatisfying.

(5) They sometimes do not care enough about a subject or problem to make the hard effort of thinking about it.

(6) In some subject areas they shut themselves off emotionally by saying, "I never did like math (or languages, chemistry, history, etc.)."

[12] For an informative chapter on student values see Marjorie Carpenter's chapter on "Stimulating Students to Make Critical Value Judgments," in Russell M. Cooper, Ed., *The Two Ends of the Log,* University of Minnesota Press, Minneapolis, 1958, pp. 86–98. See also pp. 151–152.

(7) They often lack relevant information on a subject, and they do not have reliable methods for obtaining that information nor for evaluating it once it is obtained.[13]

In a statement of policy the Association of American Law Schools said the following:

Critical power in thinking requires the development of skill in:

(1) Research: awareness of sources and types of material, adaptation to particular use, methods of fact presentation.

(2) Fact completeness: willingness to recognize all facts, avoidance of preconception and fiction masquerading as fact, disciplined ability to withhold judgment until all facts are "in."

(3) Fact differentiation: relevance of facts to particular issues, varying importance of different facts, relative persuasiveness of various facts.

(4) Fact marshalling: reduction of masses of fact to manageable proportions, arranging of facts in logical and convincing order.

(5) Deductive reasoning: use of the syllogism, spotting logical fallacies, avoiding conclusions flowing from inaccurate premises.

(6) Inductive reasoning: experimental methodology, accuracy of observation, elimination of variables, role of hypotheses, conditions essential to valid generalizations such as adequacy of sampling, strict limitation of conclusions by available reliable data.

(7) Reasoning by analogy: methods of classification, gradations of relationships, finding resemblances which justify inferences of similarity.

(8) Critical analyses: disciplined skepticism in approach, thoroughness of inquiry, keenness of mind in cutting through to essentials.

(9) Constructive synthesis: systematic formulation of principles, meaningful organization of ideas, structural relationship of concepts.

(10) Power of decision: resolution of discoverable issues in the light of short and long-term ends found preferable on explicitly identified and justified grounds.[14]

Though these statements of what is involved in critical thinking involve "a large order" for the college professor, they suggest the

[13] Roger H. Garrison, *op. cit.,* p. 135.
[14] Committee on Pre-Legal Education, Association of American Law Schools, 1955.

skills which the teaching of subject matter ought to help the student to acquire.[15]

THE PROCESS OF TEACHING

In a study conducted by Berelson, 609 college presidents and academic deans replied to the question, "Which three [of eight] qualities are most important for a college teacher?" Ninety-eight per cent listed knowledge of subject matter of his discipline; 82 per cent, knowledge of how to teach; and 68 per cent, interest in young people. Thus knowledge of how to teach was considered of great importance by more than three-fourths of those who responded.[16] Those who are preparing for college teaching need to be familiar with several methods of instruction: (1) lecture, (2) dicussion, (3) demonstration, (4) coach-and-pupil method, and (5) recitation. The "recitation" originated from the "explication of the text" in France. This method, once used in the United States, has now dropped by the wayside and will not be discussed in this volume.

It will be recalled that earlier in this book the general purposes of college teaching were discussed. Ideally, the college student should be an insatiable inquirer; his continuous curiosity to learn more and more should be cultivated. The ideal discipline to be sought is internal, which causes the individual to set for himself difficult tasks, from the achievement of which he experiences great satisfaction. We have seen that college students differ in purpose, in readiness to learn, in ways they apprehend teaching and in their responses to it. All of these points must be in the mind of the college teacher as he approaches the three aspects of all teaching—preparation, presentation and evaluation.

Preparation. It hardly seems necessary to say that college pro-

[15] For a useful discussion on this subject see Elizabeth Monroe Drews' chapter on "Helping Students to Think Critically," in Russell M. Cooper, *op. cit.,* pp. 76–85.

[16] Bernard Berelson, *op. cit.,* pp. 57 and 276.

fessors should prepare thoroughly for each teaching duty. Preparation once made for a whole course must be done over and over again. Nothing is more deadly than for college teachers to use old notes, old jokes and old stories. It is a common quip on many campuses to inquire whether Professor X has come to the part of his course where he tells the story of the bullfrog. College students are not easily fooled, and teachers who do not prepare for their teaching are soon found out.

It has been indicated that for every hour in the classroom two hours should be spent in preparation, in reading student papers and in individual conferences with students. A part of the required preparation should be spent in reading in the field in which the college teacher instructs. It is obvious that he should know the latest books and magazine articles relevant to his particular courses. Unfortunately, in many instances this is not the case. Perhaps the teacher hides behind the excuse that the college library does not buy the needed materials, but in this event the good college teacher will buy judiciously with his own funds. There is no substitute for wide reading in college teaching—not only in one's own field but in related fields. While knowledge alone does not establish the competency of a college teacher, being well informed is an absolute essential. If there ever was a time when the teacher of mathematics, science, or foreign languages and literature could assume that he knew his stuff "cold," that time is past. With the development of the "set" theory in mathematics, nuclear fission with its implication of radiation in the sciences, foreign language laboratories and new interpretations in literature, the present-day college teacher simply cannot rest on his oars. One is reminded of the quotation from *Alice Through the Looking Glass,* "It takes all the running you can do to keep in the same place."

Assuming a basis of continuous reading and study, the college teacher is ready to start preparation for a class session. As he begins his preliminary thinking about it, he needs to consider his goals. Will he aim to impart information, to change attitudes, to stimulate thinking, to develop appreciation, to help the student acquire certain skills, to encourage research? The identification of the purposes of any given class session will in part determine the nature of the preparation.

Aids in teaching. What aids does the college teacher have in achieving any or all of the aims of college teaching? Among them are tables, charts, graphs and diagrams by which he can display and clarify the relationships between facts. Then there are the traditional audio-visual aids—slides, film strips, recordings and films. If it is true, as has been said, that a picture is worth a thousand words, these devices must not be overlooked in the clarification aspect of the teaching process. In fact, a course in the history and interpretation of art could hardly be taught adequately without the showing of slide reproductions of primitive art and of masterpieces. Recordings are a necessity for a similar course in music. In the aural-oral approach to the teaching of modern foreign language, slides and tapes are used in a self-instruction laboratory. Scores of such laboratories have been installed in colleges over the nation, and hundreds in public schools. These new devices are designed not only to help students to read a foreign language, but to speak it reasonably well. Furthermore, they help the student think almost automatically in the second language. Borglum of Wayne State University says that the new teaching process bears "no resemblance to the decoding, word-learning, rule-remembering tyranny of the traditional language class."

Motion pictures are another media widely used in teaching. Combining as they do picture and sound, movies help students identify themselves with the experiences of others and thus are useful in reshaping students' values and in modifying their ways of behaving. Elsewhere in this chapter consideration is given to the use of radio and television in teaching.

More recent scientific aids in teaching are video tape recordings and auto-instructional devices. Most college teachers are familiar with audio tape recorders, which have made it possible to record, among other things, addresses given on the campus with a view to replaying them in class for analysis, interpretation and discussion. Video tape recordings have the advantage of combining picture and voice. While at this writing video-tape recorders are so expensive that only a few are available on most campuses, yet their use in teaching seems promising. For example, a course in Humanities can be recorded on tape, and each lesson played at different times of the day when class sections cannot be scheduled at the same time. This is a great saving in energy for the professor, who makes only one appearance for the original recording. Also he can view his own teaching and, if dissatisfied with it, he can erase the tape and make it over before another section sees what he considers to be teaching which is not up to his standard. Perhaps it would be helpful, if it were possible, for all college teachers to view video tapes of their own teaching at least once. It is obvious that video tape recordings require the most carefully planned preparation.

As long ago as December, 1924, Dr. Sidney L. Pressey of Ohio State University first demonstrated a teaching machine and its use at a meeting of the American Psychological Association in Washington, D.C. Descriptions of the workings of this machine and its use appeared in articles in *School and Society* on March 20, 1926, and May 7, 1927.

More recent proposals for auto-instructional devices and programmed instruction along the lines now employed seem to date from 1954, when Professor B. F. Skinner of Harvard University published an article on the subject.[17] Several types of teaching machines are now on the market, ranging in size from a simple desk model the size of a dictionary to an apparatus the size of a refrigerator. Whatever the design of the auto-instructional device, it is important to understand that neither machines nor books themselves can teach. It is the *program of class instruction* in the book or the machine that does the teaching. Both require meticulous advance preparation. Some machines require the student to write in his answers; others, only to press a button. One publisher has described programmed instruction as a system of learning in which:

[17] B. F. Skinner, "The Science of Learning and the Art of Teaching," *Harvard Educational Review,* XXIV (Summer, 1954), pp. 86–97.

(1) The subject matter is carefully organized into a logical sequence in which it can readily be learned by the student.

(2) The subject matter is broken down into small discrete steps—questions or instructions—each one building deliberately on preceding steps.

(3) The learner can progress through the sequence at his own rate.

(4) The learner is given the correct response immediately.[18]

While it might seem that instruction by teaching machines is most effective in imparting information only, its enthusiasts insist that it is effective in conceptual learning and in developing appreciations and understandings, attitudes and skills.

While the greatest use of teaching machines up to now has been in the elementary and secondary fields, they have also been used at the college level in the teaching of logic, engineering, philosophy, psychology, music, biology, mathematics, statistics and some other fields. One piece of research compared the results of the teaching of mathematics to freshman engineering students at U.C.L.A. by three different methods: teaching machines, programmed textbooks and lectures. The program groups performed significantly better than the group that received the lectures. While much more research is needed, the inevitable question arises, "Will teaching machines eventually displace teachers?" The purpose of all machines is to remove some of the drudgery from life. If programmed instruction proves to be as promising as now seems possible, it may free the teacher from many of his routine tasks and enable him to have more time to spend with individual students. It seems evident, however, that no mechanical device can replace the individual teacher in meeting student needs, answering their questions, counseling with each one and guiding and encouraging their intellectual growth. College professors will watch with interest developments in the programming of instruction and the use of teaching machines, and pos-

[18] Edward E. Booher, "Programmed Instruction in Books and Teaching Machines," McGraw-Hill Book Company, Inc., New York, 1961, 16 pp.

sibly will wish to prepare their own series of "frames" for a program of instruction.

After the goals have been identified and the media and teaching aids selected, there are several points the college teacher must keep in mind as he begins to prepare for a specific teaching situation.

(1) He may not plan carefully enough for the presentation of material he knows very well. This practice can be very dangerous, for when a person has had long familiarity with his content, he is likely to forget that some elements of it which are easy for him are difficult for the person who encounters them for the first time.

(2) It is necessary to remember that learning proceeds from the known to the unknown, from the familiar to the unfamiliar. In this connection Comenius's simple rules are worthy of study:

The few before the many,
The brief before the long,
The simple before the complex,
The general before the particular,
The nearer before the more remote,
The regular before the irregular (or the analogous before the anomalous).[19]

(3) There are two types of teaching approaches: the deductive approach, in which a law or principle is stated and then illustrated with different examples; and the inductive approach in which a number of specific illustrations are given, from which a law or principle is "discovered."

(4) There is nothing wrong with drill itself, as was indicated in the previous discussion of repetition and learning. However, the people who are required to perform the drill must see the reason for it and accept it as desirable.

[19] Vladimir Jelinek, *The Analytical Didactic of Comenius,* University of Chicago Press, Chicago, 1955, p. 123.

(5) In every class the teacher should employ a variety of activities to take into account the differing ways in which the students in his class learn.

(6) If the mastery of subject matter is the goal of the teacher, he needs to choose between one of the several kinds of organization of his material:

(a) Chronological. History is often taught decade by decade or century by century.

(b) Logical. Such an organization may be found in the presentation of such a topic as the causes of delinquency—let us say social, economic, mental, physical and spiritual.

(c) Psychological. This approach may start with a question of interest to the class and proceed from the question into the substance of the content needed to answer it. An example of this approach might be a student's question about the implications of space travel. Using this as a point of departure, a professor can delve into the scientific, sociological, political and economic implications of the subject.

(d) Developmental. Such an organization begins with a series of assumptions or presuppositions and develops the conclusions that follow from the assumptions. An example of this approach might be the assumption that immigration, the need for more agricultural production and the development of rail transportation were responsible for the westward movement in the United States. An examination of underdeveloped countries in the world could be undertaken to discover whether similar conditions exist there and if so whether a similar outcome could be predicted.

(e) Decision-making approach. The U.S. State Department in 1947 issued a publication describing its method of reaching a foreign-policy decision. This included a statement of the historic background of the problem, the identification of it, the presentation of possible alternatives for dealing with it, the arguments for and against each alternative and, finally, the selection of the alternative chosen with the reasons for choosing it in the light of the background statement.

It is obvious, of course, that since many combinations of these and other approaches can be made, the college teacher will need to make his preparation in the light of the maturity and interest of the students and the nature of the material. Advanced graduate students are likely to need far less motivation than undergraduates and are likely to be more able to deal with abstract ideas without illustrations and specific applications of the content being considered.

Presentation. The most careful preparation may be fruitless in accomplishing the goals the college teacher has in mind unless he is able to "put over," elicit or excite the knowledge, skills and attitudes he wishes his students to acquire. This ability depends on various factors: (a) the college teacher's personality, his competence in his field and his attitude toward students; (b) the academic and social climate of the group; (c) the physical condition of the meeting place, the opportunity for everyone to see and hear and freedom from possible distractions; (d) the methods used, including teaching aids; and (e) the ability of the college teacher to adapt what he has to teach to the abilities, interests and needs of the students. College teachers are not likely to be able to get college men and women to accept ideas and suggestions unless they are challenged and their interest aroused sufficiently to get them to think seriously about the substance of what the teacher is trying to teach.

Though experienced professors will find the following suggestions to be quite elementary, they may be useful to new college teachers. A vivid remembrance of one's own first experience with a class of college sophomores makes these comments seem more important than perhaps they really are. He remembers walking into the classroom where thirty-five students were waiting "to look him over." Some amount of apprehension was to be found behind the desk as well as in front. The instructor wondered if his trembling knees were visible and if he had enough material to last out a fifty-minute period. The students wondered, "What kind of prof is he? Is he tough or easy? Is he human or an

'iceberg'? Does he have a sense of humor? Is he interesting, enthusiastic? Does he know how to 'dish it out'?"

After the first session things go more easily. Presumably a text
or reading list has been assigned. The students have been given
something to do and may return with some questions of their
own. The teacher can establish a pattern of "you listen and I'll
tell," or one of participation. The assumption must be made that
the class group is interested in learning and that the members
will participate if given the opportunity.

At the beginning of every session genuine attempts should be
made to establish contact with the students. Many college teachers
make it a practice to be in the classroom while the students are
coming in and to carry on informal conversation with them before the formal class period begins. One college professor begins
every class session by asking, "Are there any questions or comments?" Sometimes these become so engrossing that the lesson is
delayed by the give and take between students and instructor and
among the students themselves. When students are unaccustomed
to this sort of participation, the teacher can usually develop it
by asking for questions and waiting two or three minutes for
some to be asked. Invariably some student will start the ball
rolling, and the pattern of class participation is set. Establishing
such contacts with students is the best way for the teacher to
sense how they are responding to the teaching.

Though these suggestions are related to all methods of instruction, they have particular significance for the lecture, because if they are not followed, the professor may be on one wave
length and the students on another without the teacher being
aware of it.

The lecture method. One author has said that "a professor is a
man who talks in other people's sleep." [20] For some college teachers the lecture is a dangerous method to use because it *is* likely to
lull students to sleep. This is particularly true if the professor has

[20] William C. DeVane, *The American University in the Twentieth Century*, Louisiana State University Press, Baton Rouge, 1957, p. 29.

a droning voice and a dispirited method of presentation. Further-more, telling is not necessarily teaching, and listening likewise does not guarantee learning. It is alleged that 85 per cent of the average person's learning comes through sight rather than through hearing. It takes a big lot of talking to get a little learning, and it must be remembered that the attention span is sharply limited. Therefore, the college teacher should not use the lecture method if he can accomplish the same purpose in about the same amount of time in another way. Also the lecture method should not be employed when the purpose is to teach students how to do some-thing. In this case a demonstration or laboratory lesson is far more effective. Nevertheless, the lecture is still a prevailing mode of instruction and can be effective under certain circumstances. It is probably the best means of covering a large amount of ma-terial in a relatively short time. It may be desirable to use it as an introduction to a lesson, before employing other methods. It may be useful in five- or ten-minute talks as a way of stimulating interest. It is a good way of summarizing material covered and ideas, attitudes and values presented.

When this method is to be used, the lecture should be carefully prepared. An organizing principle should be chosen and a psy-chological point of beginning selected as well as a psychological closing. Plans should be made to use slides, charts and diagrams to bring life to the lecture. Illustrations, anecdotes and stories should be included only if they add life and light to the presenta-tion. Delivery of the lecture should be forceful, enthusiastic and not too hurried. If the college teacher intends to read the lecture, he might better have it duplicated and distributed to the class members for them to read. Certainly he should be sufficiently in command of his material to find reading unnecessary. While he may have notes, he should be able to look his students directly in the eye, be earnest about what he is saying and speak with variety both of voice tone and in rate of speaking. At the conclusion the teacher should summarize the main points of his lecture.

While the old method of the class recitation is still practiced to some extent in elementary and secondary schools, in some private colleges and at places like West Point and the Naval Academy, a combination of the lecture and question methods is more often found at the college level. The teacher should not ask all of the questions nor answer all of them. As many students as possible should be involved in asking and responding to questions. Interchanges between students under proper control and circumstances are enlivening and stimulating to class sessions. There are several reasons for the use of questions, not all of which are equally valid. Such reasons may be listed as follows:

(1) To arouse interest
(2) To get the attention of the inattentive
(3) To learn whether students understand the content of a lecture
(4) To direct observation when models are used
(5) To help students analyze a process of some kind
(6) To develop a lesson by the inductive method
(7) To summarize the main points of a lecture
(8) To estimate the effectiveness of one's own teaching

When questions are employed in teaching, some elementary cautions should be kept in mind. For example, queries should be addressed to the whole class before any member is asked to respond. There should be no set order for having answers given—not by seating arrangement nor in alphabetical order. Dialogues with any one student should be avoided. Extensive exploration of one person's difficulties or ideas should take place during the office hours which conscientious college teachers keep faithfully. Of course, group answers should not be called for and questions need not be repeated for the inattentive. Student questions which show the interest of the group are a good sign. They may be a bad sign if they indicate that the students are not understanding the lecture.

The following suggestions relating to the form of questions, while fairly obvious, may nevertheless be helpful:

(1) Avoid asking questions that can be answered by "yes" or "no."

(2) Never ask questions that have to be answered in the words of the book or of the lecturer. Memorizing is not thinking.

(3) Ask questions in words that are easily understood.

(4) Gauge the questions to the ability of the class—make them neither too hard nor too easy.

(5) Do not ask questions for the purpose of showing the profundity of the instructor.

(6) Ask questions, if possible, that can be interpreted in only one way.

(7) Ask questions that stimulate discussion.

Group discussion method. It should be observed that several methods of presentation are generally used during the same class period, and though, for the purpose of clarity in explanation they are discussed separately as if they were discrete processes, this is not the case. In almost every class period there will be questions, the imparting of information and probably some group discussion. As indicated above, the method which will be used depends on the goals sought and the situation the instructor faces.

With the increased use of television teaching, the lecture method, supplemented with visual and auditory aids, is likely to continue to thrive. The greatest difficulty with lecturing via this electronic means of communication is that the student is not able to interrupt to ask a question when he most needs to do so. In order to meet this problem, at least partially, many television teachers provide for a period of group discussion between telecasts. Other college teachers rely heavily on group discussion in all of their teaching.

It should be recognized that certain difficulties are often encountered with the group discussion method. A discussion moves so slowly that less ground is covered. It takes time to develop skill in discussion on the part of the students. The discussion may be dominated by a few persons. It may not secure the participation of everyone. Persons who think they cannot learn from their fellows object to it. A discussion frequently becomes a pooling of ignorance. Skilled discussion leaders are difficult to find.

Nevertheless, while recognizing the validity of some of these difficulties, we must realize that they do not detract from the main purpose of group discussion—the changing of attitudes. This is not always a rational process. A college student from a conservative home environment may, in a group discussion, hear for the first time the views of a member of a minority group expressed with such sincerity and clarity that he begins to change his attitude toward liberal views. Group opinion when heard in a free and open discussion tends to influence individual opinion. Even though some student does not speak aloud during a discussion, he may be participating actively in his inner self. For many reasons it is imperative that those who plan to enter college teaching become skilled in leading a group discussion. There are several conditions which will help in achieving a good discussion:

(1) Have an informal seating arrangement. The ordinary classroom with seats fastened to the floor is not conducive to a good discussion atmosphere. Chairs placed in a circle are much to be preferred.

(2) The college teacher should sit in the circle with the group.

(3) The teacher must have genuine respect for every member of the group. Nothing quells discussion more rapidly than an expression of lack of respect for some member.

(4) The college teacher must be able to start off a discussion with a challenging statement or a question relating to an unpopular view.

(5) He must be able to listen, to ask additional questions and to follow up points of view that are expressed. He must have a good sense of humor and of timing, have a real liking for people and be determined that the discussion shall "get somewhere."

The use of film strips or a recording often provides the focal point for a fine discussion. One professor brought a radio to class and tuned it from one station to another to illustrate the trivia that were being broadcast at that particular time. He followed this "tuning in" with a reading of some of the poetry of Shakespeare, Browning and Milton. The contrast in ideas was so great that some members said during the discussion period that this experience had been a most moving one. Various discussion leaders have their own methods of achieving results. They prepare in advance, try to be impartial, avoid talking too much and keep the discussion to the point. They attempt to create an atmosphere of freedom of expression for the students, letting them know that any point of view sincerely held, whether the leader agrees with it or not, is acceptable in the discussion. From time to time the leader summarizes the points of agreement and disagreement.

The college teacher who is skillful in discussion is more rare than one might suppose. More often the practice is to tell students the facts, suggest what they should think about them and test to see if they have learned them. The reader will recognize here the contrast between the inductive and deductive methods of teaching. Much can be said for using both approaches in college teaching.

Demonstrations. Since in the various fields of science it is not always possible for students to do all experiments themselves, the college teacher must perform some demonstrations during class periods. Three steps should be followed in giving a demonstration. After the necessary preparation of materials and equipment has been made, the first step is to show the process at the normal rate of speed. This step gets the students' attention and enables the teacher to explain what is happening as the experiment proceeds. The second step is to repeat the demonstration much more slowly, carefully explaining each step in the process. The third step is to repeat the process once more, this time at normal speed, again explaining as the demonstration goes along.

It is unfortunate to note that some teachers have only seen demonstrations of experiments without ever actually handling the materials themselves. It could hardly be expected that such instructors could give good demonstrations. Moreover, college teachers who lack such experience are not likely to be able to help college students to conduct original experiments of their own.

Laboratory instruction. In Chapter 10 reference is made to an indictment of colleges for the divorce of theory from practice. One of the places where theory *is* related to practice is in the laboratory. A visitor to a medical college may sit in on a lecture in a course in human anatomy, entitled "the thoracic cavity." The lecture is well organized and delivered and is illustrated by drawings on the blackboard. This presentation is followed up shortly thereafter by a laboratory experience, in which students dissect the thoracic cavity while the professor moves from one table to another pointing out the things of which he had spoken in the lecture.

Similarly a lecture on the "diagnosis of the chest and abdomen," also well prepared and presented, is followed by a visit to the bedside of a patient in a teaching hospital. Here the lecturer and the medical students examine one by one the chest and abdomen of the patient, after which they go to a seminar room where all the laboratory data regarding the patient examined are put on the blackboard along with all the findings that the students reported hearing, feeling or seeing in their first-hand medical examination. The professor comments on each student's report of his findings, or the lack of them. Finally the group agrees on the symptoms found and turns to the task of proposing a plan of treatment. Pertinent research is quoted and many references are made to treatments that have been tried and reported in current medical literature. One who witnesses a number of such sessions is impressed with the skill of the professor in teaching in laboratory sessions. The individual attention given and the conversation between the teaching physician and the medical students quickly convince the observer that the close relation between theory and professional practice is being demonstrated to each prospective physician.

Less dramatic but equally important is the laboratory instruction associated with science, engineering and psychology courses, for here, too, theory comes alive when it is applied. While the laboratory for these courses is the scientific laboratory, in a broader sense the college and its surrounding community offer laboratory opportunities for many teachers of such subjects as history, political science, literature, sociology, music and art. Chapter 11 contains some additional discussion on this point, but it may be said here that college teachers do not usually utilize the opportunities that lie around them for relating their teaching to real situations as much as they might.

Coach-and-student method. This method of teaching is sometimes used in such fields as medicine and psychology. The college professor demonstrates how to give an individual psychological examination. Students are then paired off, one acting as subject and the other as examiner. After the examiner tests his partner, the roles are reversed. This method was used in the army in teaching the assembling and disassembling of a rifle and the use of jujitsu tactics. Obviously this method of teaching is primarily useful where specific skills need to be mastered.

Class size. An important aspect of teaching to the college professor is the size of the classes he teaches. It certainly seems true that there are courses which cannot be well taught if too many students are enrolled. In clinical medicine there might be six students; in clinical psychology, ten or twelve; in statistics possibly twenty. Customarily professors and department chairmen are asked to indicate the limit of size for a specific class, and if more than that number wish to enroll, a new section must be opened and a teacher assigned to it.

While limiting class size can certainly be defended in some areas where the nature of the subject and the mastery of materials and skills sought require it, some questions arise in regard to other areas in which teachers wish to limit the enrollment to perhaps thirty students. The data presented in Chapter 1 indicated that there is likely to be a great dearth of college professors by 1970. If college attendance continues to rise without a very large increase in the number of college teachers available, the size of classes must be increased or many qualified students will be denied admission to college.

Fortunately there is some evidence that the size of classes can be increased without serious detriment to the quality of higher education. An early study indicated that typical college instruction measured by subject matter achievement is not affected adversely by enlarging the size of classes.[21] Certainly, however, in classes like those mentioned above, the quality of student performance would be influenced. But if a professor intends to use the lecture method almost exclusively, it hardly seems reasonable to believe that he could not lecture to forty as easily as to thirty students, and if forty, why not one hundred? Some professors actually give better lectures before large classes than small ones; the increased numbers seem to stimulate them. Commenting on faculty insistence on small classes, a university president once remarked that they were a means by which a mediocre teacher could communicate his mediocrity in a more intimate fashion. At any rate, it seems likely that in some instances, depending on the nature of the course and the method of instruction, the size of classes will be increased.

It must be recognized that increasing the size of classes materially will make it far more difficult, if not impossible, for the teacher to know the students well. It also greatly increases the work of reading papers and giving grades. The latter difficulty could be met by the use of student assistants, but the loss to teacher as well as students occasioned by the lack of opportunity to know each other well is an irreparable one.

Television instruction. What, then, of television teaching? It has been estimated that about 250 colleges and universities are offering credit courses on television to about 250,000 students. In addition, some three hundred institutions have offered credit for courses taught on "Continental Classroom," a program telecast five days a week over a national network. An airplane flying 22,000 feet above a midwest state has broadcast televised instruction in thirteen subjects to about 500,000 students in schools and colleges in a six-state area. These impressive figures make one realize that television is probably destined for an important role in teaching. If a professor is going to lecture anyway, he might as well lecture to a thousand students as to a hundred. He should,

[21] Earl Hudelson, *Class Size at the College Level,* University of Minnesota Press, Minneapolis, 1929.

however, remember that television is only a conveyor—of bad teaching as well as of good teaching, of the mediocre as well as the superior. It does have the advantage of being able to allow all students to view a demonstration close up. It has the ability to give the viewer a "you are there" feeling. It can extend the reach of very superior teachers. Gradually much is being learned of what is appropriate to try to do by television, of ways in which TV instruction can be individualized by a team of discussion leaders, and of how microphones may be used for students to ask questions or talk back to a professor lecturing on closed-circuit television.

At this writing the results of TV teaching are inconclusive. Students at the college level seem to learn as much from televised as from direct instruction. If so, television may assist in solving the problem of giving good teaching to larger numbers of students. It does not, however, at present give any evidence of improving the quality of students' learning, a goal much to be sought. Some college professors may seek the opportunity to be "on-camera teachers," while others will not. All, however, should watch the developments with concern, not because television will replace the teacher, but because the medium may eventually offer great potentiality for the improvement of the learning of college students.

Evaluation. The third step in the teaching function of the college professor is that of evaluation. While he needs to evaluate himself, the kind of evaluation to be considered here is an assessment of the growth of the student—the outcome of the teaching.

No one escapes being evaluated by someone. Husbands are evaluated by their wives and vice versa. Neighbors appraise one another. Employers judge employees and the reverse is also true. The armed forces and the civil service systems have some of the most elaborate evaluation systems to be found anywhere. Certainly few students enter college without having been examined many times. Indeed, some have had such sad experiences with tests of various kinds that they have become "examination shy" and hence do not do their best in examinations. It may be observed, therefore, that though no one can expect to avoid evaluation, a variety of methods needs to be employed.

Evaluation should be a continuous process and not a single event. The wise college teacher observes and evaluates continually. He does not wait until the end of the semester and then give a pencil and paper test upon the results of which he gives a grade representing the entire semester's work of his students. The wise college teacher does not depend on only one kind of evaluation. While some persons write better than they speak, the reverse is also true. Some who can carry out in practice a worthwhile piece of professional work may have difficulty verbalizing it. Others who verbalize well and smoothly may not be able to act.

Times for giving examinations. There are at least four appropriate times at which examinations may be given. (1) At the beginning of a course. Anyone who is teaching statistics, advanced foreign language or any other subject where knowledge and skill are cumulative would be wise to find out where his students are in their accomplishments before beginning the review of old material or the teaching of new content and skills. (2) At the end of a class period. Such a test would be given to determine how well the teacher had succeeded in getting across the points he thought he had covered. (3) In the middle of the course. This progress examination should tell both the instructor and the student how each is doing. (4) At the end of a course. This of course is the final proficiency examination.

Examination variables. College teachers frequently encounter students who express apprehension of examinations of any kind. They indicate that they "forget all they know," that anxiety causes them to "freeze," to be unable to do their best. The evidence is not entirely clear on this point. Studies seem to show that on certain kinds of examinations fatigue and/or anxiety have little effect. These examinations are usually objective in character. On the other hand, McKeachie says,

. . . students who were high in anxiety about tests tended to do more poorly on the final examination than in their work during the course. Why? One clue comes from behavior during the exam period. The students who complete the exam first and leave are the most anxious students; the exam situation was so painful for them that they just couldn't stay. Students with positive motivation to succeed tended to stay in the examination room longer.[22]

The college teacher will wish to take the anxiety factor into account. He is likely to find that the emphasis he places on any examination will influence the amount of stress felt by students, and if he gives only one final examination, the stress will be correspondingly greater.

Despite the groans of students and the large amount of time required for the teacher to correct such examinations, it should be recognized that a long examination is likely to be more fair than a short one. An examination which has several different kinds of questions is also likely to be more fair. Length and variety of questions give the student a better chance to show his intellectual power than only two questions of the same kind. Teachers need to remember, too, that students differ in the speed with which they write, though those handicapped in this ability may know just as much as the others who are faster penmen. Hence, it is better to have a variety of questions so that the slow writer will not be under too great a handicap.

Purposes and kinds of examinations. Educators are generally agreed that testing has four purposes—to measure student achievement, to appraise the effectiveness of the teaching, to locate areas of difficulty or student errors and to summarize and review. A fifth purpose sometimes proposed—to challenge students, to bring them up on their toes—is less acceptable, for the argument seems to assume that students must be examined to be challenged and to do their best work. The whole point of view of this book is based on the conception that the student is eager to learn, that he is a self-starter, that, though he needs to be guided in his learn-

[22] Wilbert J. McKeachie, "How Do Students Learn?" in Russell M. Cooper, *op. cit.*, p. 29.

ing, he will do more work of his own accord than most instructors would dare ask him to do. The fifth purpose would be a valid one if it meant that students want from time to time to know how they are doing and that, in this sense, an examination would be a challenging and useful activity.

Not all examinations, of course, are written ones. Oral examinations are sometimes given by college teachers in individual appointments with their students, and they are frequently given by master's and doctoral examining committees to qualify or certify candidates for advanced degrees. In the latter instances, because of the known frailties of individual judgment, the examining committees are usually composed of five to seven faculty members when the performance of a student is to be appraised in a personal conference. One of the weaknesses of the oral examination is that a bright personality often sways the examiners' judgments favorably while a less sparkling person with ideas of equal worth is judged less favorably. Some college committees have tried to eliminate these personal factors by having a student's responses to an oral examination recorded on tape, making it possible for the examiners to listen and re-listen to answers to questions with somewhat more objectivity.

Written examinations, which are more commonly used than oral examinations, may be either subjective or objective. Subjective questions—essay or free answer—are useful in courses which deal with ideas, concepts and problems requiring analysis, organizing ability and reasoning ability. Candidates for college teaching have usually been subjected to this kind of examination for more than sixteen years of schooling and are quite familiar with it. Such an examination takes a long time to write and a long time to correct. Moreover, it is difficult to grade, and cases have been known where the same examination has been graded from "D" to "A" by different but competent college teachers. Nevertheless, there seems to be no adequate substitute for the kind of examination which calls on the student to assemble his knowledge, organize it in a specific way and write his answers in a lucid, succinct fashion.

In formulating an essay-type examination, questions should be devised which test the student's understanding, his power to organize and his ability to think rather than merely to recall what some author said. The questions also should tend to reveal a student's knowledge of the relative importance of material. Of course, each question must be stated clearly if the student is to understand and respond to it satisfactorily. In grading answers to an essay-type examination a scoring procedure should be worked out with weights assigned to each question. Experienced readers of such subjective examinations have found it desirable to read all the answers to question number one, then all the answers to number two and so on. This plan is superior to that of reading all the responses in the examination booklet of one person at a time because it enables the reader to maintain the same basis of judgment in evaluating the replies to one question all the way through the class before he adjusts his judgment to responses to a different question. Despite the inconvenience of handling each examination booklet a number of times, the wisdom of the procedure has been proved by the writer over and over again.

Objective examinations. Perhaps one of the disadvantages of the popularity of higher education is the fact that the large numbers of students make some college teachers feel that it is necessary to use objective examinations because they can be answered quickly, allow for a wide coverage of material, can be scored with a high degree of accuracy, can be used for a number of classes and are easily graded. Unfortunately, objective examinations too often test only reading power, recognition and recall rather than the analytical and integrative powers that can be evaluated only with subjective questions. However, objective examinations have their place and may be used with discretion. They usually include six kinds of questions, about each of which some illustrations and suggestions will be given.

True-false questions. Such "questions" consist of statements to be judged true or false by the student. Those which are true should be marked with a plus sign and those that are false by a zero. An example might be, "The United States Office of Education is under the direction and control of the Department of Interior." At least a hundred true-false questions are necessary to obtain a valid score. A few additional points to be kept in mind are:

(1) Avoid negative statements, such as, "It is not unusual for college teachers to refuse to accept gifts from students in their own classes."

(2) Avoid having two ideas in one statement.

(3) Avoid the use of words which tend to give away the answers. "Always" and "never" would usually indicate a false statement; "usually" and "sometimes" would usually indicate a true one.

(4) Short statements are preferable to long ones.

(5) Employ commonly used words and simple sentences.

(6) Include about the same number of true as of false statements.

(7) Scatter the position of the correct answers.

The final score is usually the number of correct answers, but to eliminate the effect of guessing, the number wrong should be subtracted from the number right to obtain the score.

Multiple-choice questions. In these questions four or five possible answers are given, from which the student selects the one he considers correct or best. The following is an example:

The first college to be founded in America was
———Columbia University
———Harvard University
———William and Mary
———University of Virginia

The alternatives should be of about the same length. The alternative answers should be plausible ones, and one should avoid the use of weak alternatives. The score is usually the number of correct answers.

Check-list. This is a variation of the multiple-choice type of question. The following is an example:

Indicate by checks which of the following are educational officers in a university:

———Auditors
———Building and Grounds Superintendent
———Comptroller
———Dean of the College of Liberal Arts
———Dean of Students
———Professor of Medicine
———Public Relations Representative
———Vice-president for Academic Affairs

The score is usually the number of correct answers.

Tabular-form test. A table set up with columns with appropriate headings and items related to them provides a quick way of disclosing the student's knowledge. The following is an example:

Place an (X) in the appropriate column after each type of gas if it is characterized by the factors listed at the top of the table.

Type of Gas	Blister Gas	Lung Damaging	Persistent Gases
Mustard			
Chlorine			
Lewisite			
Phosgene			
Titanium tetrachloride			

The score is usually the number of correct answers.

Completion test. Here a word or phrase is omitted from a statement and the student is asked to fill in the space. The following is an example:

The fundamental cause of the War between the States was as follows: ————.

A more complicated form of the completion is illustrated by the following:

By placing numbers in sequence, indicate the order in which

fuel flows from the tank to the cylinders starting with the gasoline tank as number one.

——— gasoline tank   ——— pump inlet valve
——— pump chamber   ——— intake manifold
——— carburetor bowl   ——— pump or carburetor tube
——— tank to filter tube   ——— pump to outlet valve
——— venturi   ——— sediment bowl

In most completion tests there is only one correct answer, although some credit may be given for a partially correct answer when the question is a complicated one.

Matching test. Here two columns of information related in some way to each other are given and the student is asked to match related items by placing the numbers in one column before the appropriate items in the other, as in the following example:

Place the number of the item in the right hand column in front of the item in the left hand column with which it is associated.

——— Barzun   1. The New American College
——— Bowman   2. A Student Personnel Program for Higher Education
——— Butts   3. Antioch College
——— Chamberlain   4. How to Counsel Students
——— Fine   5. The Liberal Arts College
——— Henderson   6. Are Liberal Arts Colleges Becoming Professional Schools?
——— Lloyd-Jones   7. Did They Succeed in College?
——— McGrath   8. The College Charts Its Course
——— Meikeljohn   9. The Graduate School in American Democracy
——— Reeves   10. The Teacher in America
——— Sexson   11. Democratic Education
——— Williamson   12. The Experimental College

In grading a matching test the correctly matched items are usually counted. To keep guessing to a minimum, subtract from this figure the number of incorrectly matched items.

From the examples given the reader will probably conclude that an evaluation which contains several kinds of questions might be better than one which is only subjective or only objective in character. This decision can be made only in terms of a particular course and a particular instructor. Evaluation itself should be controlled by the purposes of both. Colleges which have large departments with many instructors teaching the same course sometimes give department-wide examinations. One can understand the desire to have students reach the same point in development at the same time. However, this procedure ignores the individual differences of students and instructors. This may also, in one sense, invade the academic freedom of the professor—the freedom to have different goals, to teach in a different way, to value different outcomes. As one views the stultifying effect of the examinations prescribed by the New York Board of Regents and of the College Entrance Board examinations, he may question the extension of this approach to quality education in our colleges.

Performance tests. Ultimately the real test of learning is the ability to perform satisfactorily as a home maker, a citizen and a worker. Colleges of medicine rigorously demand that a prospective physician be competent to diagnose and to treat patients. They are not content to rely on paper-and-pencil tests; medical students must prove themselves under the supervision of competent practicing physicians. Airplane pilots must pass performance tests. Nurses and laboratory technicians must do likewise. Public school teachers are now required to take supervised practice teaching, which again is a performance test. In colleges today young teachers are frequently assigned to older staff members, who guide and counsel with them in the early months of their teaching. While few people who have studied the problem consider this arrangement entirely adequate, yet it is a kind of performance test. It is generally believed that, when the college teacher requires a performance test of his students, the college product will improve.

Grading. Evaluation of one's students results eventually in giving them grades. As was indicated at the beginning of this section, appraisal is continually taking place, though it is not always written down. The real purpose of this "writing down" is to separate the qualified student from the unqualified. It is questionable ethics for a college to keep a student in school, to take his money and his time, if there is reasonable certainty that he is not qualified for college work.

There are three sets of factors which are often involved in grading. These are the student's intellectual achievement, the performance aspects of his work and his personality characteristics. It would be desirable, if it were possible, to keep these elements separate. Usually, however, the grades given by a faculty member represent a combination of the three factors. It is well known that a winning smile and an attractive personality have a favorable influence on one's grades in college, especially since there is frequently no opportunity for performance based on actual field experience to be judged. Therefore, the performance and personality factors are likely to be intertwined with the intellectual achievement of the student in determining the grade evaluation given by most college teachers.

Several methods of giving grades are in use. Some colleges still use percentage marks ranging from 70 to 100, though it is difficult to believe that college teachers are able to make as fine distinctions as those represented in this range. Today many more colleges use the letter grades—A, B, C, D and E. When translated into percentage grades, these letters encompass the following span of achievement:

A — 93 to 100
B — 85 to 92
C — 78 to 84
D — 70 to 77
E — below 70 or failure

Other words or symbols are also used—Honors, Pass, Fail, Incomplete; or Honors, Credit, Credit-weak, Fail. Whatever the nomenclature, grades should have meaning to those who interpret them. For example, if the group is a normal one, it is likely to break itself about as follows:

A— 7 per cent
B — 20 per cent
C — 46 per cent
D — 20 per cent
E— 7 per cent

Thus we see that a "B" grade means that the college student was in the upper 27 per cent of the class in a particular subject. Such a normal curve, however, should never be applied mechanically. It is almost safe to say that no group is normal. This statement is even more likely to be true in the senior college and the graduate school. Certainly no college teacher should ever determine in advance that he would give only three "A's" no matter what the size or quality of the group; nor should he decide in advance that he would fail three students regardless of the quality of the group. He may have to fail more, or perhaps less. These percentages should be used only as a point of reference and a point of departure. On the other hand, any college teacher who turns in a great many "E's" or a long list of "A's" is likely to find it necessary to explain his actions, if not to his departmental chairman, at least to the students.

Recognizing and Rewarding Good Teaching

What is good college teaching? This is a most difficult question to answer. If we asked it of fifty different college graduates or of fifty different college teachers, we might easily get fifty different answers. And yet in these answers we could probably find some common points that characterize most "good" teachers.[23] Perhaps good teaching may be described in two ways—in terms of the experiences and growth of the student and in terms of the fundamental characteristics and methods of the teacher.

College teaching and student growth. Many college professors agree that the only real test of good teaching is what it does for the student or how it stimulates him to do things for himself. Perhaps this is the most important criterion of good teaching. In general, such instruction results in the student becoming increasingly independent of the professor and assuming progressively greater responsibilities for his own education. Certainly the ability to plan and carry out work on his own is one important mark of the capable graduate student. Perhaps the best test of previous instruction is to be noted in the *intellectual behavior* of the student when the guidance, the authority and the teaching of the instructor are left behind. Yet, while the student's continuing interest and productive work in his field are valid and much-to-be-desired over-all goals, it is difficult to judge the time at which they are likely to be achieved. The "sign-posts" which indicate if and when a student is moving in these directions are, therefore, worth considering.

Evidences of student growth. Assuming that the college has an adequate academic program, that the requirements are reasonable and the academic counseling competent, good college teaching results in an increased interest on the part of the student in the field or fields in which he is working. His choice of free activities reflects these interests, and he interprets other areas of his life experience in terms of them. He does work over and above the assignments, spends more time in the laboratory, field and library than professors might expect and voluntarily seeks counsel from persons in a position to give him help. In these and other ways the student demonstrates that he is actively interested; he works hard and likes it.

A second evidence of student growth as a result of good college

[23] A few years ago 160 college professors in a midwestern university responded to a questionnaire regarding the definition of good teaching and criteria for judging it. Their responses are given in the *Appendix.*

teaching is his increased ability in the use of problem-solving techniques. The student demonstrates the ability to collect facts, to distinguish between facts and opinions, to examine assumptions and to test hypotheses in terms of these facts and assumptions. He recognizes statements which are irrelevant and those which go beyond the data. He becomes able to identify his own and others' biases. He shows competence in delimiting a problem. He recognizes inconsistencies in his own thought and action and in those of others. He demonstrates such habits of thinking that his conclusions can be verified by others using similar procedures. He is resourceful in dealing with new or unusual situations.

Good college teaching increases the student's sensitivity to the world of physical things. He seeks to interpret natural phenomena, technological progress and change in terms of their import to himself and others. He seeks to conserve and extend physical resources to further the welfare of himself and others.

Good college teaching develops the student's ability to communicate with others in many ways. It is the responsibility of all college teachers, both by example and criticism, to develop the capacity for effective oral and written expression. In certain fields, as in music and other creative arts, the well-taught student not only has a lively enjoyment of these means of communication, but seeks as well to express himself in these media.

Good college teaching leads to a desire on the part of the student to share experiences. He seeks the association of other members of the class to talk over their present experiences, to plan and initiate new experiences, to do things together and to further the interests of the class in other ways. At the same time he recognizes the interlocking of its interests with those of other groups.

Good college teaching results in the student being able to see the relationship of what he is doing to other fields and to make application of it to them. He develops greater ability to draw material from specific fields with which he is acquainted that bears on a problem being studied. He readily sees the import of new areas of experience for the solution of other problems not included in them.

Good college teaching develops the student's intellectual curiosity. He approaches new experiences with eagerness and zest. He maintains individual creativity but exhibits the ability to make alterations or modifications for individual good in a socially acceptable pattern. He has broad interests with ability and active persistence in following certain interests.

Good college teaching leads to increased sensitivity to social problems and competency in dealing with them. The student is "at home" with groups, maintains poise in typical group activities and is generally able to get along better with people. He is increasingly more stable emotionally. He can envisage problems of groups of people and reveals consideration for individual personalities, especially for those in situations quite different from the one in which he finds himself. He takes part with others in an effective way in socially significant activities.

Good college teaching causes the student to be interested in and to maintain effectively the daily functions of community, business or profession and living in a home.

Good college teaching stimulates the student to acquire the skills, information and mental attitudes which will enable him to obtain and hold a position. He is continually developing those capacities which will permit him to make an effective contribution to society.

Good college teaching helps the student to develop a personal scale of values. It makes him conscious of his reasons for making choices. He reveals a willingness to modify previously held values in the light of new experience or information. His choices are made in terms of ultimate goals, as well as in terms of immediate necessity. In advance he relates consequences to choices. He becomes increasingly thorough, competent and responsible.

While teaching is perhaps the most complex, intricate and subtle of human enterprises, it ultimately must be measured in terms of the growth of the student.

Characteristics and methods of the college teacher. That there is no one best method of teaching is patently true. All the variables in the teaching situation are conditioning factors, among which are the teacher, the student, the subject, the equipment and the general climate of opinion or the folkways of the institution. Some of these differences may be expressed by suggesting two types of individuals whose influence may be regarded as equally valuable: persons who exert their influence chiefly upon individual students, in conferences, laboratories or the like, or upon small groups of students, mainly by example and by close association; and those who exert large-scale influence on larger groups by virtue of their stimulating personalities.

John Ciardi in a recent issue of *The Saturday Review* has this to say about one of his college teachers:

. . . English was my major and everywhere within the English Department good teachers opened doors for me. But if they were an expansion—and they were—John Holmes was an explosion. . . .

He cared. But caring only begins a teacher's work. Holmes *knew*. And what he knew was exactly what I needed. . . . What he knew about was the *insides* of a poem. What he lived was the happy excitement of each living poem as he found it. And he knew how to transmit that excitement and make it real. . . .

Praise knowledge then. But whenever has knowledge been enough for a teacher? There must be generosity, the gift of articulation, and the power to elicit enthusiasm. These are the gifts of the great teacher, and John Holmes has these gifts greatly.[24]

Would that all college graduates might look back in such a way upon at least one teacher!

With all due regard to individual differences among teachers, there are still certain general characteristics which are common to all effective approaches, and which may, therefore, be taken as fairly indicative of good college teaching. These are:

(1) A fundamental kindness of the teacher toward the student, as shown by patience and understanding in the classroom and in personal relations.

(2) Knowledge of the subject, as revealed in depth and breadth of information.

[24] John Ciardi, "A Praise of Good Teachers," *The Saturday Review,* July 8, 1961, p. 28.

(3) Clarity, logicality and vividness of statement, whether in conference, discussion or lecture.

(4) Personal enthusiasm, implying active interest in students and subject.

(5) Imagination and resourcefulness, as shown by ability of the teacher to open up a new avenue of approach to his field and to utilize various opportunities to stimulate students.

(6) Careful attention to working conditions, assignments, the organization of materials and to the development of teaching techniques which will increase the efficiency of teacher and students.

(7) A conscientious discharge of necessary duties, such as class attendance, office engagements and conferences.

It is recognized that the foregoing qualities may vary greatly in good teachers. Nevertheless, taken together, they constitute a profile which may be of service in stimulating and evaluating college teaching.

Stimulating good teaching. Many years ago Reed gave four reasons for ineffective college teaching: (1) the time-honored fallacy that the only equipment necessary for successful teaching is a thorough knowledge of the subject; (2) lack of sympathetic understanding of the student's point of view; (3) absence of any help to the teacher in improving his work; and (4) lack of knowledge of educational aims and ideals, of psychological principles which should guide him in his work.[25] Unfortunately, these conditions still exist in all too many institutions.

Some educators assert that the greatest responsibility for the improvement of college teaching lies with the administration because it selects the teachers, provides facilities for teaching, determines the teaching load, the salaries and many other conditions of work. Yet, no matter how carefully teachers are selected, many mistakes are made by the young instructor, and these come about in part, at least, because he is left to himself to sink or swim. Instead he should be given careful help and suggestions. Another point to be remembered is that no teacher can engage in too

[25] Anna Y. Reed, *The Effective and Ineffective College Teacher,* American Book Company, 1935, pp. 12–13.

many outside activities and continue to be a good teacher. Adequate salaries for moderate living, recognition of scholarly work and teaching well done and justice with respect to promotions and salaries will help to keep a teacher from becoming stagnant. But in the last analysis college teaching can be improved only as the teacher loves his work and has faith in young people and in himself.

A few years ago a Committee on College Teaching of Northwestern University suggested the following methods of stimulating good teaching:

(1) First and foremost, there should be developed throughout the University an awareness of the importance of good teaching and the conviction that good teaching will be properly rewarded.

(2) Overloading in teaching assignments and general university duties should be eliminated.

(3) The status of teaching assistants should be studied and improved, probably by elimination in some divisions, by better supervision and by higher stipends.

(4) Older and more experienced faculty members should regularly teach some of the sections of the beginning courses.

(5) Mutual help and advice should be given all staff members, especially the younger members, through more frequent consultation and staff meetings of those teaching the large beginning courses.

(6) Such interfaculty visits in courses *as will not arouse distrust or resentment* should be encouraged as a basis for increasing friendly mutual criticism as well as self-criticism.

(7) Cooperative courses, in which several faculty members assist and administer a course, should be encouraged in certain departments.

(8) Budgetary funds should be provided for teaching aids (visual materials, demonstration equipment, books, stenographic assistance, money for travel to educational conferences and to other institutions) under the control of men primarily concerned with teaching.

(9) Conferences on college teaching should be sponsored, to which members of the faculty are invited.

(10) A senior staff officer should be appointed to assist in and suggest continuous research on university teaching problems.

Upon the issuance of this report several of the faculties of the university not only distributed it among their members, but established standing committees on undergraduate teaching. These committees tended to implement the first recommendation. The fourth and fifth were followed somewhat more systematically, and in some instances cooperative teaching, as recommended in item seven, was initiated.

How reward good teaching? The belief has previously been expressed that one of the best methods of stimulating good college teaching is through proper recognition and rewards for good teachers. Here are a few of the methods by which this might be accomplished.

Good teaching should be given greater consideration in determining promotions and increases in salary. Many college faculty members feel that publication is now the determining factor. Offers from other institutions, which influence promotion and salary increases, are more likely to come to men who publish, and the effective teacher *per se* is likely to go unrewarded.

Published declarations should be made by college administrators in formal or informal communications to individual faculty members in which recognition and appreciation of good teaching are expressed. Appropriate prizes or citations should be awarded annually by the administration to the individuals who do the best undergraduate teaching. These awards should be directed especially toward the younger teachers. The University of Chicago and New York University, among others, have recognized the need for this type of award by selecting a few excellent teachers to receive a financial award each year. Methods of evaluating college teachers are discussed in Chapter 10.

The improvement of college teaching is central to the improvement of higher education and deserves more attention than it has heretofore received. Students come to college to learn from persons whose scholarship is greater than their own. They deserve the best that can be provided. The institution itself depends in great part on the quality of the faculty and the instruction given by it.

CHAPTER 7

The College Professor as an Adviser

Fundamental in all of his relationships with students is the way in which the professor regards them. In the previous chapter stress was placed on the way in which the college teacher perceives himself, but, however correctly he may see himself, he may view the young people to whom he gives instruction quite inaccurately.

Teachers' attitudes toward students. Perhaps if there is a single most important attitude that a college professor should have, it is a fundamental respect for the dignity and worth of each student, regardless of his race, color, creed, ethnic origin, economic status or social position. This statement, made before in this volume, is repeated because *it constitutes the fundamental basis for success in college teaching,* or in all teaching for that matter. On the surface it may seem so obvious as to be a truism, yet one should not lightly assume that he always feels and manifests a true respect for *all* his students. The ideal expressed is sometimes —perhaps usually—difficult to achieve. Its importance lies partly in the fact that college students are one of the nation's greatest resources; the student body *in toto* and individually has enormous potentialities. It is the task of the faculty to develop them whatever they may be. While occasionally some students not even partially qualified get into a college class, they are likely to be few in number. The professor will remember that at the college stage his students have passed through at least twelve screenings, including the admissions processes of his own institution. He ought not assume that all of the previous teachers of his students have been wrong, or that they were either incompetent or biased. The percentage of students entering the first grade who survive twelve years of schooling and are admitted to college is still relatively small. Therefore, the college teacher will wisely take the stance that the students are here and it is his task to help each develop the potential he has. It is not the teacher's role to say, in effect, "I will dish out the stuff; let the students digest it if they can." As indicated earlier, the task of the college teacher is to stimulate student growth, a process which requires knowledge and skill.

In commercial life there is a slogan that the customer is always right. Though businessmen know that the customer is not always right, it is safer to base all transactions on the premise that he is. If this is a reasonable attitude for businessmen to take, it might also be a reasonable one for college professors to assume. While the student may not always be right, it is better to assume that he may be if his real growth is to be forwarded. Certainly this attitude is superior to that of some college professors who are out to prove that the student is wrong and to exhibit the errors of his ways of thought to all other students. Ridicule, sarcasm, smart repartee have no place in student-faculty relationships; fundamental mutual respect must be displayed. Learning of significance will take place only when there is a partnership between the college student and the professor, each seeking to know more and more about life.

Informal Advising

Informal relationships with students. College professors have both formal and informal relationships with students. In the first instance it may be suggested that the student is more or less a captive, especially so in a required course. Even when a college student is being advised by a friendly professor regarding the selection of a program of studies or his progress in one of them, he is conscious of a hidden threat called "grades." Good college professors are able to minimize this influence and engage in helpful conversations with their students which lead to decision making.

There are situations, however, in which the student does not feel that he is a captive. For example, in some colleges there is a weekend freshman camp, to which the student is invited, but which he is not compelled to attend. Along with the college student personnel officers, a few professors are invited. While these camps involve a round of recreational activities, some very serious discussions take place on some such subjects as, "what a college student should expect from his education," "college and life," and "what is expected of a college graduate?" Here in the informal camp surroundings a college teacher has the opportunity to ask and to respond to some serious questions. It is true that such a weekend is both strenuous and demanding, yet the college teacher who is invited may well regard it as a compliment as well as an obligation, since only those faculty members whose attitudes and opinions are respected by students are usually invited. Under appropriate joint student and professional personnel leadership such an opportunity is one to be seized upon as the chance to influence students' values, attitudes and decisions, an opportunity which is not often available in formal situations.

Similar opportunities are available on the campus when dormitory or house groups invite college teachers to have dinner with them and to stay and talk afterward. Religion-and-life conferences held annually on many campuses also provide the opportunity for the college teacher to reach students in an informal way outside his classes.

Then there are the student extracurricular activities, each of which usually has a faculty adviser. In addition to the elected officers of each class there is a faculty sponsor. During World War II the sponsor of a junior class raised the question with those in charge of the junior prom as to whether in war time it was wise to spend five thousand dollars to obtain a "name" orchestra. This resulted in serious examination of the appropriateness of the proposal when other young people were giving their lives in the service of their country.

Athletic coaches have excellent opportunities to influence young men and women who are candidates for various teams. The same can be said for debate coaches, advisers for the college paper and yearbook, directors of musical and dramatic productions and sponsors of many clubs and societies. When students try out for an activity or voluntarily engage in it, there is an unusual opportunity to counsel and work with them.

In the more formal classroom setting—and we say it again—it is important for the teacher to remember that his students are diverse in many ways—in interests, abilities, aptitudes, goals as well as in their economic and social backgrounds, and that each must be considered and treated as an individual. He needs to realize that a student who is not doing well may have a special problem. How many professors take the trouble to become aware of situations like these:

A boy is a chronic sleeper in more than one of his classes. He is playing in an orchestra, sometimes out of town, and several nights a week he does not get to bed before two o'clock. Yet he has scheduled three eight o'clocks and is carrying a full credit load.

A girl has stayed at home to attend a junior college for two years after high school. At the beginning of her junior year she has transferred to a college away from home. All correspondence relative to her matriculation and dormitory assignment has been handled by her mother. Such a girl has a difficult time in separating herself from the interference of a capable but over-solicitous mother.

A student says, "I don't know how I can go on with biology. Evolution is all wrong, and I don't get anything else in that class." This student has a need which cannot be met in the classroom alone.

A boy does not cover his reading assignments in one of his classes and fails in a test. A conference reveals that he is in debt for his board and room. The money which his widowed mother had sent him had been spent to get a "cure" for his baldness. He cannot confess to his mother either his fear about approaching baldness nor the fact that he has not used the money she sent him to pay for his board and room.

A freshman girl seeks immediate status by relating accounts of elaborate parties given for her before she came to college, of large sums of money she has spent for clothes and entertaining. She winds up her first week in college by attempting to get into the dormitory after hours through a window.

Sometimes the problems of students are brought to light by means of a questionnaire. The following random selections from such a study made in a college a few years ago reveal the disturbance experienced by some students because of the tensions of our modern world.

"It seems that there is no use to plan for a happy future. I am pessimistic about the whole thing and believe that only the very worst will happen."

"I am physically nervous. I do not mean fear but a feeling of being on the edge of a cliff over which I might fall at any time. I want excitement but I don't particularly care for it in the way that I might get it."

"What courses do we have now and what courses could be added to our curriculum to help us live 'sane' lives both now and after the cold war is over?"

"I feel the need of maintaining a calm attitude toward life in general; of making for myself some kind of philosophy of life that will help me to understand it all."

"Having been raised in the belief that one race is as good as another, having believed all my life that racial or national hatred was the lowest form of intolerance and that intolerance was to be avoided at all costs, it is difficult for me to feel any dislike or animosity toward those nations we must consider inimical. I am not pacifistic, and I am not subversive—I am a twelfth generation American. My problem is reconciling my ideals with this present situation."

Students' needs. Perhaps more than anything else the college teacher must be aware of the needs of his students. According to a report made many years ago but still valid, students have the greatest need for the following:

(1) Adjustment to casual associations without embarrassment with members of the opposite sex.

(2) Genuine friendship with one or more adults, preferably with members of the faculty.

(3) A feeling of "belonging"—of being accepted and valued by one or more social groups in college.

(4) Encouragement and opportunity leading to wider participation and experience in a variety of social situations and activities.

(5) Development of useful social skills.

(6) Development of interest in the welfare of others and of the community.

(7) A stronger sense of personal worth.

(8) At least a few intimate friendships with persons of similar age.

(9) The gradual development of willingness and ability to accept a modest degree of social initiative.[1]

The informal relationships college faculty members have with students as well as the more formal relationships of the classroom provide the chance for them to help meet some of the needs listed. This help is important not only to bring peace and satisfaction to the college student as a human being but also to establish a basis from which real profit can be gained from the instruction offered.

Thus far we have considered the necessity for the professor to be aware of the needs of students in his informal relations with them and in his classes. However, in most colleges and universities, the teacher is involved in a formal advisement process.

FORMAL ADVISING

The student personnel program. Most colleges and universities have a student personnel program which deals with a number of phases of counseling. Recruitment officers advise with high school students in their local communities. Admissions officers frequently interview students to assess their qualifications for entrance to the

[1] Staff News Letter, "Cooperative Study in General Education," American Council on Education, Vol. 3, No. 3, April 22, 1942.

institution. Residence counselors in dormitories and houses advise college students about personnel problems that grow out of living with a group of men or women on a campus. Deans of students, or of men or women, are consulted by college students regarding personal problems, finances, life objectives and other matters. Chaplains and religious advisers, found in many colleges and in most universities, as well as clergymen in local churches, are available to students who desire religious counsel. College placement officers advise with students regarding job opportunities and set up interviews that bring a student and a prospective employer together. While in the smaller college a number of these functions may be discharged by the same person, quite an elaborate organization is to be found in others.

Academic advising. With the large amount of counseling being handled by various personnel officers, what is the function of the college teacher as an adviser? It is generally recognized that academic counseling should be carried on by members of the college faculty in the various disciplines. This is not always the case, however, for there are a number of institutions in which a staff of full-time or half-time academic advisers is maintained. The argument for the latter plan runs something like this: The member of a college faculty is inclined to believe that his own field of research and teaching is *the* most important of all fields. This attitude may disqualify him as an adviser of students, and hence it is desirable that academic advising be in the hands of a selected group of faculty members who are able to subordinate their personal inclinations and help the student choose an academic program of studies suited to his abilities and goals and in which he can make suitable progress. In spite of the seeming reasonableness of such argument, however, the more common practice seems to be to involve most college teachers in the advising of students regarding their academic programs, certainly at the senior college level. It should perhaps be pointed out that in some medical colleges members of the faculty also interview candidates for admission to their schools, a practice which is followed in some other professional schools as well. Though interviewing candidates for admission may not often be carried on by college teachers, they can hardly escape giving information about courses which they teach, and in most instances they help students plan their whole program of studies for a given year. It seems desirable, therefore, to consider this phase of the advisement function in more detail.

Perhaps two precautions should be noted. First, all college teachers need to know what kind of cases to refer to other functionaries. For example, it is obvious that a student who is physically ill should be referred to the college health service. If the student is in financial difficulties, the grants-in-aid office can give help. If the student seeks aid on a complex personal or family problem, it is usually desirable to refer him to the dean of students or to the head resident counselor. An emotionally disturbed student should be referred to the dean of students or to the director of the health service, either one of whom could put the student in touch with some psychological or psychiatric help should this seem desirable. A college teacher should not attempt to deal with problems beyond his sphere of competency, although he tries to remain the student's friend.

A recent case in a midwestern college should concern even the most sophisticated adviser. Following a conference a student committed suicide. The parents sued for damages on the grounds that the adviser should have known enough to prevent the death. The lower state court upheld the parents and awarded damages amounting to thousands of dollars, but the Supreme Court overturned the lower court's decision. This occurrence is an extreme example of the consequences that may follow from the advisory process.

The second precaution to be kept in mind by the professor who advises students on their academic choices is that different students require different programs, and he must face honestly the possibility that none of the programs of the students he advises may include courses in his own field! As an adviser he is concerned only with the welfare of his advisees; his field of special interest must be kept in the background. The writer's adviser in college was a professor of geology. Is the reader surprised to learn that *Introduction to Geology* was advised and that, this course having been pursued, mineralogy and meteorology were later recommended as desirable courses? While this professor's enthusiasm and dedication to his subject are to be applauded, his wisdom, objectivity and effectiveness as an adviser must be questioned.

Familiarity with requirements. To be helpful to students in selecting their programs the college teacher will familiarize himself with the prerequisites for various courses, as well as with the requirements for major and minor fields of concentration. He must know the requirements for graduation and for the various degrees awarded by the college, such as Bachelor of Arts and Bachelor of Science. The adviser will be familiar with the undergraduate program considered prerequisite to graduate study in such fields as medicine, law and the sciences. He should know also —and this is a point at which many advisers fall down—the occupational outlets for various programs of study. For example, advisers in liberal arts colleges should know not only the certification requirements for teaching in their state, but also in what areas there is a demand for teachers. The National Education Association each year issues a "Study of Supply and Demand for Teachers," [2] which provides this information, and the state departments of public instruction of the various states issue bulletins on license requirements. Music and art majors should be made aware that in only rare cases can they count on making a living as professional musicians and artists without taking on some immediately paying work such as giving private lessons or teaching in public or private schools.

Similarly to discharge the planning function adequately, academic advisers in engineering colleges, schools of business and schools of social work need to be acquainted specifically with the opportunities in the various fields of engineering—chemical, electrical, civil and mechanical; of business—management, marketing

[2] Obtainable from the National Education Association, 1201 Sixteenth Street, N.W., Washington, D.C.

and accounting; and of social work—case work, group work and counseling. Only in this way can advisers help the college student to choose an appropriate program of studies that is at the same time consonant with his interests and practical from the point of view of earning a living. While the sole, or even the primary purpose of going to college is not that of preparing for a job, it is best to help students avoid the dilemma of leaving college embittered because they have not been prepared to enter the world of work.

Objectives in advising. The college teacher functioning as an adviser should strive to see that each of his advisees obtains some insight into the broad fields of learning. In medieval times these would have encompassed the seven liberal arts known as the trivium—grammar, logic, rhetoric—and the quadrivium—arithmetic, music, geometry and astronomy. Today they include classical and romance languages and literature; English composition and literature; the natural, biological and physical sciences; the social sciences, including anthropology, history, economics, political science, sociology and psychology; the fine arts—music, painting, sculpture, drama; and the various other forms of the humanities—religion, ethics and philosophy. Many of these fields of learning are likely to be prescribed either by requirements for the degree or for majors and minors, but each student needs some acquaintance with all of these fields in order to acquire broad interests. He needs breadth as well as depth in his education. The task of securing both breadth and depth in *understanding* is made more and more difficult by the enormous expansion of fields of knowledge.

Recent explorations of outer space open a vast new field for learning. The rapidly developing countries of Asia, Africa, the Middle East, Malaya and Central and South America require greater knowledge and new understandings. Indeed, it seems highly probable that four years may be all too short a time in which to acquire even a reasonable amount of knowledge upon which to base political, economic and social decisions. These considerations go beyond those of making a living and concern the living of a full life. The task of helping a college student to choose a program of studies that is balanced and adequate to the times in which he will live is not easy and requires careful preparation on the part of the faculty adviser.

Mechanics of advising. Individual faculty members will have their own ways of handling the mechanics of academic advising. Among other things it seems obvious that the adviser should have a record of what the student has taken in the past and what his achievement has been. Obviously, too, if a student did not do well in a field in which he has planned to major, the situation should be studied, and perhaps a possible shift in his plans should be discussed with him. If a student fails in a required subject, it must in most colleges be repeated. If he has too low a grade point average (that is, below the average grade point required for graduation), he may need to be placed on probation, an action which constitutes a warning to the student that he may be dropped from college. Usually the college deals with the student in the first instance through his adviser, who is his friend; but if it becomes necessary for the student to be dropped, this action is commonly taken by an academic committee. In some institutions such a student would not be readmitted without first attending another accredited institution for one term or one year and achieving a satisfactory record there.

Student advising does not take place merely at registration times. Indeed, it seems unlikely that an adviser can do a satisfactory job if he tries to confine his work to this period. Good advisers keep regular office hours throughout the school year when students may visit them of their own accord. It is likely that they will set aside three or four extra hours a day during a preregistration period when their advisees will be asked to come in to reconsider their plans for the coming term. Fortunate is the adviser who increasingly finds his advisees coming to him during this period with well-formulated questions or plans. When this occurs, the teacher has the satisfaction of feeling that he has been successful in getting his students to take charge of themselves and to make their own plans intelligently—which is, of course, the goal of all good advisory work.

Thus far we have been considering the assigned adviser. This designation may have been made alphabetically or because of the student's expressed interest in some field. But the student's assigned adviser is often not his real one. Among his other professors he frequently finds someone with whom he has unusual rapport, to whom he goes for advice, subsequently taking the necessary registration cards to his assigned adviser for the latter's official signature. This relationship with another staff member should be welcomed by the assigned adviser, not only because it reduces the amount of work he has to do, but also because it shows that the student is striking out on his own. In such cases the assigned adviser need only check to see that requirements are being met. It is hardly necessary to caution college teachers against giving conflicting and contradictory counsel, which confounds and confuses the student. A telephone conversation between faculty members will often clear a situation and benefit the student.

The open-door policy. Finally, college teachers frequently find it necessary to counsel with the students in their classes. The open-door policy is here recommended in contrast to that of one professor who posted a notice on his office door that he would see students by appointment only, and only at twelve noon (the hour at which lunch was served at all dormitories and commons on the campus)! He thus succeeded in reducing his hours of advising students to practically zero. As an instructor, the college teacher is interested in a different kind of counseling relationship. Though some professors have a "take it or leave it" attitude, the professional attitude is to encourage students to come for help. This practice not only aids the students, but it shows the professor whether he is getting his work across and helps him in his evaluation of students. While the student asks him questions about the subject of instruction, the professor can also ask questions, thus learning a good deal about the questioner. Some college teachers go so far as to say to a class, "I hesitate to give top grades to people whom I have not come to know personally." Such a statement usually brings in students who seek high marks, and the teacher is able to become acquainted with those to whom top grades are given and thus to feel confident that he can defend his evaluations if necessary.

As was suggested above, the college teacher is often selected by the student as a person to whom he can talk, not only about what he is learning in the teacher's course, but also about conflicts in ideas he is receiving at college, about vague goals for the future and even about personal problems. While the college teacher should maintain both an open-door policy and a willingness to listen, it is wise, as has already been said, to refer the student to the dean of students for a consideration of his personal affairs. However, the professor is the one who should try to help the student see his way through the maze of conflicting thought that he may have encountered in one of his subjects for the first time in his life. Though some college teachers consciously try to destroy traditionally held beliefs, others try not to knock out the "pillars of belief" that a student has unless they can help him rebuild his thinking with a more substantial foundation than he had in the first place. Individual counseling on such matters is of crucial importance in the life of many college students, and professors should not turn a deaf ear to their questions.

CHAPTER 8

The Research and Writing Function of the College Teacher

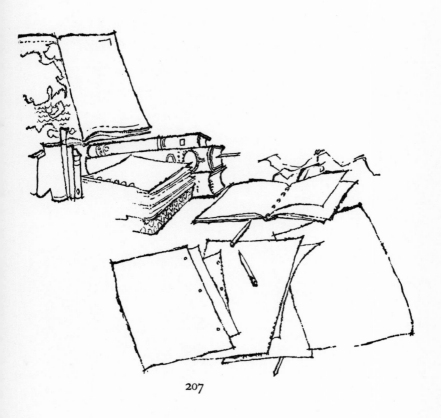

THE BEST AND MOST FRUITFUL CONCEPTION OF A UNI-
VERSITY OR COLLEGE IS THE ANCIENT ONE OF A SO-
CIETY OR GUILD OF SCHOLARS ASSOCIATED TOGETHER FOR
PRESERVING, IMPARTING, INCREASING AND ENJOYING
KNOWLEDGE.

—A. Lawrence Lowell

The teaching function of the college professor needs to be supported by research if college teaching is to be kept live and fresh. The research thus done should result in publications in professional periodicals, in monographs and in books.

Relationship between research and teaching. The importance of such research to teaching is shown in the comments listed below, which were made in personal letters from various college authorities.[1]

It is impossible to separate effective teaching from research. Research in a school . . . is a necessary part of its educational processes and current research problems going on in its various departments are regularly used to enrich and illustrate the classroom work.

I take issue with the idea that really effective teaching can be done by men who are not engaged in research. The teacher who has no intellectual curiosity of his own cannot stimulate the intellectual curiosity of the student.

The really distinguished men in research are almost always good teachers.

It is difficult, if not impossible, to find an instance of a great undergraduate teacher who was not a vigorous investigator and critic. . . . The criteria are the investigatory eagerness and the intellectual capacity of the scholar. . . . What is certain is that in most cases such qualities result in the achievement of studies worthy of publication and the absence of published work raises a natural question as to the vitality of the scholarship in the individual concerned.

[1] These letters were written to a committee of which the author was chairman.

. . . In each academic generation there will arise true scholars who do not put the results of their studies in book form. Such men are rare, we would note.

Such comments show the relationship between college teaching and research and publication, at least in the opinion of some college administrators. However, the late Edmond E. Day, when President of Cornell University, took sharp issue with some of these views. Because his opinion, expressed in a speech, represented a minority view, it is quoted at somewhat greater length:

One of the comfortable ways of dealing administratively with this situation is to belittle the idea that teaching and research are in any way competing functions at the university level. The idea is that teaching and research go hand in hand; that the successful teacher will inevitably be engaged in fruitful research and the successful scholar or scientist just as surely will be an effective teacher. This proposition in this general form is wishful thinking of the baldest sort. The eminent scholar or scientist who is also an inspiring teacher is, of course, for the university administrator an answer to prayer; but we know all too well that answers to this particular prayer appear in the flesh infrequently. . . .

Teaching and research may in a broad sense be complementary and mutually supporting functions, but they are clearly in the concrete day-to-day duties of the members of a university faculty competing and mutually excluding interests. . . . The conflict between teaching and research is barely perceptible, if it appears at all, at the level of the most advanced and specialized studies. . . .

As a rule it is desirable that all members of staff participate to some extent in both functions. But the proportions in which teaching and research are mixed in the duties of individual members of university faculties must and should vary widely . . . certainly unless or until our universities are converted into institutions for advanced study only. . . .

Our institutions are expected to treat teaching and research as coordinate functions. The two functions are in certain important respects essentially competing. The conditions of this competition appear to be definitely uneven, the function of research enjoying substantial differential advantages.

When one considers these conflicting views, it seems likely that many colleges in the future are likely to have faculties which are composed of staff members who are primarily teachers, others who are primarily researchers, along with others who divide their time somewhat evenly between teaching and research. Necessarily some college faculty members will be more effective in research than they are in teaching, and the reverse is also true.

Productivity in research and writing. While much is made of the reciprocal relationship between teaching and research, additional questions may be raised. It has been said that only about 30 per cent of the faculty of even the most highly respected institutions is really productive in research and writing. If this is true, one wonders if, in the interest of such work, it would not be socially more desirable for the members who are specially interested in research and writing to be relieved of teaching in order to contribute more in the field in which they have marked ability and are more prolific. Contrariwise, might it be better for staff members who are highly skilled in teaching and interpreting research to spend more of their time teaching at the expense of research? Many examples could be given of highly respected college professors who were creative in the sense of utilizing the research of others in their teaching, but who did little or no original research, and also of highly competent research persons, inventive of mind and capable of making fundamental discoveries, who were not able to teach effectively what they had discovered or what they knew.

RESEARCH

Research inside the university or outside? Still another question needs to be asked. Is the college or university the favorable place for research it once was? There was a period when the agricultural experimental stations in universities carried much of the burden of pushing back the frontiers of knowledge and another period when engineering and medical schools carried the same responsibility in their respective fields. But with the millions of dollars being spent today by the government for research and development, for defense and other purposes and the hundreds of millions being invested by private industry to develop its products, how can the college and university keep pace with the agencies mentioned? In state universities and state agencies there is now sharp competition for public moneys for research. Private universities also find themselves in competition with drives for many kinds of "research funds" to finance investigations carried on outside of universities. Further, these non-university research enterprises lure away some of the best research talent of the university itself.

We should not conclude that this issue of where research can best be carried on is settled. Aside from its importance for teaching, one very strong argument for its being located in the university is the necessity for freedom in doing research and in publishing the results of it. This freedom is not always available to the research worker whose talents are employed by business, industry, the armed forces, government or charitable institutions. In the university, freedom to seek the truth and to publish it is central to the real purpose of inquiring and disseminating knowledge.

Three levels of research activity. Whatever the college teacher's predisposition may be toward teaching and research, many educators feel that he would be wise to have three levels of research in progress most of the time. Perhaps the first level may be called fact-gathering, the second level a half-scale research effort and the third a full-scale project. These three steps may be illustrated by the work of an economics professor who keeps track, month by month, of the rise and fall of the stock market as related to industrial stocks, rails and utilities and compares them with the fluctuations of indices of business activity. This is an illustration of fact-gathering. Secondly, the professor makes a systematic study month by month of the major forecasts of business forecasting agencies beginning with the time of the stock market crash in 1929, with the purpose of determining which business forecasting concerns were most nearly accurate in their predictions.

This project leads to the professor's third-level study—the examination of the theories of forecasting with the purpose of determining which seems to be most nearly correct. Perhaps as a result a new theory, combining some of those studied, might be formulated. In this case the professor intends to project the theory for ten years, comparing the results of its application year by year with what actually happens and with what other business forecasters predicted would happen. He hopes that out of this research a new and better theory may emerge.

The teaching of professors of social work, psychology and education, all of whom have a special interest in people, will be enlivened if they, too, engage in research at each of the three levels suggested. First, they may gather some facts about all their students, which enable them to understand the students' interests, their previous education and their recreational and occupational experiences. Second, they make a more detailed study of a limited number—say eight or ten—students or children in the schools. This study goes beyond simple fact-gathering and includes observation and interviews of a somewhat thorough nature. Third, professors in these fields, whose skills and concern extend beyond those of other college teachers, conduct a full-scale case study of three or four persons; whether these people are adults, college students or school children is immaterial. This research includes sending the individual for a thorough physical examination, giving mental, achievement and aptitude tests, having many conferences with him, visiting his home, studying the environment and the forces that play on him, as well as securing other pertinent data.

Only when the college teacher keeps his hand in with research projects—simple or complex—does he bring the fresh insight of recent experience to his college teaching.

Occasionally a professor who advises a number of doctoral candidates becomes so interested in their research that he makes it a substitute for his own. Such advisers spend many hours of time with the candidates and, of course, contribute greatly to the quality of research and writing of the doctoral students. Yet even the best candidates—those who have written a senior thesis and a master's thesis and then taken on the doctoral dissertation—are still likely to be tackling problems in a fairly elementary fashion. Hence, the professor is almost certain to be assisting with research of a less mature nature than if he had been carrying on his own, and he misses the immense satisfaction which comes from working on a problem in which he is personally and professionally interested.

Doctoral study as the basis of subsequent research. There is considerable difference of opinion among educators and students about some phases of the doctoral dissertation. In this connection Berelson [2] reports the percentage of agreement on the part of seventy-nine graduate deans, 1,821 graduate faculty members and 2,331 recent recipients of doctor's degrees on the statements listed below:

	Percentage Agreeing		
	Graduate Deans	*Graduate Faculty*	*Recent Recipients*
Doctoral candidates are too often allowed or encouraged to attempt a major contribution as their dissertation rather than to take on a manageable topic that can be finished in a reasonable time.	64	32	32
The doctoral dissertation should be regarded more as a training instrument than as an "original contribution" to knowledge.	56	45	40
Doctoral work suffers because many students don't really want to be researchers but have to go through research programs in order to get the "union badge" for college teaching.	45	46	49

[2] Bernard Berelson, *Graduate Education in the U.S.*, McGraw-Hill Book Company, Inc., New York, 1960, p. 289.

It is interesting to note that the majority of the graduate faculty and recipients of degrees believe that the doctoral dissertation should make an original contribution to knowledge, while the majority of graduate deans believe that it should be regarded chiefly as a training instrument. Analysis made by the author of the opinions by fields of learning revealed that the dissertation was regarded as primarily an instrument for research training only by the graduate faculty and students working in the social sciences and in education. All the respondents agreed that doctoral research does not repel students from doing further research, that it is not inefficient because few recipients of the degree become researchers, and that it does not dampen enthusiasm for learning and scholarship.

Properly chosen, the college teacher's own doctoral dissertation should provide him with a first base for his subsequent research, since any worthwhile doctoral thesis turns up questions which demand further study. Who could study them better than the investigator who uncovered these questions? Here is an avenue through which a college teacher can push his way into more mature research. Further, one who closely observes a great many new college professors becomes aware of the fact that if the young teacher does no research within five years after finishing his doctoral dissertation, he is not likely to be productive research-wise in the years that follow. It is important, therefore, that the beginning college teacher continue doing research, and one of the best places to begin is with some of the questions uncovered in his doctoral thesis.

One difficulty with this proposal is the kind of sharply limited problems that graduate sponsors tend to advise for doctoral candidates. A research problem should do more for a candidate than help him obtain a doctor's degree. It should be on a subject which will be of continuing interest to him, and on which, hopefully, he can perhaps build himself a national or even an international reputation. Therefore, dissertation topics should be chosen because they contribute to the "cutting edge" of the candidate's field of learning. While the thesis itself must be manageable, the candidate should see it as part of a broader field, one in which he might like to carry on investigation for a good many years.

Research on unsolved problems. There are, of course, other ways in which a college teacher may continue his research. In every profession there are unsolved problems. In every community and state there are social problems that require study for their solution. In every discipline there are moot questions which need answering. As has been previously said, we need to realize that nothing is more important or more practical than the investigation of a good theory. Einstein's theory of relativity was formulated abstractly forty years before it was demonstrated in reality. No one needs to be told today that the events of recent years have made the outrageous theories of science fiction writers of a few years ago seem modest when compared with the realities of space penetration and orbiting satellites. As indicated earlier, one of the advantages of doing research in a university is that one is free to explore without the necessity for the research to pay off; there is freedom to dream, to posit theories and demonstrate their practicality. We can be sure that there will never be a scarcity of important problems requiring research, and for several reasons the university is the ideal place in which to carry it on.

PUBLISHING

The college teacher as a writer. Colleges and universities have a real interest in getting faculty members to write. Many administrators put considerable pressure on the teacher to get into print, and there are some institutions where "publish or perish" appears to be the policy. Where this is the case, college teachers who have no real interest in writing feel forced to resort to certain devices to meet the requirements. One of these is to attempt to get on the programs of state, regional or national conferences in their field, since the proceedings of many of these meetings are printed and thus one's name is attached to a printed document. Another device is to review books for professional publications in one's field, for the name of the reviewer is always given at the end of his appraisal of the book. However, both the conference paper and the analysis of the book are a far cry from the connected, logical, creative writing in which a scholar should be engaged.

Publication in periodicals. A better method for getting into print is to write articles for periodicals. In this category there are the popular magazines as well as the regional and national professional publications. Here it is important to know where to send the article one has written. The editor of a popular magazine with five million readers will be interested in a different kind of article than will a scientific magazine written primarily for three thousand members of a given profession. Most professional journals are bombarded with ten or twenty times the number of articles they can possibly print. Which of these journals will use a carefully reasoned article relating to a well-known policy or theory? Which will choose articles that seem to be on the "frontier" so that the magazine can advertise them as "firsts?" What do the editors of various magazines like to print? Some will seek carefully documented, penetrating analyses of philosophical arguments. Some will seek accounts of carefully controlled experiments in psychology, biology or medicine. Others will be searching for lyric poetry or writing which is beautiful in word and phrase. It is probably too strong a statement to say that almost any reasonably well-written document can secure publication somewhere, yet the biggest difficulty seems to be that the young writer does not know who publishes what.

Relatively only a few college teachers write for the large-circulation popular magazines. Those who do so are rewarded with a large number of readers of their work and usually with a check for a substantial amount of money. Since such writing must appeal to the general public, it is necessarily less scholarly than articles written for professional magazines whose readers are acquainted with the content and vocabulary of the field with which an article deals. However, writing for the large-circulation magazines requires a high degree of ability and should not be frowned upon by the writers' colleagues as unworthy of his abilities. Such periodicals as *The New York Times Magazine, Harpers* and *The Atlantic Monthly* reach a large and thoughtful public and influence the attitudes of many times the number of people reached in the professional journals. Perhaps the prime caution is for the serious writer to avoid the temptation to write only articles that will command a high price in the magazine market.

Most college teachers are more likely to secure publication of their work in the state, regional and national periodicals of their own discipline. If an article is turned down at the national level, the author may revise and re-submit it, especially if the editor of the national journal has indicated that he would consider publishing it if the article were revised in specifically detailed ways. Otherwise the writer may send it to a regional or a state journal. If rejected here, it would seem better for the college teacher to move into a different piece of writing, for making endless revisions in the hope of eventual publication is discouraging and less desirable than for the writer to grow intellectually by expressing himself on a different topic.

Publication of books. Though a college teacher reaps many advantages from publishing in periodicals, there are greater advantages to be gained in concentrating on the writing of books. The latter give the author the opportunity, not usually found in writing for magazines, of developing his ideas in continuity and in full. A book reveals the full measure of the author's thought and writing skill.

The commercial book publisher, the pocket-edition press and the university press constitute the three usual avenues for the publication of books. Because of the costs involved, the first two of these are necessarily interested in something that will sell, that is, something for which there is a demand. Too often, the demand lags behind the writer's thought and therein lies one of the difficulties in securing publication. Commercial publications are of two kinds—textbooks and books for general reading. Though a "best seller" in the general field is probably the most profitable type of writing today, a college textbook, if widely adopted, brings its author a good financial return. Though there are many well-known firms that publish college texts, the effectiveness of their sales organizations varies greatly, and there are differences, too, in the royalties offered to authors. It is important for any writer to select his publisher carefully.

Though a publishing firm hesitates to print a work that is "far out," publications which are near the frontier or the "cutting edge" of a field are to be preferred to those that tend to depict the status quo or current practice, for their future usefulness—and incidentally their future sales—will be much greater.

While "publish or perish" may seem to be a ruthless policy and perhaps not a defensible one, any college professor worthy of the name should have something to say. His ideas should be not only heard in the classroom but should be printed for others to read and criticize. For criticism is basic to the scholar's life; without it he cannot grow. Students' comments, questions and occasional criticisms are helpful to the college professor *if he will listen,* even though in most instances these are likely to be elementary or immature. The scholar may and probably will get criticism from his colleagues, or he may obtain this needed stimulation from attendance at professional meetings in his field. But only when he has written his ideas out in book form can he know the judgment of his peers on the full orchestration of his ideas and only in this way can they come to appreciate his full contribution to their thought.

CHAPTER 9

The Faculty
and
Administration

THE CENTRAL AREA OF OPERATION IS THAT CONCERNED
WITH THE EDUCATIONAL-TEACHING FUNCTION OF THE
INSTITUTION—IF ANYTHING IN ADMINISTRATION IS CEN-
TRAL, IT IS THE EDUCATIONAL DETERMINATION OF
BUDGETARY ASSIGNMENTS.
—*Lloyd S. Woodburne*

Though the college teacher's chief concern is necessarily with his teaching and research, he needs to keep in mind
that he is not exempt from certain administrative and business
matters that are of considerable importance to the successful operation of his institution.

In early American universities and in many European ones today an organized body of "masters" chooses the head of the university. On the Continent this official is called the rector. At first
his term of office was short—only three months in length—but
now he is elected for a few years. The reasoning in favor of professorial control, at least during the Middle Ages, was that since
the University was a society of masters, their social position and
self-respect required an involvement in the management of university affairs.[1] In these early years there were no boards of
trustees nor any state control. The faculty was self-governing as
well as self-respecting and the University escaped one of the unfortunate effects of the centralized college administration of today,
where decisions are made by college officers without consultation
with faculty and often without a clear understanding of the
probable effect of such decisions on classroom instruction and
student growth. Because of the effect of administrative decisions
on his students and his work, it is essential not only that today's
college teacher keep actively concerned with what is happening
in the central offices, but also that he participate intelligently in

[1] For an elaboration of this view see Charles H. Haskins, *The Rise of
Universities,* Cornell University Press, Ithaca, New York, 1957, p. 50.

university and departmental decisions whenever such a course is open to him.

Administrative role of faculty today. In 1960 a study was made of the role of the American college faculty in administration, which dealt with the various administrative posts held by faculty members in American and Canadian universities.[2] Whereas there is active participation by faculty members in executive roles in overseas universities, such participation in American and Canadian institutions seems to have been giving way to the teaching, writing and research functions. Nevertheless, in 1960 in eighty-four institutions located in thirty-two states and eleven Canadian provinces, full-time faculty members were engaged in the administrative areas shown in the following list:

Area	Number
Head of a Department	873
Committee Chairman	441
Supervisor of Practice Teaching	84
Assistant to the head of a department	32
Office of Director of Personnel	25
Project Director	25
Division Chairman	19
Member of Lay Advisory Board	17
Office of the Alumni Director	17
Assistant to the Athletic Director	17
Director of Social Activities	14
Assistant to the Librarian	13
Office of Public Relations	13
Assistant to the President	11
Assistant to the Academic Dean	11

Though there were fourteen other areas reported, none had as many as ten faculty members serving in them, and half had only one or two members.

[2] "Higher Education," mimeographed material, Department of Education, Graduate School of Arts and Sciences, the Catholic University of America, Washington, D.C., 1960.

Business aspect of the college. Before considering the faculty member's role in some of the important administrative areas listed, it may be observed that there are two separate but intertwined organizational patterns in the college or university. A college is both an academic organization and a business organization. Every college is a business and a large university is big business. It employs large numbers of people in many different categories, from the custodial staff to the president. It is composed of many departments, each with an administrative head, and the budget of a large university is frequently larger than that of a relatively large business organization. The university does, of course, differ from the business corporation in important ways. There is no profit motive in the university, and there are no bonuses at Christmas time! It has tax exemption. The most important difference, of course, is that its product is not a thing but a human being. Businesses usually have scrap heaps resulting from poor material or poor workmanship. Colleges should have no scrap heaps; they should not admit poor material nor tolerate poor "workmanship."

Except for paying his fees for tuition, board and room, the average student is unaware of the business organization of his institution. The faculty member may be aware of it only on paydays and when he wishes to requisition supplies, equipment or books or when he desires to attend a conference at college expense. However, to both faculty and student, the business organization of the college is of considerable importance, for there must be an adequate and well-run financial structure to support the academic program and make it possible for the administration and individual faculty members to achieve their own academic goals.

Boards of control. Fundamental to both the business and the academic organization of the college is its board of control,[3] most frequently called the "board of trustees," though "board of regents," "board of governors" or some other title may be used.

---

[3] Much valuable information on board members will be found in Beardsley Ruml and Donald H. Morrison, *Memo to a College Trustee,* McGraw-Hill Book Company, Inc., New York, 1959, 94 pp.

Whatever designation is employed, this board is the ultimate authority for policy decisions in both business and academic matters. It has specific control over endowments and real estate, the regulation of student fees, the granting of degrees and the conditions of employment. Final authority in decision making in the better colleges is vested in the board, However, it is generally agreed that board members themselves should seldom engage in the actual administering of the details of a policy which they have approved.

Boards of control range in size from five to 250, but the average size is twenty-four. The general belief is that small boards are more effective than large ones. There should be provision for both continuity and change in the membership. Complete changes take place slowly. This implies overlapping of terms and a possible provision that members may not succeed themselves without an intervening year. The range in length of terms is from three to sixteen years, but the average length has been twelve years. Churches often nominate members for boards of church-related colleges and sometimes may even elect them. Boards of private colleges are often self-perpetuating, i.e., members elect themselves to succeed themselves, or elect their own successors from outside the board membership without the participation of any outside group such as an alumni body or a synod. For public colleges and universities appointment by the Governor is the most common method of selection, although in some states members are elected by popular vote, often in a partisan election. Since education must be objective (non-partisan), it would seem undesirable to have members of boards of control chosen in such a fashion.

As the purposes of the colleges have changed, so has the membership of which their boards are composed. The proportion of clergymen has decreased from 39 per cent to 7 per cent, while the proportion of businessmen has increased from 27 per cent to 52 per cent. People from the professions, business and banking constitute almost the entire membership of many boards, and it is unusual to find women, union representatives or Negroes on them. Most of the large boards meet no more than twice a year, their members receiving no compensation though their expenses are paid. Smaller boards meet more frequently and do not have a standing-committee organization. Large boards customarily have four standing committees—executive, investment, buildings and grounds, and personnel—which meet to decide and report matters in these categories, thus making it unnecessary for the entire board to meet frequently.

These details come into focus when an issue arises on the campus which goes to the board for decision. Such issues may involve the requirement of a loyalty oath, academic freedom and tenure, conditions of employment, academic competence or the selection of a president. The composition of the board, the manner in which it functions and the values it holds high are of the greatest importance to the faculty as a whole and to the individual faculty member.

Types of organization of colleges. Internally, colleges may have either a multiple or a unit type of organization. Under the former, two or more coordinate officers (the president and the business manager) are separately responsible to the board for certain designated functions. Under the unit type of organization a single officer (the president) is responsible to the board for all functions. The unit type is commonly thought to be more efficient and desirable. The president should have final authority and responsibility, subject to review by the board, for all phases of college administration. Hence, the business manager should report to him, as should the academic deans, the alumni director, the director of public relations, the dean of students and the vice-president in charge of development. The board should understand that administrative officers must be given authority commensurate with their responsibilities.

Selection of a president. Boards of trustees probably have no more important task than the selection of the president of the educational institution. No pat formula can be suggested that will insure a proper choice. Following World War II a number of men who had held high rank in the armed services were elected presidents of major institutions. The assumption that they would make good educational executives was a reasonable one if a college or university organization has some resemblance to a military one. Following the depression of the thirties business men were frequently elected presidents of colleges, probably because many colleges were then in financial difficulties. The assumption that a business man could remedy this situation was a reasonable one. Clergymen also have been elected presidents of colleges and universities. Dedicated to high values and effective in public address, ministers of churches with large congregations, fairly large budgets and paid staff would, it is assumed, certainly be desirable presidents of educational institutions.

A fourth category is the academic man. He is the person who has worked up through the various professional ranks, established himself a scholar, been influential on university committees and professional societies in his discipline and is well known and liked for his balanced judgment and qualities of leadership. No one can say from what previous position the president of a college should come. There have been shining examples of success as well as some notable failures from each of the categories mentioned. If the understanding, confidence and respect of the faculty is a key factor in the selection, then the academic man is in the most advantageous position from which to be plummeted into the presidency. He understands the necessity for academic freedom, he believes that criticism is important to a college community and he knows that, while a college must be run in an economical and efficient manner, it cannot be operated like a business or a military organization.

The first step in the selection of a president is the appointment of a committee by the Board of Trustees to make a canvass and present a nomination. At least one faculty member should be invited to serve on this committee, and he should have a faculty committee to advise him. One of the first functions of both committees is to draw up a set of criteria for possible candidates. These should include age qualifications, academic preparation, professional experience, leadership qualities, executive ability, the capacity to command public support and to raise money, and desirable personal characteristics. Both the faculty and board committees should agree on whatever criteria are adopted, but it should be realized that the criteria are not likely to be met in every respect by any of the candidates.

Prospects for the office of college president do not usually apply for the position. They must be sought out and persuaded to accept. Canvassing for eligible persons is therefore a very time-consuming task. Appeals for recommendations of people should be made to university presidents, presidents of foundations and prominent people in educational organizations, professional societies and in church, business and public life. As many as thirty or forty names may be received from these sources. The board committee should have a secretary whose task it is to obtain information about the people whose names are brought to the attention of the board through the canvass. This is done usually by writing to each person nominated, telling him that he has been recommended for the presidency and asking whether he is interested in it. If so, he is asked to send a vita sheet. Quite often the person's reply will consist of a request for more information about the position.

When the data concerning each interested nominee are compared with the criteria agreed upon, all but eight or ten names will probably be eliminated for one reason or another, Perhaps the board committee will visit the four or five most promising of these in their own locale for interviews. Then comes a final check on the two or three candidates being most seriously considered—perhaps a second visit to them in their present posts and telephone calls to many people who know them. The final step is the campaign to secure the acceptance of the person elected to the position. This campaign would include a visit of the person chosen and his wife to the campus (if they have not made a previous visit) and a meeting of the nominee with the faculty committee and the whole Board of Trustees. He may also receive letters from the governor of the state and from other college presidents in the state, as well as from the persons who first recommended him.

Though the selection of a new president is an involved process, no other activity of the Board of Trustees will ever be more important to the faculty, the students and the institution itself, for the president will leave a lasting impress on all concerned.

THE FACULTY AND BUSINESS MANAGEMENT

Business administration. A short definition of the business function of a college is that it is any activity involving money. It is not the purpose of this volume to discuss all the functions and procedures normally assigned to the business office, but they may be listed as follows: (1) financial accounting, (2) assistance in the preparation of an annual budget, (3) preparation of financial reports and statistics, (4) expenditure of institutional funds, (5) collection of revenue, (6) maintenance of financial relations with students, (7) management of investment funds, (8) purchasing, (9) employment and supervision of non-academic personnel, (10) management of business phases of auxiliary activities, (11) control of sales of materials, (12) financial promotion, (13) planning for the financing of special projects, (14) research on financial problems and (15) supervision of physical plant. In a large university there will be an accounting office, a purchasing office, a bursar's office, a non-academic personnel office, a book store and a division of buildings and grounds, each with an executive officer and a staff. Each of these officers is responsible to the business manager who, in turn, is responsible to the president. In smaller colleges several of these functions are combined under one person.

All business processes should point toward the educational service to be rendered. It is most important for all concerned to realize that the whole purpose of these operations is to enable the college professor to meet the student under conditions that promote the growth of each. It may be more economical to have classes of 250 in size, but if this class size does not promote academic excellence, it is undesirable. It may be possible to serve poor quality food in the dining rooms, but in the long run this economy will drive students away from the institution. Good health and good teaching are both examples of services to be promoted by the business organization.

The income of a college. Later in this chapter reference will be made to the business function of the college teacher. Here we are interested specifically in how the business practices of an institution can be appraised. A college professor will be interested in how an institution in which he might consider being employed secures its income. The percentage of income received from three sources in three privately supported liberal arts colleges is shown below:

		College	
Income from	*A*	*B*	*C*
Tuition	55.7%	56.7%	67.9%
Endowment	36.2%	8.8%	16.3%
Gifts	8.8%	34.0%	15.7%

It is apparent from the above that the students paid different fees at these institutions, depending on the amount of income received from endowment and gifts. These figures may be contrasted with those of a large state-supported university, which obtained 20.2 per cent of its income from tuition, 4.5 per cent from endowment and 75.3 per cent from the state government.

A rule of thumb is that the college should have a stable income of $400 per student in addition to the fees paid by him. If the return on the investment of the institution is about 4½ per cent, an endowment of approximately $9,000 per student would be required. Hence, the college with an enrollment of 500 should have an endowment of about $4,500,000, and if it does not have sufficient endowment, it may not be a desirable place in which to be employed. The general understanding is that an endowment is a fund to be maintained inviolate, the income alone being used. The prospective employee who finds that the college under consideration is spending its endowment for operating expenses would do well to look elsewhere.

However, many colleges are not able to achieve a stable income of $400 per student from this source alone. Some colleges have instituted what they call "living endowments," a term which means that alumni and patrons pledge sufficient gifts each year to equal $400 per student. If all of this amount were to come from such sources for a college of 500, annual giving to the college would have to reach $200,000. Most private, church-related colleges obtain some stable income from their endowment as well as some from private gifts and from churches.

Costs per student. The college teacher is interested also in the amount the college spends for educational and general expenses per full-time student. Among forty-five four-year colleges in 1960–1961 the median weighted educational and general expenditure per full-time student was $733.94, but the range was from $410.70 to $1,446.27. It would seem clear that it would be more advantageous to work in a college whose educational and general expenses per student were $733.94 or above. While costs vary between the different state-supported institutions, they vary also within the institutions themselves. In one such institution the average cost per student was $1,300, but the cost per medical student was $4,000 while that of a liberal arts student was $900.

As a general rule it is thought wise for auxiliary enterprises and non-educational activities of colleges to be operated on a non-profit, break-even basis. If the college has an expensive "big-time" athletic program, the teacher will need to discover whether or not it breaks even. In some institutions the faculty have had to take a cut in salary to help meet such non-educational expenses. Some colleges follow the dubious practice of making a profit on lodging and meals provided students. While this profit is often diverted to the educational program to avoid raising tuition, the practice is a questionable one since the student does not receive full value for what he pays for his living expenses. The faculty member also has an interest in the student fees charged because authorities generally believe that income from this source should be expended substantially for instructional purposes. While these include library expenses and the cost of instructional materials and laboratory supplies, the major item is faculty salaries. If the tuition fee is $650 per year and the ratio of students to faculty is fifteen to one, the average salary of faculty members will be a little less than $9,750 annually (since the other educational expenses must be deducted from the total fees collected from the students).

Analysis of expenditures. The view discussed here relates not so much to the details of the business organization of the college as to the outcomes of its functioning. Is too much being spent for buildings and grounds? Is the cost of administration excessive? Are endowment funds being conserved for educational purposes? Are appropriate amounts being spent for educational and general expenses?

The following figures show the percentages of the total expenditures of five colleges that were devoted to six specific categories:

TABLE 4

PERCENTAGES OF TOTAL EXPENDITURES OF FIVE COLLEGES
DEVOTED TO SPECIFIC ITEMS

Item	Institutions				
	A	B	C	D	E
Administration and general	34.1	35.2	43.7	31.3	28.6
Instruction (total)	49.8	48.6	40.2	44.4	47.4
Faculty salaries	(39.6)	(44.9)	(30.1)	(36.6)	(44.4)
Other	(10.2)	(3.6)	(10.1)	(7.8)	(3.0)
Library	4.0	4.6	3.4	2.6	1.6
Maintenance and Operation	12.1	11.6	12.7	21.7	22.4
	100.0	100.0	100.0	100.0	100.0

After a quick scanning one might suggest that college C spent too much of its budget on administration and general expenditures, too much on maintenance and operation and not enough on faculty salaries. College E also spends too much, comparatively, on maintenance and operation and not enough on the library. How a business administration spends the college income is of significant concern to all of its faculty.

Tax exemption. One other matter remains to be discussed in this section, and that is tax exemption for collegiate institutions. Tax laws apply equally to all persons and property except as expressly exempt. College property may be tax exempt either (1) by clauses in the general statutes of the state or (2) by unalterable provisions in the college charter. Most colleges are tax exempt under the first of these provisions. The general belief is that they render a public service to the state and therefore should not be taxed. Thus property is taken off the tax roll and the real estate taxes of local residents are increased. If, however, the college engages in profit-making enterprises, it is likely to be subject to a tax levy on them. One college once owned a profitable spaghetti company and sought to escape taxation on it on the grounds that the business profits and the taxes saved on them were used to support the college program. The courts, however, ruled that the college had to pay taxes in this instance. Northwestern University and Washington University of St. Louis are examples of institutions of higher education which hold unalterable provisions for tax exemption in their charters. The U.S. Supreme Court has held that provisions in these charters were granted without reservation and are not subject to change by state authority without the consent of the institution. A minority view of such a decision is that no legislature can be conceded the power to bargain away the taxing power for all time.

THE FACULTY AND THE EDUCATIONAL ADMINISTRATION

The faculty member in academic administration. While all faculty members are or ought to be concerned with the financial administration of a collegiate institution, their assignments, their morale, their real satisfactions are likely to reside in the academic organization. Nevertheless, as was said early in the chapter, the college faculty member cannot enjoy these without accepting some responsibilities in academic affairs. When he participates actively in these, some of his time is taken up with academic committees and councils and he has less free time for his own study and research. There is also in such participation the possibility of encountering the tyranny of faculty colleagues over his actions if not his opinions, from which there may result conflicts in ideology affecting academic policy making and administration. Morale-wise this may be quite as devastating as to have a board of trustees who regard faculty members as employees instead of appointees and who prevent the teachers from being included in academic policy making and administration.

On balance it seems that the college teacher should be willing to take time off from his classroom duties, his reading and research to give his judgment and assist his colleagues in formulating academic policy. It should be remembered that the tenure of college presidents and deans is relatively short, the composition of boards of trustees changes and the student body changes every four years. The persisting factor in the academic life of the institution is the faculty, and its members must be concerned with the long-run academic policies of the college.

The college professor functions within two or more frameworks which he can influence and by which he is in turn influenced. These are college-wide frames of reference and departmental areas, and the college teacher must live responsibly within each of them. It would seem desirable, therefore, to consider each briefly.

The professor as a member of the college. There are three areas of educational policy making which are generally considered to be of great concern to all faculty members. These are policies with regard to admission, the academic program and standards for graduation. Faculty members are also concerned with salaries, working conditions, secretarial help and retirement policies, and their advice should be sought on all such matters. The latter, however, are primarily administrative in character, and though they greatly affect the effective functioning of the professor in his academic duties, the making of policy with regard to them is usually left to administrators.

Admission policies. It is a truism to say that the quality of work a teacher will be able to achieve depends basically and in the first instance on the caliber of students sought and admitted to the college. While a superior college teacher can do much for inferior college students, he can do more for those with superior abilities. If the quality of an institution is judged by the quality of its academic product, it is self-evident that much attention should be given to the criteria actually employed for admission.

Admission policies vary with the type of institution. At one extreme there is the instance of the small private junior college whose officials solicited prospective freshmen who had been rejected by a neighboring private institution. This private junior college needed students in order to operate economically, and apparently the policy was, "Admit any student who is a high school graduate and has the money to pay." Some highly reputable private universities admit students only from the upper quarter, or even the upper tenth, of their high school classes, but these students must also be able to pay at the rate of thirty-five or forty dollars per credit hour taken. Here two criteria are employed—ability to pay and rank in high school class. Other private institutions prescribe these two, plus a successful score on the College Entrance Examination Boards. Still others require all of the foregoing plus a designated pattern of high school studies, such as four years of English, four years of mathematics, four years of science, four years of foreign language, two years of history, plus art, music and physical education.

When such criteria are employed for admission, the college teacher is likely to find in his college classes students from the economically and socially privileged classes who have successfully met the academic standards of the institution. It is disquieting to assume that only young people from the privileged classes should attend college, even though generous scholarships do admit a few whose parents cannot afford to pay. When one recalls the early lack of interest in schooling on the part of some of the world's greatest leaders, it is also disquieting to realize that the admission policies of some colleges tend to exclude the nonconformist, the non-memoriter learner and the "late bloomer." Whatever the admission policy may be, the college professor will be affected by it; hence, as a faculty member, he should assert an interest in modifying or improving it if he feels a change is necessary.

State colleges and universities face many, though not all, of the problems mentioned, and they have a few of their own. For example, the state typically bears about two-thirds of the cost of the student's higher education, whereas in private institutions the student and his parents bear this proportion of the cost. State institutions tend to be less selective in admission than private institutions. The argument runs, "As all taxpayers pay state taxes to support state higher educational institutions, the sons and daughters of these taxpayers should be permitted to attend them." In at least two states the courts have ruled that any graduate who has been recommended by his high school principal for college (and such a recommendation is often easily obtained) must be given a chance to try himself at college. It is true that if he fails, he need not be kept in college, and hundreds of students are dropped at mid-semester or after the first semester and sent home with what their parents sometimes lamely call "sore eyes."

Private institutions often try to attract students from all regions of the country, thus securing a cosmopolitan college population. State institutions, on the other hand, often feel obligated to serve the people of the state first, admitting students from outside the state only in limited numbers. Some taxpayers and legislators object to any out-of-state students even though they pay a higher tuition than state residents, and hence, state institutions sometimes fail to achieve the heterogeneity of culture in the student population that most educators deem desirable.

Colleges may be facing a most serious problem by 1970. After World War I almost everyone began to go to high school, and now a very large percentage of students finish. By 1970 will we be facing a situation where almost everyone desires to go to college? If they do, will there be anything remaining which resembles the higher education of past years? There are only a few years left in which college faculties may face these questions and adopt admission policies with which they will want to live. To fail to adopt such policies or to drift into their formation is the road to irresponsibility for any college or university in the years ahead. From personal, professional and social points of view, every faculty member should interest himself in his institution's policy with regard to admissions.

Academic program. The readers of this volume will have pursued at least twelve years of elementary and secondary education. Some will have completed four years of college and be well on the way toward the completion of their graduate studies. At whatever point they may be on this continuum, they will have formed some opinion with regard to the education to which they have been exposed. Whether their reactions are favorable or unfavorable, college teachers should consider the aims of the whole college program as far as the student is concerned. Here they should try to put aside their own fields of specialization and any vested interest they may have in them and consider from an unbiased point of view two important questions: what will the world of tomorrow require of the educated person, and what does he need to live fully and richly and to contribute to this rapidly changing world?

It is already apparent that the academic program of the past will not be comprehensive enough for this next generation. A liberal arts program which included ten semester hours of English, eighteen of social studies, twelve of laboratory science, twelve of foreign language, eight of mathematics and three each of psychology, philosophy, art and music, plus a major of twenty-four hours, a minor of sixteen hours and electives amounting to eight hours may have been adequate for the years that have passed. However, it should be noted that such a program lacked unity, being rather a collection of relatively independent and unrelated subjects. Today much more stress is being placed by the public on the physical sciences, mathematics and foreign languages. While agreeing that greater emphasis on these fields may be needed, other segments of the public assert that, however necessary these fields may be in the short run, it will be the humanities and social sciences that will help mankind gain and maintain peace in the long run. The exploration of outer space and the explosions in Africa and Asia constitute further evidence of the need for a more comprehensive and better college curriculum. It is the effective use of knowledge in improving the relations between men on this planet that seems most imperative. Most civilized men insist that they wish to live at peace with one another, but problems of religion, race, ethnic origin and of social and economic status interfere. What is needed is the development of generations of people better able to handle these problems as well as their own personal relationships and to deal with international problems of vast importance to the world.

General education. While any teacher functioning as a member of a college faculty may dislike to envision any other pattern of college education than the one he has himself experienced, yet upon reflection he knows that in the introductory courses in most of the academic fields there will be (1) those who expect to concentrate in a particular department, (2) those who do not expect to do so but want a general education, and (3) those who have not yet decided on a field of concentration. If the first group is given the rigorous grounding it needs, the other two groups may not achieve their purposes unless additional courses are especially designed for their needs.

As a result of these conflicts of interest there have been attempts to reorganize content to emphasize fields of learning. A description has already been given of broad-field courses which cut across departmental lines and attempt to give students a total view of life's problems in place of the scattered-parts view. It will be noted that, although these offerings are not without value to the first group mentioned above, they are designed primarily for the last two groups listed.

As a faculty member the college teacher is likely to have to vote to install, retain or eliminate such general education courses. In considering how he will vote, he will wish to consider the problem of integration. Is it desirable for the student to see the relationship between the natural sciences and the social sciences? If each of these fields is taught in discrete parts, will he see the connection? Should students be expected to integrate fields of knowledge when their professors do not do so?

If the college teacher accepts the idea that such integration is desirable, there still remains the question of whether the student should be oriented to the whole field of knowledge prior to the study of many specific fields, or whether such an integrating seminar might well come at or near the end of his college studies. Valid arguments can be stated for both positions. Possibly, if time were available, the student would profit from orientation courses at the beginning of his college studies and a synthesizing seminar near the close of his study.

Method of curriculum change. Most college professors join the faculty of an institution after its curriculum has already been determined. How is this curriculum modified? How are new offerings installed? New single courses or new patterns of courses are usually proposed by a member of some department to its staff. If the proposal wins favor in the department, it is presented to an all-college curriculum committee. Here the debate is likely to be one of two kinds. If the new offering is not competitive with the subject matter of any other department, the main question is likely to be, "Can we afford it?" However, if the new offering is competitive with or replaces a course presently being given, the question will be debated more vigorously, perhaps even acrimoniously. Eventually, however, the curriculum committee reaches a conclusion. Their decision is recommended to the whole faculty, which may either adopt or reject its committee's report.

Degree requirements. Another problem of policy which the college teacher may be asked to help decide relates to requirements for a degree. Though the requirements for a degree in most colleges remain relatively constant, history shows us that they are subject to change. The shock of the first Sputnik, the requirements of our national security and the developments of the space age probably account for the present demand by a large number of educators and laymen for the requirement of four years of mathematics, four years of science and four years of foreign language. But if four years of work in each of these subjects are to be required for graduation, what is to become of English and American literature, philosophy, psychology, history, political science, economics, art and music? And what should constitute the core of knowledge and skills to be possessed by the person on whom the college, by granting him a degree, confers the label of "an educated man?" These are questions which require a high degree of understanding of the contributions of the various branches of the curriculum and at the same time a high degree of objectivity regarding the teacher's own special field.

The first of these requires that the teacher be well informed as to both the content and aims of all the subject fields listed in the catalog. Since he knows that much of the content of the courses students take will be forgotten, he must give thought to such questions as: Do the physical sciences really cause students to see relationships between cause and effect? Does the study of history give young people a better understanding of the problems of the present day? Do music and art as taught in the particular college contribute to the development of creativity in the learner? From what subjects will the student obtain a sense of values to guide his future decisions?

Departmental versus college-wide interest. Because the college teacher knows that the opinion of the members of his department is important to his promotion and his future, he frequently hesitates to vote and act independently when he comes to vote as a college faculty member. It is almost inevitable that every faculty member should feel that some course in his field should be among the graduation requirements. After all, each staff member has devoted much time and money specializing in his field, and he is vitally interested in it. However, this very fact may disqualify him from considering impartially what should be required today for tomorrow's citizens. But suppose that such a college teacher did believe his field less important than some other. In such a case there is a good possibility that his colleagues in the department would not agree with him and it would be difficult for him to vote in opposition to them. It would be to his own interest as well as to the vested interest of the department to insist that their introductory course be required. This would be true not only from the standpoint of intellectual interest, but from an economic one as well. If the department's course is required, all students will take it, there will be a high enrollment and hence a job for every member of the department and eventually probably a larger staff. Does not every department wish to expand? One can understand why it is so difficult to achieve significant change in the college curriculum! But if a college teacher is to pass intelligently on curriculum issues that come before the faculty, especially with regard to requirements for degrees, he must develop the ability to see his own field in the perspective of the curriculum as a whole. Within limits the academic program is for him to determine.

The Professor and Departmental Administration[4]

The college teacher as a member of a division or department. If it is true that the college professor sometimes appears not too interested in the over-all college framework for his teaching and research, he is likely to be quite concerned with the functioning of the smaller units—the division and/or department which touch him more closely. Whether a college teacher is working in a department of political science, for example, or in a division of the social sciences may depend on curricular organization or on administrative convenience. If, for example, the faculty believes that integration of knowledge is very important as opposed to its discreteness, then a divisional organization may be adopted to help the faculty to move in this direction. Or the faculty may disavow this concept and discourage such a structural plan for the college, despite the three advantages mentioned in Chapter 4.

Divisional organization. Sometimes a change in organization

[4] Theodore Caplow and Reece J. McGee have an interesting chapter on "The Strategy of the Department," in *The Academic Marketplace*, Basic Books, Inc., New York, 1958, pp. 94–108.

is made for the wrong reason. Perhaps the administrator—president, dean of faculties or dean of the college—feels that it is not feasible to deal effectively with fifteen or twenty department chairmen. In this case he may, for reporting, executing and other administrative reasons, establish a divisional organization. The top educational executive then deals with the directors of the divisions—e.g., humanities, physical sciences, social sciences, communicative arts—which reduces the number of his contacts from twenty to four. Such "administrative convenience" seems to be a poor excuse for changing a structural plan. Organization should grow out of a program that will best serve the learning and researching of students. While there are legitimate grounds for debating the different ways in which students can best mature intellectually, socially and spiritually, their best welfare is the test—not the convenience of the administration or even the predispositions of the faculty.

Departmental status. For the purpose of this discussion it will be assumed that a college teacher is thinking favorably about accepting an offer in an institution that has a departmental organization. Before he accepts, he will do well to inquire into the department's status. Is it large or small? Is it one of the strong departments of the college or university? All departments are likely to need strengthening in some ways. Would his acceptance of the position offered tend to make the department stronger? Presumably the president or dean believes so, or the offer would not have been made, but what does the candidate himself think the department needs, and does he believe that he can fill the bill? Candidates for teaching positions in colleges should remember that it is most likely that there are some obstacles or disadvantages in every teaching post, though frequently they do not become aware of these until a few months after they are on the job. Therefore, one should rarely take a new position just to escape the difficulties in his present one; for if he does so, he merely changes a known set of problems for one that is unknown. There should be positive challenges in the new post which are likely to offset any unknown difficulties.

The candidate for a position in a particular department should assess not only the strength of the department but his probable rank-in-succession in it. For example, the department may be small but strong, and the candidate may see an uncovered area of teaching and research to which he could contribute strength. However, he may find that of five good men in the department, four are of approximately his own age and, assuming equal competence, these four have seniority and therefore priority for promotion over him. In such a situation he might have to wait many years for either resignations or retirements before he could expect to reach either his maximum salary or opportunity to serve. Contrast this probability with an opportunity to step into a department where one man will retire the next year, one the following year and the other two within five years. While it is likely that one could move out of the college department first described into another position, any college teacher who accepts a post should ask himself if he would be content to stay with it for the rest of his life. If not, he should probably not accept it. Hence, along with assessment of the departmental program should go an appraisal of the staff and his relationship to the members of it.

Departmental factions. It would be useless to deny the fact that faculties and departments have groups within groups. Usually there are the older group and the younger group, the conservatives and the liberals, the humanitarians and the strict constructionists, those who have spent their professional lives in the department and the newcomers. Any department chairman, dean or faculty member who believes that all is sweetness and light within the college or department just does not know what is going on.

A strong argument can be made for having differing points of view in a department or a college. A single viewpoint tends to become a "party-line," a method of indoctrination of the student which is unfair to him. On the other hand, one department of philosophy has as members of its staff an idealist, a pragmatist, an experimentalist and a reconstructionist. A student majoring in this department is thus exposed to each philosophy and, after recognizing the merits of each, can decide for himself the one he will choose. Likewise, psychologists, political scientists, economists, sociologists and natural scientists hold differing views. While each view cannot be represented on the faculty of the small college, the various theories should be fairly presented to the student.

The heart of a scholarly community is scholarly criticism. Progress in advancing thought results from critical analysis and examination of assumptions and conclusions. Therefore, these must be tolerated. What should be avoided like the plague, however, is the degeneration of scholarly criticism into personal criticism and animosity. Simply because one holds a different view from that held by a fellow faculty member ought not cause dislike between the two. Rather, each should stimulate the other to develop and express his own best thinking in defense of his viewpoint. One might even hope that such an exchange would result in a modification of the more extreme views of both professors. So, while the faculty members appraise the candidate for a position, he would do well to probe for evidence of unhealthy factionalism in the department or college.

Role of a new department member. The new college teacher often goes through an orientation experience. Some institutions set aside a day for the induction of new faculty members. Here they again meet the hiring officers as well as other important functionaries of the college, such as the business manager, the dean of students, the chairman of the faculty council, the chairman of the committee on faculty welfare, the librarian, the director of audio-visual services and other all-college personnel with whom they need to become acquainted quite soon. This general orientation day is all-college in character. Beyond this, each department often has an induction plan of its own. An older member is often asked to take a new staff member "under his wing." If the new teacher is to teach one of the required introductory courses, he is provided with an outline and a bibliography of the course. He is likely to try to keep in touch with his new colleagues, and if invited he may visit a few classes. If there are several sections taught by different people, occasional meetings are held to exchange experiences.

Evaluation at the departmental level. In large departments in which introductory courses are required of most students, there is often a single common examination. Presumably all instructors contribute to the preparing of the examination and all help in the grading of the papers, although not necessarily those of their own students. Here the reputation of the new teacher is often made or broken, for unfortunately, his colleagues too often judge the effectiveness of the college teacher on the scores his students achieve on such a department-wide examination. If his students rank above the median on the examination for the whole group of students taught in the course, he may be favorably regarded; if below the median, unfavorably. While department-wide examinations are one method of assessing college teaching, there are others that may be more dependable.[5] Despite similar course outlines and bibliographies, teachers vary in their emphasis on the importance of specific items of knowledge, depending on the values and interests of the instructor.

Nevertheless, it is at the departmental level that more careful appraisal of the faculty member can be made. The stimulus given to the ablest students is particularly significant. The opinions of departmental colleagues, under normal circumstances, are fairly reliable when they can be obtained. Some departments also look into the kinds of examination questions given, the grades recorded and the course syllabi used. Through some or all of the means cited the department appraises the college professor's teaching; from his public lectures and his publications it assesses the quality of his thinking and his ability in research.

Introductory versus advanced level teaching. Since we are here considering the department as the basic unit of operation, the question should be raised as to whether it is desirable for the department to develop some teachers who specialize in lower-division teaching and others who work primarily in upper-division teaching and research. A survey of the opinions of one faculty showed that 63 per cent said "yes" to the first half of the question while 75 per cent said "no" to the second half! An actual

[5] For a discussion on the evaluation of college teaching, see Chapter 10.

survey of its teaching load showed that the teaching of most faculty members was divided about equally between upper- and lower-division teaching. There seems much to be said for having fine teachers at both elementary and advanced levels. Without them in the elementary courses there are likely to be too few students taking the advanced courses; and if this happens, it will be uneconomical to offer these courses and perhaps majors should not be offered. With so many considerations to be taken into account, a college professor must have a good deal of dedication to youth, balanced judgment and vision and the willingness to sacrifice in order to consider objectively the educational problems of both the college and the department.

Faculty morale. In a survey made of the attitudes of faculty members in a medium-sized university, they were asked what factors they considered most serious in weakening the morale of the staff. Their judgments are given below by weighted rank; i.e., if a factor was given first place, it was given a five; if second place, a four, etc.

(1) Overloading in teaching assignments and general university duties 470

(2) The lack of a clear definition of what they should do in teaching and scholarly work to merit promotion 451

(3) Lack of physical facilities and secretarial help 359

(4) The conviction that the definition sought in number two above is not carried out consistently in practice 353

(5) Financial need for outside employment 217

Though these items were considered briefly in Chapter 1, they are re-introduced here because it is at the departmental or divisional level that they are controlled. Three of the factors mentioned as detrimental to faculty morale will be briefly considered.

Service load. Many colleges and universities are trying to determine a "service load" which will include most of the duties undertaken by members of the staff. The following formula was worked out by a faculty committee in one institution:

General Policy:

1. Faculty load should be computed in terms of "service units." A "service unit" is defined as a proportion of time required to carry out basic professional services. What should constitute a full load should be determined and modified from time to time according to funds and faculty resources available and in terms of the quality of work possible under varying loads.

2. "Service units" should be allowed on faculty load for teaching services including:
   a. on-campus lecture-discussion courses
   b. off-campus lecture-discussion courses
   c. laboratory, shop, physical education
   d. directed research, independent study, essay, thesis, dissertation
   e. teaching via television
   f. teaching foreign students

3. Additional "service units" should be allowed on faculty load for:
   a. supervision of laboratory experiences including student teaching, cooperative work studies, practica, et al.
   b. counseling and advising students at all levels of professional preparation above and beyond the first fifty active, currently enrolled advisees. Thereafter, for each fifty active, currently enrolled advisees one "service unit" should be allowed on faculty load.
   c. leadership responsibilities encountered through assigned research projects within a given curriculum area, within the college and/or the university
   d. individual writing under contract and/or assigned writing
   e. chairmanships of major work committees
   f. administrative responsibilities

4. Where two or more persons are involved in teaching a class, the service unit value of the course should be divided equitably among the faculty members concerned.

5. Minor adjustments, up or down, in determining the service unit value of a course should be made for:

   a. very large classes (plus value, unless compensated for by reader assistance)
   b. very small classes (minus value)
   c. new courses in the process of development (plus value)
   d. multiple sections of the same course (minus value)
   e. experimental courses (plus value)
   f. excessive travel time (plus value)
   g. amount of reader and other assistance given (minus value)
   h. laboratory-type courses in terms of actual teacher-pupil contact hours per week (plus value)

Examples of the Application of the Above Policy:

1. Three service units should be allowed on faculty load for each two-semester-hour course taught.

2. Two service units should be allowed on faculty load for supervision of laboratory experiences, cooperative work studies and practica.

3. One and one-half service units should be allowed on faculty load for each ten semester hours of credit in directed research, independent study, essay, thesis and dissertation direction.

While one may not agree with this rather complicated plan, it seems clear that the college professor's total work load cannot be represented by any single factor such as hours taught per week.

Lack of physical facilities and secretarial help. In most institutions there is a severe lack of physical space—office space, for example—as well as lack of needed laboratories, books and audio-visual aids. These seriously handicap the college teacher and the department. If the teacher has no office in which he can work quietly or interview students privately, he is likely to come to the college only when he has classes or to attend called meetings, and the student, the college and the staff member all suffer because of this situation.

While it is probable that the demand for secretarial help on most campuses is insatiable, there is no doubt that some well-paid staff members are forced to divert their energies from constructive professional endeavors to do their own filing, write their own letters or make their own appointments. Secretarial help is usually assigned to the department in some such ratio as one secretary to every four staff members, depending on the department and the volume of activities carried on by the staff.

Outside employment. Assuming adequate salaries, faculty members ought to devote their full time to departmental and college duties. Exceptions are made when the outside employment is good for the public relations of the college or is an experience which will enrich the college staff member's teaching and research. An example of the latter is that of a political science professor who was employed to survey the public administration of a small city. This experience put money into his pocket, but, what was more important, it put more vitality into his teaching and enriched his research. Such outside employment, however, should be engaged in only with the knowledge and consent of the departmental chairman and other appropriate collegiate authorities. College teachers are cautioned against accepting outside assignments, whether they be studies or addresses, merely because there is a stipend attached. Worthwhile projects should be engaged in without the requirement of monetary reward. Financial return should not be the criterion for accepting or rejecting outside employment.

It is necessary that outside employment be kept under strict control. If it is overdone, teaching, research and publication will suffer because of its limitation of the professor's time. The writer knows personally several persons who gave bright promise of a research career, but who never lived up to the promise because they accepted so many offers of outside employment that they became almost itinerant lecturers. The department chairman has a great opportunity and a responsibility to advise members of his staff in this area.

The departmental chairmanship. There are two divergent views about the importance of the departmental chairman. One is that this post should command the highest salary, carry the greatest prestige and therefore secure the services of the most competent person in the area. The other view is that the most competent person in teaching, research and writing should not be saddled with the chores of making schedules, handling requisitions, dealing with secretaries and working on scores of other administrative details. There are valid arguments in support of each of these views. It would indeed be too bad to cut down on the writing and research of a creative scholar by making him a department chairman. Further, it would seem unwise to attach more salary to this post and thus, in effect, to say to younger staff members that the only way to get a high salary is to become a department chairman. This kind of motivation seems highly questionable.

On the other hand, when it comes to securing a new staff member, the question of the person for whom he is going to work looms large. Few men of stature wish to work for a junior staff member called a department chairman. Though general practice seems to lean toward a status person as department chairman, a middle ground between these two views seems to be developing. This is an elective, rotating chairmanship held for a minimum of two years and a maximum of three, with a provision against immediate re-election. This plan avoids taking a competent person out of his research for so long that he loses touch with it entirely. It assures some continuity of policy and development. It makes possible orderly change without severe dislocation and the dissipation of any petty tyranny that may have developed. Since the department is the basic administrative unit of the college and has such a marked effect upon the work of the individual faculty member, its role and that of its chairman should receive the careful attention of all college teachers.

Future patterns of administration. What of the future of the administration of our colleges? Will it be concentrated in the hands of academic officers or will there be greater decentralization? A recent study [6] throws some light on these questions.

[6] "A Study of the Role of the American College Faculty in Administration," mimeographed material, Department of Education, Graduate School of Arts and Sciences, The Catholic University of America, Washington, D.C., January 11, 1960.

Among recent changes showing greater faculty participation in administration were the following: increase of faculty committees, increase of participation of faculty in policy formation through academic Senate or committees, greater faculty membership on the administrative board and more faculty responsibility for curriculum and all matters dealing with educational policy.

The study also shows a slight trend in the opposite direction as evidenced by the relief of administrative members from classroom duties, reduction of the teaching load of persons engaging in administrative areas to less than nine hours and addition of full-time personnel in college development, public relations and the office of the dean of students.

Obligations of the college. A great deal has been said in this volume concerning the obligations of the faculty member to his department and to the college as a whole. There is of course the other side of the coin. The obligations of the college to the college teacher have been summarized by Justman and Mais as follows:

(1) To employ wise policies of teacher selection, retention and promotion

(2) To afford adequate remuneration

(3) To foster a climate conducive to good teaching and learning

(4) To assign teachers to instruction and other service in ways that take account of their special capabilities, interests and needs for growth

(5) To maintain a reasonable work schedule and satisfactory conditions of work

(6) To orient the new teacher to his job

(7) To give every teacher the benefit of constructive supervision

(8) To protect the teacher in the exercise of his professional duties [7]

[7] Joseph Justman and Walter H. Mais, *College Teaching,* Harper and Brothers, New York, 1956, pp. 67–75.

In institutions where all of these obligations are conscientiously met, the work of the teacher is greatly facilitated.

The teaching and research faculty have a vital interest in the administration of the college—whether it be financial or academic. They are greatly affected by the decisions made. Without becoming full-time administrators, faculty members need to maintain an interest in the decision making. If they do so, this would seem to assure less authoritarianism in institutional policy making and management.

CHAPTER 10

Evaluating the Services
of the College Faculty Member

. . . EVALUATION, WHETHER RECOGNIZED AS SUCH OR
NOT, GOES ON CONTINUOUSLY IN ALL EDUCATION.
—*Troyer and Pace*

In a statement made in 1957 the Educational Policies
Commission said, "No matter what may be its material resources
and programs, a college or university cannot rise above the level
of quality of its faculties." In an earlier chapter it was said that
no one escapes evaluation, and in Chapters 6 and 9 consideration
was given to the evaluation of teaching and of a faculty member's research and writing. The present chapter is concerned with
the over-all evaluation of the faculty member by the administrator.

A rather slight study made by a graduate student in 1959
brought seventy-three replies from teachers in nine colleges and
universities. One of the questions asked was, "Which of the following factors do you consider to be the most important in
establishing a basis for promotion of a college teacher?" The
following table gives a tabulation of the returns on this question.

TABLE 5

FACTORS CONSIDERED MOST IMPORTANT BY 73 COLLEGE TEACHERS
IN ESTABLISHING A BASIS FOR PROMOTION
(in terms of percentages)

Factors in Promotion	First Factor	Second Factor	Third Factor
Committee work		5.4	9.6
Membership and activity in professional organizations		2.8	23.3
Membership and activity in community organizations		1.4	4.1
Research		28.8	27.4
Teaching ability and effectiveness	97.3	1.4	1.4
Publications	1.4	8.2	17.8

TABLE 5 (cont.)

FACTORS CONSIDERED MOST IMPORTANT BY 73 COLLEGE TEACHERS

IN ESTABLISHING A BASIS FOR PROMOTION

(in terms of percentages)

Factors in Promotion	First Factor	Second Factor	Third Factor
Aggressive support of administration policy	1.4		6.8
Student counseling and guidance		52.1	9.6

From this informal investigation we see that in these nine institutions teaching ability and effectiveness constituted the most important single factor in the promotion of a college faculty member. The second most important factor was student counseling and guidance and the third was research. However, the number of institutions involved was quite small.

A more substantial study is reported by Gustad.[1] The number of institutions he queried is listed by type below.

Type of Institution	Number Included
Liberal arts colleges	272
Private universities	68
State universities	62
State and municipal colleges	90
Teachers' colleges	29
Junior colleges	25
Professional and technical institutions	38
Total	584

In view of Berelson's findings reported earlier,[2] it may seem surprising that in this study of evaluative factors, college classroom teaching was given first rank in every type of institution except teachers' colleges. In the latter a category called "other

[1] John W. Gustad, *Policies and Practices in Faculty Evaluation,* American Council on Education, Washington, D.C., 1961.

[2] See page 141.

factors," which included such items as cooperation, loyalty, Christian character, church membership and activity, and compatibility, ranked first, and "other factors" ranked second in all other types of colleges. Thus it is clear that the factor of personal attributes ranked either first or second (after classroom teaching) in all of the institutions replying. The combined ranking for all types of institutions reporting is given below.

FACTORS CONSIDERED IN EVALUATING FACULTY MEMBERS
(in order of importance)

(1) Classroom teaching
(2) Personal attributes
(3) Student advising
(4) Research
(5) Publication
(6) Committee work
(7) Activities in professional societies
(8) Length of service in rank
(9) Public service
(10) Supervision of graduate study
(11) Consultation
(12) Competing offers
(13) Supervision of honors work

Six of these factors will be considered in this chapter. They are evaluated about the same by various types of institutions. As would be expected, some place more emphasis on research, supervision of graduate study and of honors work, and these same colleges tend to place less emphasis on personal attributes, student advising and committee work.

Substantially, these two studies corroborate each other, for they are in agreement that classroom teaching, student advising and research are the most important factors considered in evaluating faculty members. By whom is this evaluating done? In reply to this question, Gustad says,

It is apparent that, in the large majority of institutions those principally responsible for evaluation are the president, the dean, and the department (or division) chairman. Of the three, presidential involvement appears to have the greatest variation, from 100 per cent in the case of the teachers' colleges to just over two-thirds among the state universities. In the case of the other two officers, the deans are more often involved than chairmen in all but the technical and professional institutions. Only in the case of the junior colleges does chairman involvement drop significantly.[3]

The usual procedure is for the department or division chairman to make a recommendation concerning promotions to the dean; and if he approves, it is forwarded to the next higher officer—usually the president in the small college or his representative in a larger institution. The president ultimately must recommend all promotions to the board of trustees for its approval and hence, he must either review the matter personally or rely heavily on the judgment of his staff since he is not likely to have any substantial amount of knowledge about each candidate recommended to him.

Of the 584 institutions queried by Gustad, 246 had department or faculty committees on promotions, and these were found most commonly in universities. It is generally observed that faculty members hold stricter standards for promotion than do the administrative officers. There are some institutions in which promotions are secured or refused by a vote of the department. In such colleges there is likely to be a small amount of "political pulling and hauling," which may be represented by the statement, "You vote for my candidate and I'll vote for yours."

A better plan is the one followed in a highly rated department in a large western university. Here four criteria are considered in the evaluation of each individual teacher—publications, professional competence, teaching and university and community service. These are not necessarily ranked in their order of importance. The individual is ranked in attainments in each of the four categories by a departmental committee of his seniors; i.e.,

[3] John W. Gustad, op. cit., pp. 4–5.

associate professors judge assistant professors and full professors judge associate professors. A committee of three then reports to the department as a group, recommending promotion or retention in rank. Rarely are committee recommendations repudiated, but they sometimes are. In the end, everyone in the department has the opportunity to pass on the individual's qualifications, and the final recommendation is a departmental decision.

An elected faculty committee on promotions in another university has drawn up some rules of procedure which seem to produce desirable results. Some of these are stated here.

(1) No member of the faculty committee is eligible for promotion or special recognition during his two-year term as a member of the committee.

(2) A teaching faculty member on an academic year assignment is eligible for consideration for promotion under the university's schedule of automatic annual increments (a) when he has served a year at the maximum salary of his rank, or (b) when he has served five years in a rank, whichever occurs first.

(3) Each faculty member eligible for promotion is responsible for providing the committee with an up-to-date record of his education, experience, teaching, research, publication, public service, professional society activity, student advising and committee work.

(4) The Promotions Advisory Committee desires to receive information and/or recommendations from departmental chairmen, from any member of the faculty, or from any person who considers himself eligible for promotion.

The involvement of faculty members in promotions and merit recognition seems desirable if the committee is elected by the faculty, if it is entirely professional in its work and if it is not given either the blame or the credit for the recommendations eventually approved by the president. In large institutions a faculty committee, through its many contacts with students, with other faculty members, professional societies and publications, is in a better position than an administrative officer to know the quality of work actually being done by a teacher. While no dean should commit himself to carry out every action recommended by such a committee, he will be well advised to consider each one with care.

Ways of evaluating college teaching. In Chapter 6 reference was made to ways of stimulating and rewarding good college teaching. Ability in classroom teaching was, it will be recalled, the second most important factor in the minds of hiring officers and the most important single factor considered in recommending for promotion. It therefore deserves more attention than it usually receives. Unfortunately, the most frequent source of information about the teaching of any staff member seems to be hearsay, which may be either complimentary or derogatory. It is to the faculty member's interest to get this important factor in the evaluation of his work out of the realm of rumor. Perhaps the best way for him to do this is to find out for himself what his strengths and weaknesses in teaching really are. In most cases he himself is much aware of these, but he can obtain more information from his students, his colleagues and the alumni of the college. If he makes such a careful study of his own abilities, he will not be surprised when the department chairman or the dean reports that there have been either compliments or complaints about his teaching.

To obtain the evaluations of his students, one college professor hands a blank sheet of paper, folded in the middle, to each of his students at the end of a course. He asks them to write above the crease one or more things they consider good about the course, and below it ways in which they think the course might be improved. In this way he receives a good many valid criticisms and some good suggestions and comments. Since, as has been previously said, students constitute a "captive audience," in a limited sense, and are the ultimate objects of instruction, their opinions should be sought.

A more formal method of obtaining student evaluation is to use one of the printed rating scales that are on the market. There will probably always be some criticism of the practice of having students evaluate their professors because so many irrelevant factors may enter into such judgments. When students are asked to rate their teachers, certain questions should be considered before too much faith is placed in their judgments. What qualities of the teacher are students really competent to express opinions about? Are they qualified to judge his mastery of subject content? If one teacher makes legitimate but heavy demands on their time and effort while another does not, how will their judgments be affected? Another question which merits consideration relates to whether all students should be asked to fill out the opinionnaires, or only the more mature ones. Perhaps a more important point is whether the administration should require the use of the opinionnaires by all teachers or limit their use to those who request them. And should their results be made available to administrative officers, to a faculty committee or only to the college instructor?

In some institutions department chairmen distribute and collect such opinionnaires without the instructor's consent. There is a very real question as to this practice and also as to whether the results should be furnished to the higher administrative officers. Probably the better practice is for the institution to make such opinionnaires available to the instructors who wish to use them, but not require their use by those who do not wish to do so. And the instructor should be the one to decide what should be done with the results.

How frequently should such opinionnaires be used? Probably at mid-term and again at the end of the term. Mid-term evaluation is suggested to permit improvements suggested by the class to be made before it is too late, and end-of-term appraisal is necessary to secure a final evaluation from the students after the course is over.

Exchange visits. Another way in which a college professor may secure an evaluation of his teaching is through an exchange of classroom visits with some of his colleagues. Contrary to the customary practice in elementary and secondary schools, college classrooms are not visited regularly. Indeed, the classroom has been referred to as the college professor's "castle." Some deans never visit classes unless invited to do so, and such invitations are rarely received. On the other hand, there has been developing a practice of interclass visits by college teachers. Gustad found a larger amount of such intervisitation than he had expected, with 286 institutions reporting it. With regard to such visits he says,

In using classroom visitations, of course, one must ask about the competence of the observer. Years of experience are not in themselves any guarantee that the observer is competent. There is even some reason to believe that the younger faculty member *may* actually be a better teacher, on the average, than his older colleagues. Also, there is the question of stage fright, which may afflict the visited teacher. The matter of sampling—how many and at which times to visit—must also be dealt with.[4]

Gustad concludes, however, that classroom visitations seem superior to informal student comments. Where these can be made between faculty members on a basis of "you visit my class and I will visit yours," this practice would seem to be a good one.

In spite of the means of evaluation which have been discussed, the evidence seems to indicate that, though classroom teaching is regarded as the first criterion for promotion at the college level, in most institutions of higher education little or no valid evidence is gathered concerning the matter. College professors should be encouraged to gather whatever evidence they can regarding their teaching which will protect their being evaluated by hearsay, innuendo, rumor or the campus "grapevine."

Evaluation and the administration. The conclusion seems inescapable that the farther the individual is removed from the faculty member he is trying to evaluate, the more difficult and the more precarious the task becomes. The person in the best position to improve his work is the teacher himself, and hence, the emphasis up to this point has been on cooperating with the faculty member in the interest of securing improvement, where

[4] John W. Gustad, *op. cit.,* pp. 11–12.

necessary, rather than checking up on him. However, when the administration undertakes to determine the quality of work done by individual faculty members, there should be a clear recognition of the personal nature of the factors involved, as well as of the great tact required in appraisal. The lack of research publications, for example, cannot be taken as evidence that one is a superior teacher. On the contrary, a continuing scholarly development appears to be one of the almost universal characteristics of a good teacher and, properly appraised, published research is one useful index of such development.

Conferences with students. With appropriate safeguards, an administrator may gather a good deal of valuable information about a teacher's ability in the classroom from his students. To guard against possible injustice in judging staff members in this way, one department chairman suggested the following procedure in a personal letter to the writer:

I asked my secretary to make a list of all the honor students in the department. I talked to each student for about fifteen minutes, making clear that the purpose was to ascertain our ablest teachers and give recognition. I then asked for the names of all members of the department with whom the student had taken work, and then asked him to name half of the group who in his judgment were the better teachers. In drawing up my final statistics I took into account (1) the number of students who had been in the classes of Professor X and (2) the number of them who felt him to be an excellent teacher. A proportion was ascertained. I may say I feel strongly the value of such personal interviews.

Alumni opinion. Sometimes the alumni of a college help in evaluating the general work of the institution as well as that of specific professors who have been with the college for a period of years. Twelve relatively small liberal arts colleges several years ago sent out nearly four thousand questionnaires to the graduates of classes spanning more than sixty years beginning with 1890. Almost 1,300 replies were received, a percentage response of 32.5. It is likely, of course, that the most loyal, most satisfied and most competent alumni responded to the inquiries. Their judgments as to the ways in which they had received preparation for later work life were as follows:

Specific courses	354
General preparation	143
Well-rounded, solid educational foundation	86
Broadened mental, spiritual, cultural, social horizons	67

While the foregoing items do not bear directly on the quality of college teaching, they do suggest that the results of it had persisted a long time. More pertinent to our present topic is the fact that the canvass brought out many such comments as, "I owe a great deal of an enriched life to Professor X and his inspiring courses."

The teacher's personal attributes and activities. Much has already been said about the qualities desirable in a college teacher, and they do not need to be repeated here. When it comes to promotions, the college administrator is likely to consider them, and perhaps some additional points as well. One of these is the teacher's outside activities. Unfortunately, there are some college teachers for whom being a professor is merely a job. A social program carried on with his wife is of greater importance to him. Such hobbies as collecting, fishing, hunting, golfing, boating, painting and the like absorb the time of other staff members to such an extent that their work in the college seems to be only a sideline. Business activities, begun as small "extra-curricular" enterprises, sometimes develop to the point where they become the chief activity of the teacher, relegating his teaching to second place. Social life and hobbies are desirable, of course, but not when they take precedence over the professor's commitment to his work with students.

A teacher who must have a good deal of special consideration when promotion time comes is the one who is "different." He may be essentially negative, or habitually silent, or find it impossible to work with others. Perhaps one of the most important tasks of the college administrator is to cherish and nurture college faculty members who are different, *providing* that each of them has a unique contribution to make to the student and the institution. Their contributions must be evaluated in a different way than are those of the average teacher.

Another point which, unfortunately, many administrators seem to consider in making promotions is whether or not the individual faculty member has given "aggressive support to administrative policy." This ought not to be so. If the administrative policy is in error and can be demonstrated to be so, the faculty ought to resist it. Certainly this is true if the faculty is to be regarded as appointees rather than as employees. The early view of the American Association of University Professors was that they are appointees, and this view remains in effect to a greater or less degree today, especially after the teacher has passed the probationary period and achieved continuing contract status or tenure. Sometimes a faculty member who has been delegated to carry a complaint to the executive officer of a college is regarded by the latter not as a delegate from the faculty group, but as a "troublesome character." He, therefore, is listed as lacking in some desirable personal attributes and certainly not as one who "aggressively supports the administrative policies." A college faculty group who thus delegates a professor should support him as their representative and resist any attempt by the administration to discipline him because he sought to discharge a responsibility imposed on him by his colleagues.

More positively then, what personal qualities are especially valued? Commitment to students, faithful discharge of whatever assignments are given, judicial temperament, objective judging of college policies apart from his own interests, optimism in the face of difficulties and ingenuity in carrying out his own professional tasks as well as those of the college are among those favorably considered. Since research, publications and advising of students have been considered in previous chapters, they will only be noted here as important factors to be considered in evaluating the faculty member.

Committee work. In deciding on promotions, most administrators give some consideration to the time spent in committee work by faculty members. A faculty of more than a hundred people was recently found to be devoting an average of 4.6 per cent of its time to this activity. This is a small percentage, but since it represents an average, some members spent more and some less time than this percentage in committee service. In deciding on the amount of weight to be given this factor, the administrator needs to make some evaluation of the services rendered by different committees. There are three committees which are of greatest importance in a college—the Committee on Admissions Policy, the Committee on Curriculum and Instruction and the Committee on Standards and Graduation Requirements. These three committees deal with the central academic policies of the institution, which are the prime concern of the faculty. Service on any one of the three can be arduous and time-consuming. If the services rendered move the institution toward a higher and higher quality instead of consolidating the status quo, their members surely deserve recognition when faculty members are being evaluated. There are other committees which absorb a good deal of time on the part of faculty members but which are probably less fundamental to the college than the three previously listed. Among these are the Committee on Student Life, the Committee on Honorary Degrees, the Committee on Athletics and the Committee on Non-Academic Discipline. No one, however, would doubt the necessity for the work of these committees.

A third category of committees consists of those which are advisory to the administration. Among these are the Promotions Advisory Committee, the Committee on Salaries, the Committee on Grievances, the Committee on the Library, the Committee on Space and the Committee on Registration and Records.

It is possible, of course, that the same faculty member will be involved in committees in all three categories. If so, this would suggest that his help and judgment are sought and respected, and also that he may need to decide where to put his energies. There are many faculty members who are "quadruple threat" people, that is, they teach well, advise well, write well and are effective committee members. Yet if they try to distribute their energies into too many channels, something suffers, and too often this is the teacher's research. The question for such a professor to answer is what fundamental contribution he will make in the long run. He may decide that he has spent too much time on committee work to make a fundamental research study and so will limit his activities in this direction. Regardless of the type of committee on which a faculty member serves, most administrators will give this factor some weight in making their decisions on promotions.

Activity in professional societies. It is valuable for any institution to have a faculty member active and holding office in a professional society. If this is to be achieved, the institution must send him to regional and annual conferences regularly. He must accept service as a member of some committee and through his own diligence and competence become sufficiently well known and respected to be nominated for higher office. Such recognition by the society of an academic discipline or profession at least suggests—though it does not necessarily prove—that the college has a faculty member approved by his peers in his discipline elsewhere in the nation, and this factor deserves recognition in considering him for promotion. Like all other factors considered in this chapter, it must be weighed in connection with other competencies.

Length of service in rank. Public utilities, labor organizations and industry generally utilize seniority as a factor in recognizing service. The theory is that the person who has been permitted to serve for some years should be recognized, for if he were unworthy of recognition his services would have been terminated earlier. Many college administrators will not accept this line of reasoning because they have "inherited" faculty members whom previous administrations mistakenly allowed to build up seniority. Consequently, they do not feel bound to recognize seniority as an important factor in the promotion of these individuals. On the other hand, these same administrators say that, if two fine faculty members seemed to have similar demonstrable competencies and personal attributes, they would recognize the person with seniority first. Length of service, then, cannot be ruled out as a realistic factor in evaluating faculty service.

Public service. Since the following chapter contains a section on the faculty member in his community, the nature of this service will not be discussed here. It may be noted, however, that because of its visibility, this factor represents one of the easiest ways of achieving recognition. Good teaching and careful advisement of students receive little publicity. High quality research and publication may be on the library shelves and go unnoted by the administrator. Committee work is likely to be unpublicized. But public service usually gets the headlines. As this is written, a number of faculty members from Harvard University have been called to public service in Washington. These appointments are a compliment to the university as well as to the men involved and a challenge to the professors. They may, indeed, mark the beginning of new larger opportunities for college professors to serve the public. Of course, most faculty members will serve in much more modest ways in their state, region or community, but whatever the service rendered, it should be considered in the evaluation of the faculty member.

Supervision of honors work and graduate study. Students in honors work and graduate study are supposed to be able to work independently, though prior to this point in their education, they have probably taken the more traditional course work. The mere fact that students have been admitted to honors work at the undergraduate level or to graduate study shows that a judgment has been made that the student is qualified to pursue studies on his own. The ability of a professor to encourage and guide such students may be significantly different from that required in classroom instruction. The question for the administrator to consider is with what facility does the teacher perform this function. In every institution there are those who have turned out, one after the other, graduate students who have produced imaginative studies in depth, while others have settled for pedantic, repetitive and unimaginative pieces of research. If it is possible to distinguish between these extremes, it is more difficult to do so in the middle ranges. Nevertheless, providing the inspiration for honors and graduate students to tackle new and difficult problems, to construct new instruments, to solve them and to carry through a research to a conclusion, whether the results are positive or negative, is most important. Here the faculty member is working with the most able students, pushing back the frontiers of knowledge. If he can do this well with even a few students, this ability deserves high recognition in the evaluation of his services.

As the reader has observed, there are many factors to be considered in the evaluation of faculty members. The respective weights given to each will depend on the kind of institution and the purposes emphasized. Of course, the best evaluation is one in which the professor conscientiously assesses himself. However, the institution cannot escape making some appraisal, and it is important that the professor knows what the administration considers to be of highest importance. This it has an obligation to make clear.[5]

[5] Theodore Caplow and Reece J. McGee have an interesting chapter on "How Performance is Evaluated," in *The Academic Marketplace,* Basic Books, Inc., New York, 1958, pp. 81–94.

CHAPTER 11

The College
and Its Community

THE COMMUNITY INDEED IS THE BASIS OF WHATEVER
UNITY KNOWLEDGE, VALUES AND BEHAVIOR HAVE. IT IS
THE SOIL FROM WHICH THEY GROW.
—*Baker Brownell*

When a cordial and cooperative relationship exists between an institution of higher learning and the city or town in
which it is located, each makes a very large contribution to the
other. Fortunately, such cooperative relationships usually do exist.
Back in the early days of the American college, cities and towns,
realizing the prestige value as well as other advantages of having
a college, vied with each other to secure such institutions for
themselves. When it was announced recently that a new college
was to be built in a southern state, eighteen communities offered
substantial inducements for its location. The community finally
selected presented the college with a campus of 220 acres and more
than two and a half million dollars to be used in the construction
of buildings or as endowment. Such an offer, which was approxi-
mated by several of the other communities, provides ample evidence that a city considers a college an economic asset.

Community characteristics desirable for a college. Of course,
no group looking for a site for a college or university would locate
it in the community offering the greatest material inducements
unless it also met most of the other requirements for a favorable
location. The following criteria, which were recently used in
selecting a place in which to build a liberal arts college, suggest
other considerations to be kept in mind:

(1) The city and county governmental authorities should actively
aid and support the coming of the college. They should be willing
to enact necessary legislation or make physical improvements important to the welfare of the college and its students.

(2) The leaders of the business and financial affairs of the community should manifest interest not only initially in the location of
the college, but also interest and concern across the years in its maintenance and financial and moral support.

275

(3) The community as a whole also should have interest in and provide general support for the college.

(4) The community should make available a well-located campus site (of at least 500 acres). If all utilities are not available and the site does not have full fire and police protection, these also should be provided.

(5) The area should contribute not only a substantial initial gift, but also generous annual financial support.

(6) The community should provide a wholesome moral and cultural environment for the students and also make it possible for the college to render the largest possible service to its immediate region as well as to the state and the nation.

(7) The population of the community should be not less than twenty times the size of the anticipated enrollment (since 600 is the minimum enrollment for the economical operation of a college, the population of the community should be at least 12,000).

(8) There should be annually a pool of at least one thousand high school graduates within a radius of fifty miles.

(9) The community should be recognized as a progressive and growing one.

(10) The area should be served by adequate transportation facilities.

(11) The community should have adequate restaurants, hotels, motels, stores, recreation facilities and good dental, medical and hospital care.

(12) Good public schools should be available to the children of the college community.

(13) Housing should be available for faculty, staff and students at reasonable rates and in sufficient quantity.

(14) The area should be free from distractions and nuisances which might interfere with college work, such as smoke, dust, odors, noises and contamination.

Probably no college would find a community that offered all of the fourteen points, but the list indicates that the characteristics of the community in which a college is located are important to the institution. It seems quite likely that colleges founded a hundred or more years ago would not today be located where they now are. Indeed, in many instances it was then deemed desirable that a college be placed some distance away from a population center in order to provide better opportunities for study, reflection, meditation and communion with nature and the Deity. Today colleges are more likely to be located in towns than in villages, in cities than in towns and in urban centers rather than in smaller cities.

Services provided by the college. If the size and other characteristics of the city are important to the college, the activities of the college are also of importance to the city. The college brings to the city a large group of consumers who add substantially to the income of shops, restaurants, bookstores, hotels, theaters, building contractors, food markets and other business establishments. It also provides a great inducement for people to move to the community who are interested in securing a college education for their children. Perhaps more important even than the economic advantages is the raising of the educational and cultural level which occurs when the college is an integral part of the community. This results largely from the many informational, musical, dramatic and other cultural activities and programs provided by the college not only for the students but for the townspeople as well. Indeed, the college in many cases becomes the heart of the community, and its president frequently outranks the mayor in local as well as in regional and national prestige.

"Corrupting principles" of college life. Many of the services provided the college by its community are suggested by the criteria given above for the location of a college. There are other services of the greatest importance to the college that can be provided only by the community and which may greatly strengthen the college program if college and city cooperate in them. These services are related to the "three corrupting principles of college life," identified by Brownell and mentioned earlier,[1] which could be at least modified in those cases where a resourceful college faculty is aided by cooperative relationships with people and organizations in the community. The first of these is the principle of delayed function, a term which refers to the fact that college

[1] Baker Brownell, *The College and the Community,* Harper and Brothers, New York, 1952, pp. 34–39.

students commonly spend four years storing up knowledge before they return to the stream of life's activity and utilize it. This practice corrupts knowledge itself as well as the student, who must wait, so to speak, on the sidelines. According to Brownell, "the pseudojuvenilism of the college, the postponement of function and mature responsibility can only result in decay." [2]

The second corrupting principle of college life—that it takes place in a social vacuum—is somewhat similar to the first. In this connection Brownell says,

The college is set up on the assumption that the student should be abstracted from his home and work community, placed in a special environment called the campus and segregated so far as the process of education is concerned from normal relationships within his community. His community, both past and future, his occupational milieu, and his mature patterns of political and social behavior are largely ignored. In the irresponsible freedom and emptiness of a vacuum he is taught the easy doctrines of a philosophy that has no continuing contact with the operationally real. . . .

[Campus life] is irresponsible, highly selective, usually snobbish. It is socially frivolous and inept because the basic functions of mature life are carefully excluded. [3]

The student who lives at home and attends college in his home town probably experiences less of this sense of isolation from real life, for many of his activities within his community—social life, church and club relationships, perhaps a part-time job—are not necessarily broken off by his attendance at college. But even such a student is likely to find little connection between his classroom learning and his community life.

The last of the corrupting principles is the divorce of theory from practice. If theories taught on the campus are to have real significance for young people, they should be acted upon almost immediately. Every theory should eventually be carried over into action, and every activity should have a theoretical base. To quote Brownell once more:

[2] Brownell, *The College and the Community*, p. 35.
[3] *Ibid.*, p. 36.

It is an easy game, this guiding toy boats across a bathtub. But steering a ship is a different matter. Until the college moves off the campus and centers the significant behavior patterns of the individual during all of his life and of the community during all its history, it will continue to be more of an influence toward decadence than health. It makes play problems, stage situations, it forever rehearses life, with life itself denied admittance.[4]

If the college student is to be "saved" from the decay of delayed functioning, of living in a social vacuum and of divorce from significant practice, it is the community surrounding the college that must help him by providing opportunities for him to relate his learning immediately to the world about him in some useful way. And the one who must provide the imaginative leadership for such a relating is the college teacher. If he, too, feels remote from the community and its problems, the case is hopeless insofar as his own students are concerned. It is not difficult to find instances in which a professor has led his students into meaningful experiences which transform their classroom learning into reality. The trouble is that these instances are so comparatively rare as to excite surprised comment. It would be impossible, obviously, for every student in every class to be immediately putting his learning into practice in the community. But every student should have during his entire college career some facet which entices him out of the social vacuum of the college into the reality and problems of the life about him.

Community service of college students. Meeting this vital need of the college student is not, however, the only part of the picture. In every community there is a host of problems which are unsolved, or only partially solved, because there is no one with the interest and time and energy to devote to them. A sociology class in an eastern university uncovered some of these needs by conducting a survey in the city in which it was located. The students called at every fourth house asking the same questions at each one. In doing so they gained first-hand contact with some of the theoretical problems discussed in their class sessions, and the sum-

[4] *Ibid.*, p. 38.

mary of their interviews revealed a good deal about the community.

Compilations were made of the answers obtained to the following questions:

(1) What do you like about our community?

(2) In what ways could our city be improved?

(3) Who could help most in making the necessary improvements?

The summaries showed that, though the citizens liked the climate and the general atmosphere of this particular college town, there was a wide variety of ways in which they felt the city could be improved. However, of particular interest were the names of the persons most often mentioned as those who could do the most to help bring about the desired changes. Well down on this list were such status persons as the college president, county judge, bank president, mayor of the city and the owner of the largest manufacturing establishment in the city. High on the list were the names of housewives, a small grocer, a scout leader, a justice of the peace and ministers of little churches. Through this one project the sociology professor helped his students to obtain experience working on a practical problem, and the community to discover some of the local problems of which they had been only partially aware and some of the human resources available for doing something about them.

The Program of Community Dynamics inaugurated at Earlham College in 1947 represented an outstanding effort on the part of a college to relate its students to the problems and activities of nearby communities. The program on the college side is developed through inter-departmental seminars set up with the double purpose of encouraging students to aid nearby cities and towns in projects of community betterment and in so doing to have worthwhile experiences in real situations along with their academic classroom work. All projects undertaken are at the request of people in the communities and many of them involve students not enrolled in the seminars. As many as two or three hundred students may work on a cleanup campaign or a community survey. Others help with recreation programs or make a series of soil tests to help improve agricultural methods. During the summer vacations the program is extended to service in foreign countries with students paying their own expenses in order to participate in the work. In describing this program, Biddle expresses the beliefs of its founders as follows: "A college might make an essential contribution to the civic and cultural growth of a region. But in the process it might also find its own soul, discover its own peculiar usefulness." [5]

As an instance of a tie-up between a college class and the students' own communities, a political science teacher requires all of his beginning students to investigate the governmental and social structure of their home towns and to write rather substantial papers on the subject. Many years ago an economics professor who was asked to draft an income tax law for his state, was able to involve his senior students in the project. A southern university has a working relationship with a research organization, in which the students participate by doing analyses that contribute to the discovery of new oil wells.

If community projects are to seem significant to the students who participate in them, it is important that they be real rather than contrived for the purpose of giving the student an outlet for his training. The community survey mentioned above would have been mere "busywork" for the students who conducted it if it had not been undertaken at the request of community leaders, and if they had not followed up on the results discovered and sought solutions to the problems that had been uncovered.

The programs found in most universities which probably get the largest number of students to relate their classroom work to actual community situations and problems are those in distributive education, student teaching, agricultural extension and medical education. Here the student, under supervision, attempts to focus all of his previous training obtained in the classroom.

[5] William W. Biddle, *The Cultivation of Community Leaders,* Harper and Brothers, New York, 1953, p. 12.

Through work with people in the larger world he not only becomes familiar with the community, but gains awareness also of the educational, social, economic, health and agricultural problems in the district. While it is true that the opportunities mentioned are found for the most part in professional schools, yet we have seen that many smaller colleges have established an organic relationship between the college and the community.

The college professor as a consultant. Another way in which the college can be an asset to its community is in providing the know-how of highly trained faculty members to help with community activities and problems. A professor of finance may be called upon to consult with city officials regarding the financial policies of the city. A sociology professor may advise regarding community welfare problems as well as provide trained workers for the local welfare program. A psychology professor may be asked to help in organizing a child guidance clinic. Professors of education are frequently asked to conduct surveys of particular educational systems in order to uncover their weaknesses and suggest ways of improvement. The results of such research work tend to feed back to help both the college and the community, and when students as well as faculty can be involved in them, the benefits are greatly increased.

Such college-community projects, of course, can be successfully undertaken only when a feeling of mutual trust and cooperation exists. In some cases, unfortunately, the feeling between town and gown is chiefly one of tension and conflict. The scholarly community may be either looked up to or looked down upon by the practical community. In the latter case the intellectual or the "highbrow" is disdained as being inferior to the men and women who carry on the practical work of the area. Young people, perhaps because of their immaturity and inexperience, often tend to be overly idealistic and optimistic, sometimes even "radical," and hence, may grate upon the sensibilities of the townspeople. In many cases the community taxpayers resent the fact that no taxes are paid by the college on the substantial amount of property it owns. Where ill feeling exists between town and gown, the leaders of both must work together to overcome it for, as has been observed, each community needs the other to accomplish its highest purposes, and cordial and cooperative relationships are essential to the best interests of both.

The college teacher is the key person in the situation. If he centers his social as well as his professional life only in the college community, he contributes to the separation between town and gown. If he becomes an integral part of the community by participating wholeheartedly in its civic and religious as well as its social life, he helps to bridge the gap between the two. In so doing he not only gains in the breadth of his personal relationships but helps in securing acceptance for actual participation in community life and work by his students.

CHAPTER 12

The College Professor's Life

THE GREAT USE OF A LIFE IS TO SPEND IT FOR SOME-
THING THAT WILL OUTLAST IT.

—*William James*

It may be unwise and presumptuous, even foolhardy, to attempt to present any adequate picture of the life of the college professor. Certainly there is no uniform pattern and no model that can be described here.

Demands of the college teacher's work. Perhaps one of the most outstanding differences between college teaching and other vocations is that the college teacher's work is never done. The increasing amount of leisure predicted for other kinds of workers will not come true for him. He brings his work home with him, literally as well as figuratively, and probably thinks about it most of the time. Those who choose college teaching in order to avoid the "hurly-burly" of an active life in business, public administration or military service will learn that they have only exchanged one set of demanding services for another set of a different kind. The conscientious teacher will find that he has much less leisure time than do most of his friends who are in business enterprises.

Moreover, his conditions of work are different. As has been said, no competent and committed faculty member can escape the necessity of many hours of reading each week in order to keep up with his field. Yet, generally speaking, his college office is not a suitable place in which to pursue this task. If the library does not provide carrels or cubicles for individual faculty members, they must do their reading at home. Probably the work a college teacher must do at night will require that he have a study at home no matter what the college provides. This situation imposes some restrictions on his family, but even during the years when the children are growing up, the family will need to accommodate themselves to his need for a quiet place to study and carry on his research. Moreover—and this point may constitute a real trial to the professor's wife—his study is a workroom, not a beautiful library, and it is likely to be filled with bookshelves, filing cabinets, desk and comfortable, if a bit shabby, chairs. However, such a workroom will contribute materially to the ease and convenience with which he does his work at home.

Another way in which the work of a college teacher differs from that of his business acquaintances is that he is not required to spend eight hours a day in an office. Except for the times he meets his classes, his office hours for students and the hours he devotes to committee meetings, examinations of doctoral candidates and the like, he makes his own schedule of work and decides where he will do it.

The professor's wife and his work. One important contribution a professor's wife can make to her husband's work is in entertaining his students occasionally. Unfortunately, this practice is followed so seldom that, when a group of students recently did receive such an invitation, they were heard to remark, "We have attended this college for three years, and this is the first time any professor has invited us to come to his home." The purpose of such a gathering is larger than the social one—something important seems to happen to a college class or group that has had a social evening in a professor's home. The students see one another differently, and relationships between them improve in the informal setting. Then, too, they come to know the teacher in a different way, and closer relationships develop with him. When the students themselves help in planning and carrying out such a social affair, the advantages that carry over are increased.

A faculty wife has a unique opportunity for a working partnership with her husband, for she may act as his assistant in carrying on research and in writing books and articles. In both of these activities she can help greatly by locating important references and data. When a publication is in preparation, she can help by checking footnotes, securing permissions from authors and publishing houses to quote from their works, preparing indices, reading proof and typing. If she is knowledgeable in her husband's field, she can in addition act as a "sounding board" for the ideas he is putting into his publications. Thus, in a sense quite different from that of a business executive, the professor's home and his family can be a real source of strength to him and can thus improve his contribution to the college community.

Progress in career. The candidate for a college professorship needs to see his career in perspective. Berelson found that doctoral students usually complete their studies in about eight years.[1] Thus if a person received his Bachelor's Degree at age twenty-two, he would be about thirty when he received the Ph.D. The trend seems now to be toward a retirement age of seventy, so that the average professor can count on about forty years of active work. To achieve the greatest satisfaction from his work both professionally and salarywise, he should do everything possible to reach a full professorship between the ages of forty-five and fifty. Moreover, by age fifty he should be in a position where he will be content to remain. Caplow and McGee say, "An academic man's career is normally only half over at the age of fifty . . . yet, unless he is widely known, his mobility after fifty is very, very limited." [2] This lack of mobility is due in part to the limitations of retirement systems, and partly to a question about the person's further productivity.

In view of these facts the safe career plan for a candidate is to work very diligently for fifteen or twenty years after obtaining his degree. Assuming that he obtains an assistant professorship soon after completing the doctorate, the college teacher should be sufficiently well thought of to be promoted to an associate professorship between ages thirty-five and forty and to merit the rank of full professor six or seven years later. The factor of productivity varies from one field to another. Historians, for example, do not reach their peak until they are quite mature, while mathematicians are said to make their greatest contributions in their thirties.

If one is not very productive in research and writing, he can

[1] Bernard Berelson, *Graduate Education in the U.S.,* McGraw-Hill Book Company, Inc., New York, p. 157.
[2] Theodore Caplow and Reece J. McGee, *The Academic Marketplace,* Basic Books, Inc., New York, 1958, p. 87.

often obtain a raise in rank by moving to another institution. In fact, two moves might be required before a full professorship was forthcoming. However, with the scarcity of college teachers in this decade, one cannot be certain that former standards or practices will be maintained, but it is important for the young college teacher to consider his career in something other than short-range terms.

Service in the community. Earlier in this chapter reference was made to the use of the community as a laboratory for students. In addition, the college professor should give some time on his own to public service in the community. As intellectual leaders, college teachers will probably choose to associate themselves with activities in which intellectual concerns are dominant over those which are merely entertaining or set up for physical exercise of various sorts. Many college teachers become school board members, or they serve on mayors' committees on housing, welfare and education, or they become members of the governing boards of community churches.

Satisfactions. What are the outstanding rewards of the college professor's life? One of the greatest of these has already been mentioned—the opportunity for continuous association with generations of intellectually eager young people. Such an association is not only a constant source of joy, but it serves also to keep the professor young in spirit and in outlook. Youth with its optimism, its new and stimulating ideas and boundless hopes for the future can be a source of inspiration and delight to the teacher who really likes young people (and if not, why would he choose the profession?).

Moreover, in his association with young people, he has the opportunity to exercise a lasting influence upon them—on their thinking, their ideas and ideals and on the way in which they see their future vocations—at a most critical stage of their maturing. The Alumni Opinion survey, mentioned earlier, contained many comments like the following:

My whole life is different because of college. My friends are a different kind of people, my interests are different, my home is different.

Liberal arts education has been invaluable in my work in the bank.

The excellent teaching I received in college was an inspiration for me to become a teacher.

When one remembers that college young people are likely to become leaders in their communities, their states and perhaps the nation, the importance of the professor's influence stands out even more clearly. The college teacher should recognize that for some young people he may represent the finest influence ever to be felt in their lives. This is indeed a great privilege—and an overwhelming responsibility.

Along with the privilege of working with young people the professor has the added stimulus of being constantly in touch with new ideas, particularly those in his own field, but also, through his fellow staff members, with those in other fields. He is continually involved with the cutting edge of knowledge and with the relating of the new to the old and familiar. Akin to this reward is that of working with other faculty members who are intellectually alive because they, too, are constantly working with new ideas. Recently two young men—one a successful business man and the other a successful professor in a western university—were discussing their relative work. In the course of the conversation the business man said to the college professor, "It must be wonderful to be working all the time with people who know something!"

And so, though the work is demanding of one's very best, the rewards are high. The conscientious college professor who teaches well, who seeks to know and understand his students, who engages in research, writing and public service finds himself fully occupied and richly rewarded in the satisfactions that emerge from these pursuits. It is a challenging life.

A P P E N D I X

Bibliography

American Council on Education, *Cooperation in General Education*. Washington: American Council on Education, 1947.

——, *Letter*, August 12, 1958. Washington: American Council on Education.

——, "Cooperative Study in General Education," *Staff News Letter*, Vol. 3, No. 3, April 22, 1942. Washington: American Council on Education.

Axt, Richard G., *The Federal Government and Financing Higher Education*. New York: Columbia University Press, 1952.

Barzun, Jacques, *The House of Intellect*. New York: Harper and Brothers, 1959.

——, *The Teacher in America*. Boston: Little, Brown and Company, 1945.

Beck, Hubert Park, *Men Who Control Our Universities*. New York: Kings Crown Press, 1947.

Berelson, Bernard, *Graduate Education in the United States*. New York: McGraw-Hill Book Company, Inc., 1960.

Biddle, William W., *The Cultivation of Community Leaders*. New York: Harper and Brothers, 1953.

Bloom, B. S. and Broder, Lois J., *Problem-Solving Processes of College Students*. Chicago: University of Chicago Press, 1950.

Bogue, Jesse P. (ed.), *American Junior Colleges*, 3rd ed. Washington: American Council on Education, 1952.

——, *The Community College*. New York: McGraw-Hill Book Company, Inc., 1952.

British Council, *Higher Education in Great Britain and Ireland*. London: Longmans, Green & Company, 1948.

Brownell, Baker, *The College and the Community*. New York: Harper and Brothers, 1952.

Brubacher, J. S. and Rudy, W., *Higher Education in Transition*. New York: Harper and Brothers, 1958.

Bruner, Jerome S., *The Process of Education*. Cambridge: Harvard University Press, 1960.

Burns, Norman and House, C. L. (eds.), "Community Responsibilities of Institutions of Higher Learning," *Proceedings* of the Institute of Administrative Officers of Higher Education, 1948.

Butts, R. Freeman, *The College Charts Its Course*. New York: McGraw-Hill Book Company, Inc., 1939.

Capen, Samuel P., "Seven Devils in Exchange for One," *Coordination of Accrediting Activities*, American Council on Education Studies, Series 1, Vol. 3, No. 9. Washington: American Council on Education, 1939, pp. 16–17.

Caplow, T. and McGee, R. J., *The Academic Marketplace*. New York: Basic Books, Inc., 1958.

Carmichael, Oliver C., *The Changing Role of Higher Education*. New York: The Macmillan Company, 1949.

——, *Universities: Commonwealth and American*. New York: Harper and Brothers, 1959.

Ciardi, John, "A Praise of Good Teachers," *The Saturday Review*, July 8, 1961.

Clark, Burton R., *The Open Door College*. New York: McGraw-Hill Book Company, Inc., 1960.

Commission on Financing Higher Education, *Nature and Needs of Higher Education*. New York: Columbia University Press, 1952.

Cooper, Russell M. (ed.), *The Two Ends of the Log*. Minneapolis: University of Minnesota Press, 1958.

Corson, John J., *Governance of Colleges and Universities*. New York: McGraw-Hill Book Company, Inc., 1960.

Cronbach, Lee J., *Educational Psychology*. New York: Harcourt, Brace and Company, 1954.

Cronkhite, Bernice B. (ed.), *A Handbook for College Teachers*. Cambridge: Harvard University Press, 1950.

Cubberly, Ellwood P., *Public Education in the U.S.*, Rev. ed. Boston: Houghton Mifflin Company, 1934.

Dashiell, J. F., "Contributions of Scientific Knowledge about the Psychology of Learning," *37th Yearbook,* N.S.S.E., Part II. Bloomington, Illinois: Public School Publishing Company, 1938.

Deferrari, Roy J. (ed.), *Functions of the Dean of Studies in Higher Education.* Washington: Catholic University of America Press, 1957.

———, *Guidance in Catholic Colleges and Universities.* Washington: Catholic University of America Press, 1949.

———, *The Philosophy of Catholic Higher Education.* Washington: Catholic University of America Press, 1948.

Deutsch, Monroe E., *The College from Within.* Berkeley: University of California Press, 1952.

DeVane, William C., *The American University in the Twentieth Century.* Baton Rouge: Louisiana State University Press, 1957.

Dewey, John, *Democracy and Education.* New York: The Macmillan Company, 1916.

———, *Experience and Education.* Tiffin, Ohio: Kappa Delta Pi, 1950.

Diekhoff, John S., *Democracy's College.* New York: Harper and Brothers, 1950.

Dressel, P. L., Mayhew, L. B. and McGrath, E. J., *The Liberal Arts as Viewed by Faculty Members in Professional Schools.* New York: Bureau of Publications, Teachers College, Columbia University, 1959.

Eckert, Ruth E., "Ways of Evaluating College Teaching," *School and Society,* 78, February 4, 1950, pp. 65–69.

———, "When Teachers Join College Faculties," *North Central Association Quarterly,* 34, October, 1959, pp. 161–166.

Eddy, Edward D., Jr., *The College Influence on Student Character.* Washington: American Council on Education, 1959.

Educational Policies Commission, *Higher Education in a Decade of Decision.* Washington: National Education Association, 1957.

English, Mildred E., *College in the Country.* Athens: University of Georgia Press, 1959.

Feindel, William, *Memory, Learning and Language.* Toronto, Canada: University of Toronto Press, 1960.

Fine, Benjamin, *Democratic Education.* New York: Thomas Y. Crowell Company, 1945.

Fowlkes, John G., *Higher Education for American Society.* Madison: University of Wisconsin Press, 1949.

Garrison, Roger H., *The Adventure of Learning in College.* New York: Harper and Brothers, 1959.

Gleazer, Edmund J., Jr. (ed.), *American Junior Colleges.* Washington: American Council on Education, 1960.

Grueningen, John Paul von (ed.), *Toward a Christian Philosophy of Higher Education.* Philadelphia: Westminster Press, 1957.

Gustad, John W., *Policies and Practices in Faculty Evaluation.* Washington: American Council on Education, 1961.

Gustavson, Reuben G., "An Introduction and a History of the Relationship of University and College Organizations to Accrediting Agencies," *Excerpts from Addresses,* January 8, 1952. Washington: National Commission on Accrediting.

Hancher, Virgil M., "Liberal Education in a Professional Curricula," *Proceedings* of the 67th Annual Convention of the American Association of Land Grant Colleges and State Universities. Columbus, Ohio, 1953.

Hardee, Melvine D., *The Faculty in College Counseling.* New York: McGraw-Hill Book Company, Inc., 1959.

Harris, Seymour, "College Salaries, Financing of Higher Education and Management of Institutions of Higher Learning," *A.A.U.P. Bulletin,* 44, September, 1958, pp. 589–595.

——, *How Shall We Pay for Education?* New York: Harper and Brothers, 1948.

——, *The Market for College Graduates.* Cambridge: Harvard University Press, 1949.

Harvard Committee, *General Education in a Free Society.* Cambridge: Harvard University Press, 1945.

Haskins, Charles H., *The Rise of Universities.* Ithaca, New York: Cornell University Press, 1950.

Henderson, Algo D., *Policies and Practices in Higher Education.* New York: Harper and Brothers, 1960.

—— and Hall, Dorothy, *Antioch College.* New York: Harper and Brothers, 1946.

Highet, Gilbert, *The Art of Teaching.* New York: Alfred A. Knopf, Inc., 1950.

Hill, Alfred T., *The Small College Meets the Challenge.* New York: McGraw-Hill Book Company, Inc., 1959.

Hillway, Tyrus, *The American Two-Year College.* New York: Harper and Brothers, 1958.

Hofstadter, Richard and Hardy, C. D., *The Development and Scope of Higher Education in the U.S.* New York: Columbia University Press, 1952.

—— and Metzger, W. P., *The Development of Academic Freedom in the United States.* New York: Columbia University Press, 1955.

Hudelson, Earl, *Class Size at the College Level.* Minneapolis: University of Minnesota Press, 1929.

Hudson, Hoyt H., *Educating Liberally.* Stanford University, California: Stanford University Press, 1945.

Hungate, Thad L., *A New Basis of Support for Higher Education.* New York: Bureau of Publications, Teachers College, Columbia University, 1957.

Hutchins, Robert M., *The Higher Learning in America.* New Haven: Yale University Press, 1936.

——, *The State of the University, 1929–1949.* Chicago: University of Chicago Press, 1949.

Jacob, Philip E., *Changing Values in College.* New York: Harper and Brothers, 1957.

Jelinek, Vladimir (ed.), *The Analytical Didactic of Comenius.* Chicago: University of Chicago Press, 1953.

Johnson, B. Lamar, *General Education in Action.* Washington: American Council on Education, 1952.

Johnson, Roy I., *Explorations in General Education.* New York: Harper and Brothers, 1947.

Jones, Barbara, *Bennington College.* New York: Harper and Brothers, 1946.

Justman, Joseph and Mais, W. H., *College Teaching.* New York: Harper and Brothers, 1956.

Kallen, Horace M., *The Education of Free Men.* New York: Farrar and Straus, 1950.

Keezer, Dexter M. (ed.), *Financing Higher Education, 1960–70.* New York: McGraw-Hill Book Company, Inc., 1959.

——, *The Light that Flickers.* New York: Harper and Brothers, 1947.

Koos, Leonard V., *The Junior College.* Minneapolis: University of Minnesota Press, 1924.

Limbert, Paul M. (ed.), *College Teaching and Christian Values.* New York: Association Press, 1951.

Lowry, Howard, *The Mind's Adventure.* Philadelphia: Westminster Press, 1950.

Marvin, C. H., "National Commission on Accrediting," *Bulletin,* Association of American Colleges, No. 36, March, 1950, pp. 53–54.

Mayhew, Lewis B. (ed.), *General Education: An Account and Appraisal.* New York: Harper and Brothers, 1960.

McGlothlin, William J., *Patterns of Professional Education.* New York: G. P. Putnam's Sons, 1960.

McGrath, Earl J., *Toward General Education.* New York: The Macmillan Company, 1948.

——, *The Graduate School and the Decline of Liberal Education.* New York: Bureau of Publications, Teachers College, Columbia University, 1959.

—— and Russell, C. H., *Are Liberal Arts Colleges Becoming Professional Schools?* New York: Bureau of Publications, Teachers College, Columbia University, 1958.

Medsker, Leland L., *The Junior College.* New York: McGraw-Hill Book Company, Inc., 1960.

Millett, John D., *Financing Higher Education in the U.S.* New York: Columbia University Press, 1952.

——, "The Role of Student Charges," in Keezer, Dexter M., *Financing Higher Education, 1960–1970.* New York: McGraw-Hill Book Company, Inc., 1959, pp. 162–182.

Moberly, Walter H., *The Crisis in the University.* New York: The Macmillan Company, 1949.

Morison, Samuel E., *The Founding of Harvard College.* Cambridge: Harvard University Press, 1935.

Morrill, James L., *The Ongoing State University.* Minneapolis: University of Minnesota Press, 1960.

N.E.A. Research Division, "Does It Pay to Teach in Colleges?" *Research Bulletin,* May, 1960, p. 36.

N.E.A. Research Report, "Teacher Supply and Demand in Universities, Colleges and Junior Colleges, 1959–60 and 1960–61," May, 1961, pp. 7, 23.

Newman, John Henry Cardinal, *The Idea of a University.* New York: The American Press, 1941.

Nyquist, Ewald B., "National and Regional Development in Cooperative Evaluation and Accrediting Activity," *Journal of Engineering Education,* 44, May, 1954, pp. 533–538.

Ortega y Gasset, José, *Mission of the University.* Princeton, N.J.: Princeton University Press, 1944.

Pace, C. Robert, *They Went to College*. Minneapolis: University of Minnesota Press, 1941.

Peterson, Houston (ed.), *Great Teachers*. New Brunswick, N.J.: Rutgers University Press, 1946.

President's Commission on Higher Education, *Report,* Vols. I, II, III, IV, V, VI. Washington: Government Printing Office, 1947–1948.

President's Committee on Education beyond the High School, *Second Report to the President*. Washington: Government Printing Office, 1957.

Reed, Anna Y., *The Effective and Ineffective College Teacher*. New York: American Book Company, 1935.

Ruml, Beardsley, *Business Financial Cooperation,* an address printed by The Seventh Company, New York, 1951.

—— and Morrison, D. H., *Memo to a College Trustee*. New York: McGraw-Hill Book Company, Inc., 1959.

Russell, John Dale, *The Finance of Higher Education,* Rev. ed. Chicago: University of Chicago Press, 1954.

Schmidt, George P., *The Liberal Arts College*. New Brunswick, N.J.: Rutgers University Press, 1957.

Selden, William K., *Accreditation*. New York: Harper and Brothers, 1960.

Shuster, George N., *Education and Moral Wisdom*. New York: Harper and Brothers, 1960.

Shyrock, Richard H., *The University of Pennsylvania Faculty*. Philadelphia: University of Pennsylvania Press, 1959.

Skinner, B. F., "The Science of Learning and the Art of Teaching," *Harvard Educational Review,* XXIV, Summer, 1954, pp. 86–97.

Skinner, Charles, *Elementary Educational Psychology*. New York: Prentice-Hall, Inc., 1945.

Smith, Huston, *The Purposes of Higher Education*. New York: Harper and Brothers, 1955.

Snow, C. P., *The Two Cultures and the Scientific Revolution*. New York: Cambridge University Press, 1959.

Stoke, Harold W., *The American College President*. New York: Harper and Brothers, 1959.

Swarthmore College Faculty, *An Adventure in Education*. New York: The Macmillan Company, 1941.

Taylor, Harold, *On Education and Freedom*. New York: Abelard-Schuman, Inc., 1954.

——, *Essays in Teaching*. New York: Harper and Brothers, 1950.

Tead, Ordway, *Administration: Its Purpose and Performance*. New York: Harper and Brothers, 1959.

——, *The Climate of Learning*. New York: Harper and Brothers, 1958.

——, *College Teaching and College Learning*. New Haven: Yale University Press, 1949.

——, *Trustees, Teachers, Students: Their Role in Higher Education*. Salt Lake City: University of Utah Press, 1951.

Thelen, Herbert A., *Education and the Human Quest*. New York: Harper and Brothers, 1960.

Thomson, Ruth H., "An Experimental Study of Memory as Influenced by Feeling Tone," *Journal of Experimental Psychology*, 13, 1930, pp. 462–467.

Thornton, James W., Jr., *The Community Junior College*. New York: John Wiley & Sons, Inc., 1960.

Tickton, Sidney G., *Teaching Salaries Then and Now*. New York: Fund for the Advancement of Education, May, 1961.

Tilton, J. W., "A Psychological Basis for Learning," in Gruber, F. C. (ed.), *Foundations of Education*. Philadelphia: University of Pennsylvania Press, 1957, pp. 36–54.

Trueblood, Elton, *The Idea of a College*. New York: Harper and Brothers, 1959.

Tyler, Ralph W., *Basic Principles of Curriculum Instruction*. Chicago: University of Chicago Press, 1950.

U.S. Department of Health, Education and Welfare, *Higher Education Planning and Management Data, 1959–60*, Circular #614. Washington: U.S. Government Printing Office, 1960, pp. 2–4.

——, *Opening (Fall) Enrollment in Higher Education, 1961: Institutional Data*. Washington: U.S. Government Printing Office, 1961.

White, Lynn T., *Educating Our Daughters*. New York: Harper and Brothers, 1950.

Whitehead, Alfred N., *The Aims of Education*. New York: The Macmillan Company, 1929.

Wilson, Woodrow, "Should an Antecedent Liberal Education Be Required of Students in Law, Medicine and Theology?" *Proceedings* of the International Congress of Education, 2nd ed., World's Columbian Exposition, Chicago, 1893.

Woodburne, Lloyd S., *Faculty Personnel Policies in Higher Education*. New York: Harper and Brothers, 1950.

——, *Principles of College and University Administration*. Stanford University, California: Stanford University Press, 1958.

Wriston, Henry M., *Academic Procession*. New York: Columbia University Press, 1959.

1940 Statement of Principles [1]

The purpose of this statement is to promote public understanding and support of academic freedom and tenure and agreement upon procedures to assure them in colleges and universities. Institutions of higher education are conducted for the common good and not to further the interest of either the individual teacher [2] or the institution as a whole. The common good depends upon the free search for truth and its free exposition.

Academic freedom is essential to these purposes and applies to both teaching and research. Freedom in research is fundamental to the advancement of truth. Academic freedom in its teaching aspect is fundamental for the protection of the rights of the teacher in teaching and of the student to freedom in learning. It carries with it duties correlative with rights.

Tenure is a means to certain ends; specifically: (1) Freedom of teaching and research and of extramural activities, and (2) a sufficient degree of economic security to make the profession attractive to men and women of ability. Freedom and economic security, hence tenure, are indispensable to the success of an institution in fulfilling its obligations to its students and to society.

ACADEMIC FREEDOM

(a) The teacher is entitled to full freedom in research and in the publication of the results, subject to the adequate performance of his other academic duties; but research for pecuniary return should be based upon an understanding with the authorities of the institution.

(b) The teacher is entitled to freedom in the classroom in discuss-

---

[1] "Academic Freedom and Tenure," *A.A.U.P. Bulletin,* Vol. 33, Spring, 1947, p. 74.

[2] The word "teacher" as used in this document is understood to include the investigator who is attached to an academic institution without teaching duties.

ing his subject, but he should be careful not to introduce into his teaching controversial matter which has no relation to his subject. Limitations of academic freedom because of religious or other aims of the institution should be clearly stated in writing at the time of the appointment.

(c) The college or university teacher is a citizen, a member of a learned profession, and an officer of an educational institution. When he speaks or writes as a citizen, he should be free from institutional censorship or discipline, but his special position in the community imposes special obligations. As a man of learning and an educational officer, he should remember that the public may judge his profession and his institution by his utterances. Hence he should at all times be accurate, should exercise appropriate restraint, should show respect for the opinions of others, and should make every effort to indicate that he is not an institutional spokesman.

ACADEMIC TENURE

(a) After the expiration of a probationary period teachers or investigators should have permanent or continuous tenure, and their services should be terminated only for adequate cause, except in the case of retirement for age or under extraordinary circumstances because of financial exigencies.

In the interpretation of this principle it is understood that the following represents acceptable academic practice:

(1) The precise terms and conditions of every appointment should be stated in writing and be in the possession of both institution and teacher before the appointment is consummated.

(2) Beginning with appointment to the rank of full-time instructor or a higher rank, the probationary period should not exceed seven years, including within this period full-time service in all institutions of higher education; but subject to the proviso that when, after a term of probationary service of more than three years in one or more institutions, a teacher is called to another institution, it may be agreed in writing that his new appointment is for a probationary period of not more than four years, even though thereby the person's total probationary period in the academic profession is extended beyond the

normal maximum of seven years. Notice should be given at least one year prior to the expiration of the probationary period, if the teacher is not to be continued in service after the expiration of that period.

(3) During the probationary period a teacher should have the academic freedom that all other members of the faculty have.

(4) Termination for cause of a continuous appointment, or the dismissal for cause of a teacher previous to the expiration of a term appointment, should, if possible, be considered by both a faculty committee and the governing board of the institution. In all cases where the facts are in dispute, the accused teacher should be informed before the hearing in writing of the charges against him and should have the opportunity to be heard in his own defense by all bodies that pass judgment upon his case. He should be permitted to have with him an adviser of his own choosing who may act as counsel. There should be a full stenographic record of the hearing available to the parties concerned. In the hearing of charges of incompetence the testimony should include that of teachers and other scholars, either from his own or from other institutions. Teachers on continuous appointment who are dismissed for reasons not involving moral turpitude should receive their salaries for at least a year from the date of notification of dismissal whether or not they are continued in their duties at the institution.

(5) Termination of a continuous appointment because of financial exigency should be demonstrably bona fide.

INTERPRETATIONS

At the conference of representatives of the American Association of University Professors and of the Association of American Colleges on November 7–8, 1940, the following interpretations of the 1940 Statement of Principles on Academic Freedom and Tenure were agreed upon:

1. That its operation should not be retroactive.

2. That all tenure claims of teachers appointed prior to the endorsement should be determined in accordance with the principles set forth in the 1925 Conference Statement on Academic Freedom and Tenure.

3. If the administration of a college or university feels that a teacher has not observed the admonitions of Paragraph (c) of the section on *Academic Freedom* and believes that the extramural utterances of the teacher have been such as to raise grave doubts concerning his fitness for his position, it may proceed to file charges under Paragraph (a) (4) of the section on *Academic Tenure*. In pressing such charges the administration should remember that teachers are citizens and should be accorded the freedom of citizens. In such cases the administration must assume full responsibility and the American Association of University Professors and the Association of American Colleges are free to make an investigation.

TABULATION OF THE RESPONSES OF 160 COLLEGE PROFESSORS
IN A MIDWESTERN UNIVERSITY TO A QUESTIONNAIRE
ON "GOOD" COLLEGE TEACHING

	Liberal * Arts	Professional * Schools	Total
A. Definition of "good" teaching			
1. Must enlist active interest of students	48	37	85
2. Logical organization and clear presentation of subject matter	29	31	60
3. Stimulates thinking	19	25	44
4. Emphasis on fundamental elements	10	9	19
5. Adjusts subject matter to capacities of students	9	9	18
6. Thorough mastery of subject on part of teacher	11	1	12
7. Stimulates intellectual curiosity	6	3	9
8. Friendliness and genuine interest in student	3	5	8
9. Promotes maximum learning, growth achievement	5	3	8
10. Must have enthusiasm for subject	7	1	8
11. Integrates materials with other fields	5	2	7
12. Inspires students	5	1	6
13. Develops ability to solve problems, educate oneself	4	2	6
14. Need to keep abreast of field	6		6
15. Results in desirable changes in behavior		5	5
16. Results in social intelligence	3	2	5
17. Availability to students for conferences	3	2	5

306

	Liberal* Arts	Professional* Schools	Total
18. Avoids sensational techniques	4	1	5
19. Varies techniques	2	3	5
20. Results in desirable attitudes	2	2	4
21. Is based on educational philosophy	4		4
22. Develops tools essential to work in field	1	3	4
23. Demonstrates techniques		4	4
24. Should not propagandize	3	1	4
25. Should not be confined to textbook	3	1	4
26. Student in principal role; teacher the guide	2	1	3
27. Relates subject to professional work		3	3
28. Mutual respect between students and teacher	1	1	2
29. Human point of view without softness		2	2

B. Criteria by which "good" teaching should be judged

	Liberal Arts	Professional Schools	Total
1. Response of students	32	26	58
2. Achievement of students	11	17	28
3. Judgment of colleagues	11	7	18
4. Work of students in advanced courses	2	13	15
5. Judgment of better students (B or above)	8	6	14
6. Records of graduates	3	9	12
7. Objective examinations (or exams conducted by outside examiner)	3	7	10
8. Number desiring to register for courses	2	7	9
9. Personal relations with students—willingness to help		7	7

308

TABULATION OF THE RESPONSES OF 160 COLLEGE PROFESSORS
IN A MIDWESTERN UNIVERSITY TO A QUESTIONNAIRE
ON "GOOD" COLLEGE TEACHING

	Liberal* Arts	Professional* Schools	Total
10. Judgment of administrators	2	5	7
11. Judgment of mature students	1	4	5
12. Judgment of alumni	1	3	4
13. Degree to which student behavior is modified		4	4
14. Publications and research	4		4
15. Grades	2	2	4
16. Frequency of personal conferences on student initiative	2	1	3
17. Few failures		3	3
18. Type of student attracted to course		2	2
19. Effect on students' thinking		2	2
20. Absence of disciplinary difficulties	1	1	2

* Eighty liberal arts faculty members and eighty professional schools faculty members (medicine, law, dentistry, education, engineering, business) responded to this inquiry. Since more than one definition or criteria often were given, more than eighty responses are shown in each column.

Index